MARRIAGE
IN
CANON LAW

Texts and Comments

Reflections and Questions

MARRIAGE
IN
CANON LAW

Texts and Comments

Reflections and Questions

LADISLAS ÖRSY, S.J.

Michael Glazier
Wilmington, Delaware

ABOUT THE AUTHOR

Ladislas Örsy, S.J., is internationally respected as a leading expert in canon law. He has written several books and over 200 articles on canonical and theological questions. He holds his doctorate in canon law from the Gregorian University, took his degree in civil law from Oxford University, and did his graduate theological studies at Louvain University. He is presently on the faculty of The Catholic University of America.

Imprimi potest. February 20, 1986.
Joseph A. Novak, S.J., Provincial
New York Province of the Society of Jesus.

First published in 1986 by Michael Glazier, Inc., 1935 West Fourth Street, Wilmington, Delaware 19805.

Library of Congress Catalog Card Number: 86-80421
International Standard Book Number:
  Marriage in Canon Law: 0-89453-582-X
Cover design by Florence Bern.
Printed in the United States of America.

CONTENTS

ACKNOWLEDGMENTS

All quotations from the Bible are from *The Oxford Annotated Bible with the Apocrypha*, Revised Standard Version (New York-Oxford: Oxford University Press, 1965).

The Latin text of the canons is from *Codex Iuris Canonici*, promulgated by the authority of John Paul II (Vatican City, 1983).

All translations of the documents of Vatican Council II are taken from *Documents of Vatican II*, ed. by Walter Abbott (New York: Herder and Herder, 1966).

All other translations from official documents or of various works are our own unless otherwise noted.

ABBREVIATIONS

AAS	Acta Apostolicae Sedis
ABBOTT	Documents of Vatican II, Abbott ed.
CAPPELLO	Cappello: De matrimonio
CDF	(Sacred) Congregation for the Doctrine of Faith
CIC	Corpus Iuris Canonici, Friedberg ed.
CIC/17	Codex Iuris Canonici, 1917
CIC/83	Codex Iuris Canonici, 1983
CLD	Canon Law Digest
CLSA	Canon Law Society of America
CLSGBI	Canon Law Society of Great Britain and Ireland
COC	(Sacred) Congregation for the Oriental Churches
COD	Conciliorum Oecumenicorum Decreta, Alberigo ed.
COMS	Communicationes
COM-USA	The Code of Canon Law: A Text and Commentary by the CLSA
CPM	Contemporary Perspectives on Christian Marriage, Malone and Connery eds.
CS	(Sacred) Congregation for the Discipline of the Sacraments
DDC	Dictionnaire de droit canonique
DH	*Dignitatis humanae*, VC II: Declaration on Religious Freedom
DTC	Dictionnaire de theologie catholique
D-SCH	Enchiridion Symbolorum, Denzinger and Schön-metzer eds.

7

GASPARRI	Gasparri: De matrimonio
GEL	Greek-English Lexicon, Bauer ed.
GS	*Gaudium et spes*, VC II: Pastoral Constitution on the Church in the Modern World
HO	Sacred Congregation of the Holy Office
IND	Index verborum ac locutionum Codicis Iuris Canonici, Ochoa ed.
JUR	The Jurist, Washington, DC
LE	Leges Ecclesiae, Ochoa ed.
LG	*Lumen gentium*, VC II: Dogmatic Constitution on the Church
LTK	Lexikon für Theologie und Kirche
NCCB	National Conference of Catholic Bishops
NCE	New Catholic Encyclopedia
OLD	Oxford Latin Dictionary, Glare ed.
REL/81	Relatio complectens synthesim animadversionum ... 1981
SC	Studia Canonica, Ottawa
SCH/75	Schema documenti pontificii ... de sacramentis, 1975
SCH/82	Codex Iuris Canonici: Schema Novissimum, 1982
SCH/80	Schema Codicis Iuris Canonici, 1980
SRR	Sacra Romana Rota
TRL-USA	Translation of the Code, CLSA
TRL-GBI	Translation of the Code, CLSGBI
TS	Theological Studies, Washington, DC
UR	*Unitatis redintegratio,* VC II: Decree on Ecumenism
VC II	Vatican Council II

Fides quaerens intellectum
Faith seeking understanding
St. Anselm of Canterbury

PREFACE

The purpose of this book can be accurately stated with the words of St. Anselm of Canterbury: faith seeking understanding, *fides quaerens intellectum*. He, of course, was describing the goal of theological reflection. But his famous dictum can be applied also to a search for the meaning of laws of the church: faith in the church seeks the understanding of its laws.

The laws of the church, however, do not have an autonomous existence; their scope is to uphold theological and human values and to help the community to appropriate those values.

It follows that no intelligence of the laws is possible without the understanding of the particular values which they are meant to serve. The text and immediate context of the canons can never be the full and adequate sources of their interpretation. Paradoxically, to find the meaning of the canons, the commentator often must go out of the world of legal meanings and enter that where theological and human values are revealed and defined. There, within a new horizon, the true significance of the words of the law may unfold.

Such an inquiry could well be called critical, provided the term is not used in the sense of irresponsible criticism, but it is given the widely respected meaning that it has acquired in biblical sciences: all the available resources of human intelligence enlightened by faith are brought to bear on a passage or on a book of the Scriptures in order to find its message. If such method is correct in the search for the meaning of the word of God, it must be correct also in the inquiries for the meaning of our laws.

Precisely because canon law under many aspects reflects the humanity of our church, it is in need of such scrutiny — in a spirit of faith. If it is correctly done, it cannot take anything away from the authority of the laws; the fact that they can be reformed does not mean that they are not binding. The church could never grow in wisdom and grace (as the parable of the mustard seed indicates) unless it has the authority to revise and improve whatever is of human origin in its organization.

To discover the theological values behind the legal texts and to assess how far the norms correspond to them, is an immense task that must go on always but cannot be completed ever. The mysteries behind the norms will never be translucent to our eyes. The questions that future generations will raise we cannot anticipate. Accordingly, this book is no more than an effort to contribute to this process. It is not conceived however as an introductory textbook in canon law: its scope is much broader than that.

All my interpretations are based on the official Latin text, which remains the only authentic one. For this reason, I reproduce it. My translation of the canons is more literal than interpretative; to facilitate the work of comparing the two, I kept the translation as close to the original Latin as it was possible without sacrificing intelligibility in English.

The greatest help toward the composition of this book came over many years from those who brought me problems and questions and thus compelled me to reflect not only on the laws but on the values that the laws intended to cover. More directly, it was Michael Glazier who approached me with the suggestion of publishing a commentary on some part of the new Code; I accepted his offer and chose the canons on marriage. During the period of the preparation, he knew how to combine encouragement with patience. Finally, my colleagues, James Conn, S.J. of Fordham University, New York City, and Joseph Koury, S.J. of Weston College, Cambridge, Massachusetts read the manuscript and helped me to improve its content. To them all, I am grateful.

Ladislas Örsy S.J.
The Catholic University of America
Washington, DC

A HISTORICAL SURVEY: CHANGING HORIZONS AND DEVELOPING CATEGORIES

The purpose of this survey: history for reflection.

The purpose of this historical introduction is not to give a comprehensive account of the development of the doctrine and legislation concerning Christian marriage. Its aim is more restricted: to look in this history at those factors and movements which contributed significantly to changing horizons and developing categories. By horizons we mean the frameworks, with their particular breadth and length, height and depth, within which the community, especially its theologians and lawyers, perceived marriage; by categories we mean the interlocking pattern of concepts through which they expressed themselves in construing their theories and defining their practices. The knowledge of such changing conditions and articulations not only can give us some clues for a better understanding of what we have today but it can also reveal to a significant degree what is the permanent core of our beliefs and what should be regarded as historically and culturally conditioned accretions. That is, it can provide us with a great deal of material for critical reflections.[1]

[1]For this historical summary we are indebted to the works listed in our Bibliography under the heading "Historical Works," especially to the authors of the article on Marriage in DTC, which remains the most detailed and the most comprehensive study on the subject. We have profited also from the more general surveys of Joyce and Schillebeeckx. On several issues (development of the classical

Such critical reflections concerning the doctrine and law of marriage are sorely needed. To insist that more historical research is necessary before we can raise major questions is a fallacy; it can delay critical thinking forever. The main facts of history and the principal lines of doctrinal developments are well known; they offer abundant material for reflections. Besides, we have pressing contemporary problems that demand answers; answers that do not break with our authentic traditions yet provide fresh responses to new needs. Each generation is called to draw its own lessons from history, leaving it to the next one to bring in the necessary corrections.

As it is the case with every single Christian mystery, so it is with marriage: there is a core of belief about it that has been handed down incorrupt from generation to generation. But while the core has been preserved, much has been added to it as well. Explanations and opinions, customs and regulations accumulated over the substance, sometimes to the point that they appeared more important than the core. To separate the two, the permanent gift of God, "the mystery," and the fragile human structures around it is not easy; nor can it ever be done perfectly. But, easy or difficult, we should not recoil from doing it. Even if our efforts lead to a partial success only, there is a rich reward. As soon as some layers are cleared away, the mystery reveals itself with greater clarity and we are in a better position to understand it.

Admittedly, in the case of the sacrament of matrimony the layers laid on the core are numerous and heavy. The work of separating the permanent from the transient can be attempted but certainly not completed by individual persons. Apart from the magnitude of the task, there is the problem that we all are historical beings. In surveying the flow of past events, we cannot situate ourselves on a platform of observation that is untouched by the currents of our own times. We too are enclosed in our own horizons; we, too, operate with our own categories. Therefore, no matter what conclu-

doctrine, consent, indissolubility), we found a mine of information in the works of Gaudemet; he supplements and brings up to date the articles in DTC. We gained valuable information also from the monographs of Bressan (Council of Trent, Eastern church) and Sequeira (contract and sacrament) and others who are mentioned in the principal part of the book in connection with specific issues. To all of them, we are grateful.

sions we reach, it is not likely to be the full truth. Thus, the work can go on from generation to generation.

Old Testament origins: the human couple in a sacred universe.

There is not a "systematic doctrine of marriage" in the books of the Old Testament. We have only fragments that describe the beliefs and practices of the Hebrew people; but those fragments speak of a highly developed understanding and of long-standing observances. They are important for our purposes because they influenced and inspired the beliefs and practices of the early Christian communities.

In the Hebrews' understanding of marriage, the institutional aspect dominated: the family was the primary source of the strength of the tribe. To have children in abundance was a great blessing; the survival and the future prosperity of the people depended on them. Yet, side by side with the appreciation of the institution, we are told also touching stories of marital relationships; that of Abraham and Sarah is one of them.

The creation narratives, as we have them, are the fruit of a long maturation; they contain a culturally advanced, even sophisticated understanding of marriage. The first human beings appear in a sacred context: they are part of a universe that has been created by God. They appear as a couple, as equals, in conversation with their Maker.

In the more primitive "Yahwist" tradition "the Lord God formed man of dust from the ground, and breathed into his nostrils the breath of life" (Gen 2:7); then "God said, 'It is not good that the man should be alone; I will make him a helper fit for him,'" (Gen 2:18). So "God caused a deep sleep to fall upon the man, and while he slept took one of his ribs and closed up its place with flesh; and the rib which the Lord God had taken from the man he made into a woman and brought her to the man" (21-22). The story implies that man and woman are different, thus they can complement each other; yet it points also to their unity: the flesh of the one is the flesh of the other.

The more developed "sacerdotal" tradition completes and corrects the Yahwist one. It places the origin of both, man and woman, in the creative strength of God's word: "So God created man in his own image, in the image of God he created him; male and female he created them." (Gen 1:27)

The source of their equality and unity is now placed directly into God's own powerful word. He gave them also the task of continuing his work in this creation: "And God blessed them, and God said to them, "Be fruitful and multiply, and fill the earth and subdue it; and have dominion over the fish of the sea and over the birds of the air and over every living thing that moves upon the earth" (Gen 1:28). This task they received together.

The ideal put forward in the creation is that of a monogamous marriage; a remarkable fact because the sacred books tell us about the polygamous unions of several outstanding personalities in the history of Israel. This orientation toward monogamy was certainly supported and strengthened by the developing symbolism attached to marriage: Israel used the image of the human couple to describe and to understand with increasing depth the nation's relationship to Yahweh; he was the "bridegroom," they the "bride." It was a jealous relationship: as Yahweh was the God Israel, Israel had to be the people of Yahweh.

This symbolism has been often recalled by the prophets; it inspired many poetic texts of the Old Testament, and it may well be the reason why the Song of Songs was received into the collection of the holy scriptures.

The horizon, then, in which a theology of marriage developed in the Old Testament times was very broad; it stretched from the visible universe to the invisible divinity who made it. The human couple was seen as embedded in this world that was altogether sacred even if under some aspect it has been distorted by the Fall. The unique relationship of a man and a woman in marriage has become the symbol of the relationship between Yahweh and his people. So, marriage has became the carrier of a second meaning: it represented God's dealing with Israel. In such a horizon marriage could be understood only as good and holy. The categories used in the inspired books are of the the existential kind; the authors speak in symbols and images, in prose and poetry; they do not offer analytical abstractions.

New Testament revelations:
the place of marriage in the new creation.

Again, we have fragments, not a systematic exposition. The principal pieces are found in the synoptic gospels, in John's gospel and in the Pauline writings.

The doctrine of the Synoptic gospels is rooted in Israel's tradition. When the disciples asked about divorce, Jesus simply referred them to the story of the creation: the first man and woman were made one by God, so no human being had the power to touch that bond: "What therefore God has joined together, let no man put asunder" (Mt 19:6).

The clause in Mt 19:9 containing the words "except for unchastity [adultery?]," *porneia* in Greek, has been variously interpreted. Many modern exegetes see in it a permission or perhaps an injunction to terminate an already illegal union, such as one forbidden by the Mosiac law by reason of kinship. Today, the Roman Catholic church does not read this clause as establishing an exception from the law of indissolubility; the Orthodox church, however, understands it as authorizing divorce and remarriage in the case of adultery by one of the partners (cf. Mt 19:9).

Jesus recalled the traditional symbolism of the bridegroom and the bride but he gave it a new and pregnant meaning: he was the bridegroom. "And Jesus said to them, 'Can you make wedding guests fast while the bridegroom is with them?'" (Lk 5:34).

He spoke also of marriage as a reality that belongs to this passing world: "For when they rise from the dead, they neither marry nor are given in marriage, but are like angels in heaven" (Mk 12:25).

Yet, his deeds spoke of his esteem for marriage. According to John, the first solemn act of Jesus' public ministry took place at the wedding feast of Cana: "the first of his signs, Jesus did at Cana in Galilee, and manifested his glory." There he changed the water into wine, and those present at this messianic entry were given a new wine of no earthly origin (cf. Jn 2:1-11).

In the Pauline literature we find the first elements of a reflective theology. Marriage is not only good but it can be a source of sanctification even for the unbeliever: "For the unbelieving husband is consecrated through his wife, and the unbelieving wife is consecrated through her husband. Otherwise, your children would be unclean but as it is they are holy" (1 Cor 7:14).

Also marriage is a relationship that expresses the perfection of love; it is the symbol of the relationship of Christ to his church: "Husbands, love your wives, as Christ loved the church and gave himself up for her. . ." (Eph 5:25); and "'For this reason a man shall leave his father and mother and be joined to his wife, and the two shall become one.' This is a great mystery, and I take it to mean Christ and the church" (31-32).

Hence, the model for determining the ethical demands of marriage must be taken from the image of the relationship of Yahweh to his people, or of Christ with his church.

But Paul, too, following the teaching of his Lord, asserted that marriage was a reality of this world, therefore it could be subordinated to higher values. For him, there are individual vocations; he wrote that each one should "lead the life which the Lord has assigned to him, and in which God has called him." (Cf. 1 Co 7:17). Also, the imminence of the parousia or the apostolic calling itself may counsel a person not to marry: "I think that in view of the impending distress it is well for a person to remain as he is." (1 Cor 7:26) And "The unmarried man is anxious about the affairs of the Lord. . ." (32).

Moreover, if in a given case, married life with an unbeliever becomes destructive of that peace to which a "saint" is called, "in such a case the brother or sister is not bound. For God has called us to peace" (15). This is the passage that from fairly early times (fourth century?) has been invoked as granting the special privilege of divorce and remarriage to Christians whose unbelieving partner wished to separate.

But side by side with the substantial teaching, there are also culturally conditioned directions in the Pauline writings, especially concerning the position of women in the family and in the community. They should be handled as such; they were not meant to be proclamations of belief.

The coming of the Kingdom brought with it an expansion of the horizon in which marriage was understood. It was seen not only as part of this sacred universe but also in the context of Christ's relationship to his church. Human love has become the symbol of God's redemptive love. Marriage has never been exalted any higher in Christian literature than it has been in the Pauline corpus. But we cannot say that Jesus imposed new categories on marriage. There is no evidence that he would have prescribed any specific formality for bringing it into existence, or would have initiated any specific legislation for it. The community understood him well: the formalities have not changed, only persons changed. Christians married "in the Lord."

The first three centuries: domestic celebrations.

In the early centuries Christians lived and moved within the traditional religious and secular horizons in understanding marriage and accepting binding norms for it; they married as everybody else did. They have not introduced any specifically Christian pattern for marrying but simply followed the customs of the place where they lived or of the ethnic group to which they belonged.

Some new concerns, however, emerged and were voiced by ecclesiastical writers: parents should respect the freedom of their children in choosing a marriage partner; also, those who marry unbelievers should be aware that their faith may be in danger. Such preoccupations were of a pastoral character; they did not lead to protective legislation. In fact in the first three centuries there was not any official legislation concerning the marriages of Christians.

There was, however, some dialectical development in the attitudes of the community that prompted a certain amount of reflection — not always in the right direction. Christians made an effort to distance themselves from the sexual excesses of the pagan world around them, and by doing so they became vulnerable to another extreme that saw marriage as all too material for spiritually enlightened persons.

Although the scriptural understanding of marriage as a sacred reality was never lost, some writers and teachers tended to impose a rigoristic interpretation on the sayings of Jesus and Paul. They exalted virginity and abstinence beyond measure, independently from the eschatological context in which they were first mentioned in the New Testament. Some saw marriage as unbefitting for the "saints": a state of life of lesser values. Such change for the worse is well exemplified in some of the writings of *Tertullian (160-220)*; he gradually abandoned the balance of the traditional doctrine and moved into a position of extreme rigorism. Even if the community at large was protected by its own healthy instinct against the excesses of similar writers and preachers, the discussions created a climate which obscured the clarity of the scriptural vision. The material creation was looked upon as defective in some way, and marriage was part of it.

The fourth and fifth centuries: ecclesial dimensions.

This was the age of local councils, which have become increasingly preoccupied with pastoral problems concerning marriage; they initiated a legislative process. The norms they enacted concerned themselves mostly with the impediments and warned about the dangers inherent to marriages with heretics and unbelievers.

Also, the first elements of marriage liturgy began to appear. It was customary to hold the ceremony at the home of the family of the bride. A priest was often invited to be present at the wedding, and once there he was requested to pronounce the blessing over the couple, which otherwise was the task of the father of the bride.

It did not take long before the celebration of marriages was transferred to church buildings; people could participate in the eucharist as well. Quite naturally, the role of the priest increased. In the church, he alone invoked God's blessing over the spouses; in the East he also "crowned" them and he let them join their hands. The symbolism of it all was not lost on those who interpreted the role of the priest: he came to be regarded as the "giver" of the sacrament —not to be identified with the more technical scholastic concept of "minister".

The theological speculations about marriage continued to affirm its fundamental goodness — with cautions and caveats. *Jerome (c.345-420)* certainly went well beyond the parameters of the biblical tradition in exalting virginity and devaluing marriage. Parallel with such developments, the doctrine of the equality of the sexes suffered also; women were consistently regarded as inferior and subordinate to men.

As regards indissolubility, the overall stress was on the duty of fidelity, yet the inevitability of a separation was accepted more easily when a man wanted it than when the woman asked for it. If a man separated from his wife married against, there were indulgent voices in his favor (e.g. *Basil of Cesarea (c.329-379), Ambrosiaster (wrote between 370-384).*

Augustine (354-430): the shadow of sin over marriage.

Augustine was the first among the Fathers of the church to work out a systematic theology of marriage. His ideas inspired and dominated much of the development to come, in preaching, teaching and legislating — well into the Middle Ages and beyond. Undoubtedly, his experience with his own sexuality has influenced his speculations; he remembered well how his unruly passion was an impediment in his search for God. But he was moved also by a more objective and intellectual factor: he wanted to oppose the simplistic claims of the Pelagians, who believed that human beings can save themselves by their own effort. They preached a logically coherent system of ideas which accounted for sin and grace, for the incapacities of our lapsed nature, and for God's power in rescuing us.

Augustine answered by a much more sophisticated theory. His intention was to explain the revealed truth; his starting point was the history of our salvation. God created the first couple immortal and innocent. Through their disobedience, they not only lost the original gifts but also lapsed into the state of original sin. As their immortality and innocence were to be shared by all human beings, so their posterity had to inherit their sinful condition. Their lapsed nature was to be transmitted by the act of human generation. But due to the Fall, that act has become tainted with sin since it was dominated by concupiscence. For Augustine the words of Psalm 51, "Behold, I was brought forth in iniquity, and in sin did my mother conceive me" (5), were the proclamation of our true condition. In order to stress the importance of grace, he devalued our nature. Unconscious memories from his Manichean past may have played also some role in the construction of his theories.

The consequences of his reflections for the theology of marriage were far reaching. Since the sexual act could hardly ever be performed without sin, to be in the married state was to be permanently exposed to the danger of sin.

Understandably, in such circumstances, for a Christian to choose marriage, some justification was necessary; the inherent dangers had to be compensated by immanent good things, the *bona matrimonii*. They were the children, *proles*, the virtue of fidelity, *fides*, and the sacred commitment for life, *sacramentum vinculum*. The last one is not to be confused with the modern concept of sacrament.

The idea of a sacred commitment, *sacramentum vinculum*, led Augustine to speculate on the sign value of marriage, *sacramentum signum*: it expressed the fidelity of Christ to his church. He reached back to the Pauline doctrine for inspiration but unfortunately never explored it to the point where the sanctity of marriage would have become the focus of his speculations.

In the matter of indissolubility, he displayed some hesitations. On the one hand, he regarded a man who has dismissed his wife and married again as guilty of a "light" transgression, *venialiter* lapsed, hence, not to be excluded from the eucharist; on the other hand he confessed that he found the problem a perplexing one and that he was not fully satisfied with his own solution.

By the end of the fifth century, a narrowing of the horizon in which marriage was viewed has taken place. Its original sacredness has become obscured by the undue exaltation of the soul and the devaluation of the body; the harmony that was so obvious between the two in the creation stories has become disturbed. Even divine redemption did not heal the ravages of sin fully; concupiscence remained a dominant force in all sexual activity.

Developing liturgy, new ecclesial dimensions, from the fifth century onward.

Perhaps the only field that remained substantially untouched by the Augustinian pessimism was the field of liturgy. The evidence available, fragmentary as it is, shows that the celebration of a marriage remained a joyous event in the spirit of the scriptures, no matter what gloomy picture some writers and preachers may have painted of the dangers inherent in married life.

The liturgical celebration of marriage with the participation of a priest not only conferred a visible ecclesial dimension on the sacrament but also contributed toward bringing marriage under the jurisdiction of the church.

In the West *Leo the Great (pope 440-461)* was the first to insist on the duty of a public celebration, which as yet did not mean that the wedding had to take place in the church; it meant only that the ceremony was not to be performed in secrecy; it was not hidden from the community. Later, *the pseudo-Isidorian decretals (c.847-*

c.857), by stressing the need for discipline, contributed greatly toward the church assuming veritable jurisdiction over the marriages of the faithful. This gradually led to an increased legislation and, by the tenth century, to the beginnings of a judicial system.

In the East, the instrument of evolution remained the liturgy. There, the public celebration of marriage received a greater emphasis than in the West. By the end of the first millennium, the only way a couple could marry was through a public liturgical celebration. It would be idle to speculate whether or not according to our western categories (of later origin) the ceremony was for validity. It was the only way of marrying.

From the tenth century onward, the ecclesial dimension was part of the horizon in which marriage was understood. The pessimistic views of Augustine continued to dominate theological speculations.

The penitential books on marital problems, *c. 500 - c. 900.*

The importance of the witness of the penitential books should not be overrated; they certainly do not reflect "what has been believed everywhere, always and by all," *quod ubique, quod semper, quod ab omnibus creditum est* (— to quote Vincent of Lerins; Commonitoria, ch.2); yet, in their own limited way they speak of the grant of pardon in the church as no other documents do. By listening to them, we can learn something about how the duty of marital fidelity, that is, the indissolubility of marriage, was understood by their authors.

The Irish and Breton penitentials permitted the separation of the spouses but they did not permit remarriage while the former partner was alive.

The Anglo-Saxon and Frankish penitentials permitted the following persons to divorce their spouses and remarry, but if they were guilty after the completion of a severe penance only:

— both spouses after adultery by one of them,
— the husband maliciously abandoned by his wife,
— the wife of a man condemned to slavery,
— the spouse who obtained freedom while the other had to continue in slavery,
— the spouse of one who was taken into captivity,

— the spouse who converted to Christianity while the other remained in paganism,

— the wife of a man who was impotent (infertility was not enough).

The same penitentials did not permit divorce by consent, and the practices listed above have been terminated by the Carolingian reforms between 813 and 900. (*See* Cyril Vogel, *Les "Libri Paenitentiales"* [Turnhout: Brepols, 1978], pp. 107-8.)

The early Middle Ages: what makes marriage?

With the advent of the Middle Ages, the attention of the theologians and lawyers began to shift to a new focus, following a general pattern that was taking place in the intellectual life of the church: they became more interested in the institution of marriage than in the personal problems of those who were married. Thus, new questions arose, centered on the institution. Among the first of such questions, there was a fundamental one: what is it that brings marriage into existence, or, what is it that "makes" marriage, *quid facit matrimonium?*

The search for an answer took a long time and it was not devoid of hesitations and doubts, due to the lack of a critical methodology and of a commonly accepted terminology. Both had to be developed — not an unusual situation when a new paradigm of understanding is arising or when the horizon of the researchers is changing.

According to classical Roman law marriage was a fact, sustained by the marital affection of the parties. According to the customs of Germanic peoples, marriage came into existence by subsequent stages: betrothal, solemnization, consummation. While it was certain that at the end of the process there was a marriage, the role of each stage in "making" it was rather vague. The pressure to decide the issue, through a universally valid rule, came from practical cases brought before ecclesiastical authorities.

Hincmar of Reims (805-882), was bishop of Reims, and as such had to handle marriage cases of important families. He understood and answered the question about "what makes marriage" in the Germanic categories: betrothal apart, both the solemnization and the consummation played a role in perfecting marriage. After the solemnization, if a marriage could be consummated, it was not to be dissolved. If it could not be consummated, it could be dissolved. That much may sound to us like a clarification of the impediment of impotency. But the importance of Hincmar is that he was the first to state firmly that once a marriage was consummated, it obtained a new status; it represented the union of Christ to his church, therefore it could not be dissolved. Thus, Hincmar established the principle that indissolubility is intimately linked to consummation; a position that modern canon law continues to hold. Whether or not he was of the opinion that marriage comes into existence by consent alone remains uncertain.

Nicholas I (pope 858-867) addressed himself to the question of "what makes marriage" in his letter to Bogoris, Prince of the Bulgarians. He stated authoritatively that the consent of the parties is required and is enough to bring an authentic marriage into existence. Without consent, even if sexual intercourse has taken place, there cannot be a marriage. He quoted Chrysostom: "Marriage is not brought into existence by intercourse but by consent," *matrimonium non facit coitus sed voluntas.* Thus, Nicholas I articulated the principle that consent made marriage; he was the first pope to do so. (*See* D-SCH 643)

The dispute, however, continued into the eleventh and twelfth centuries, and there was no uniformity in resolving practical cases. Two divergent opinions were defended and represented by two schools: they are usually referred to as the school of Paris and that of Bologna.

* The Parisian school was of the opinion that marriage was brought into existence by consent, not by sexual intercourse. An outstanding doctor of this school was *Ivo of Chartres (1040-1116),* another *Hugh of St. Victor (1098-1141).* Hugh in particular, intending to uphold the opinion that Mary and Joseph were truly married, stated unequivocally that marriage was brought into existence by the consent of the parties, given freely, according to the law, and intended to take effect immediately. The object of this consent, for Hugh, was mutual love and help, not the procreation of children. Thus, he could conclude that Mary and Joseph were truly married. But his doctrine had broader implications: the existence of a marriage depended on consent and consent alone. He affirmed also that marriage was not only a holy thing but had a sanctifying power — he anticipated the classification of marriage among the sacraments.

Unfortunately, his doctrine concerning the object of the marital covenant was lost on succeeding generations and was not recovered until Vatican Council II.

* The Bolognese school held that consent alone was not enough for marriage to come into existence; sexual intercourse between the spouses was necessary as well. *Gratian*, a Camaldolese monk from Bologna, about whom little is known but whose work under the title *Decretum*, or *Concordance of Discordant Canons (composed around 1140)*, became the best known collection of canon law in the middle ages and beyond, defended this theory. He taught that marriage became perfect and indissoluble when it was consummated. Consenting could only initiate a marriage, and that in a fragile way: if a union formed by consent alone was superseded by another one that was consummated, the first one was canceled out.

To the two schools of opinion corresponded two ways of handling marriage cases in France and Italy.

Alexander III (pope 1159-1181) was the one who "canonized" the consent theory. Before his election to the papacy, he belonged to the Bolognese school. But as pope he modified his views and held that once consent was given, there was marriage. The bond was firm to the point that the parties themselves could not dissolve it anymore (this has become known as "intrinsic indissolubility"). After the marriage had been consummated, it could not be dissolved at all ("extrinsic indissolubility") — to be understood, by any human power. He did not decide the subtle question whether or not the church may have some radical power to touch even such marriages. With the decision of Alexander III, the main elements of modern canon law were in place. *Innocent III (pope 1185-1216)* confirmed the same doctrine, and so did *Gregory IX (pope 1227-1241)* by including the relevant documents into his official collection of decretal letters.

A legal model for the institution: marriage as contract; twelfth century.

The new and relatively sophisticated developments demanded a better defined and uniformly acceptable legal framework through which marriage cases could be handled. The church was already in possession of full and exclusive jurisdiction over marriages; it was also developing complex theories about its "essence," yet it did not have a good legal "instrument" that the newly developing judicial system needed. To find it, the canon lawyers turned to Roman law, recently rediscovered in the West. They found the model they were looking for in the law of contracts.

In ancient Rome, the law of marriage was part of the law of persons because for the Romans marriage was a fact that determined the status of a person in their society. If a man and a woman were living together with marital affection, *affectu maritali*, and if they were legally capable of being married, they were married in the eyes of the law. The Romans did not think of marriage as a contract since the marital state did not generate legally actionable obligations. This is not to say that there were no legal effects to marriage; there were, but not by way of obligations, which arose from contracts and delicts only. For a long time, Christians, too, had the same understanding of marriage: it was a state of life. They did not think of it as a contract.

Classical Roman law admitted different types of contract. The one that was chosen as the model on which the marital agreement could be patterned, was the consensual type. They came into existence by consent alone, without any prescribed formality. So did marriage. But they had a well determined internal structure of rights and duties. So had marriage. Thus, the model was eminently suitable to handle marriage cases.

There was a new expansion of horizon, now with the help of law. The institution of marriage was seen as a contract, surrounded by all kinds of legal relations and explainable in juridical categories.

The recovery of the Greek philosophy and the theological speculations of the twelfth and thirteenth centuries: what is marriage?

Aristotle's thought penetrated into the medieval world through the translation of his works, mainly by the efforts of Islamic philosophers; his impact on the mind of Christian theologians was immense. He gave them a broader vision of the universe: he helped them to understand and explain all beings — created and uncreated. His ideas appeared to blend well with their traditions. Out of this meeting of philosophical insights and evangelical beliefs new theological systems arose; they were complex, carefully built and enduring, not unlike the medieval cathedrals. After all, the same type of mind created them both. From the union of reason and faith, a new harmony emerged.

One of the foundational ideas of Aristotle was that in this universe all things were good, be they spiritual and material. Besides, there was a beautiful order in the universe; everything existed for a purpose. To this the theologians (in the process of being liberated from the Augustinian ideas) added that the whole creation and everything in it mirrored the image of God and participated in his perfection. There was a new horizon for a fresh understanding of marriage.

Human nature, too, was good. Although it has been wounded by sin, it has not become radically corrupt. The human soul was not an unwilling prisoner in the body, but the two together formed a harmonious union, each contributing to the unique beauty and perfection of the human person.

In this perception, sexuality could not be wrong either; it belonged to human nature that was essentially good. Its use was meritorious provided it was done according to the dictates of the right reason and the precepts of faith.

The belief in the ordered structure of the universe led the theologians, however, to search for a hierarchical structure everywhere, which they did not fail to find. So, although nothing in this visible universe equalled the dignity of human persons, there was no perfect equality among them. Man was an image of God directly, woman indirectly, through man. Hence, immortal as they both were through the grace of Christ, the man held a subtly superior position to the woman.

In theory, at least, all blemish had been removed from marriage. It took its rightful place among the seven sacraments. This new and strong articulation of its sanctity was also a rejection of the heresy of the *Cathari* and *Albigenses*. They preached a revived form of Manicheism that claimed that the "sensible" world was the creation of the devil, therefore it was intrinsically evil. Marriage, being an institution of this sensible world, could not be a way of life for spiritual persons. Such attacks, by prompting more reflections, contributed indirectly to a healthy development of the Catholic doctrine.

Parallel with the progress in the understanding of the sacramentality of marriage, there was also an advancement in the perception of its indissolubility; in the mind of the theologians the two were closely connected. Marriage was a sacrament, they said, because it contained the mystery of Christ and the church; that is, it was a symbol of that relationship. Since that relationship could not be broken ever, the marriage bond could not be dissolved either.

In all such considerations the primary issue was more the nature of the institution than the spiritual welfare of Christian persons; a shift from the approach of the authors of the New Testament and of the writers of the patristic age. It was a new level of abstraction that generated its own categories, inspired by Roman legal science and Greek philosophy.

Here are some of the outstanding contributors to these developments:

Anselm of Canterbury (c. 1034-1109) was the first to counter Augustine's theory of sin and grace, and thus to rehabilitate human sexuality. For Anselm, the original sin did not consist in concupiscence, transmitted and inherited through the act of human generation, but in the absence of God's sanctifying grace. Thus, he lifted marriage out of the shadow of sin.

Peter Lombard (1095-1160) was probably the first to formulate the doctrine of the seven sacraments; marriage was one of them. They were not only the signs of a specific grace granted but also the mysterious instruments of that grace. Thus, marriage, too, was a carrier of grace.

Once the theological community accepted that marriage was a sacrament, the discussions centered on identifying its internal structure: the matter and the form that constituted its substance, the person of the minister, and so forth — a discussion that continued for centuries. Those who claimed (a minority) that the form was in the blessing, held also that a second marriage after the death of the first partner was not a sacrament because the ceremony did not allow a second nuptial blessing. The interesting point is that they allowed that a non-sacramental valid marriage could exist among the baptized. Their opinion did not prevail.

Walter of Mortagne, Bishop of Laon (c. 1090-1174) defended the position that the sacramental marriage, consummated or not, could not be dissolved by the church. In his argumentation he followed the general line that many others accepted: marriage is a sacrament because it is the sign of Christ's union with the church; that union cannot be broken, hence the sacrament of marriage cannot be broken either. All other marriages that are non-sacramental could be dissolved. Walter saw the symbolism as already present in a merely soleminized marriage.

Thomas Aquinas (c. 1225-1274), who so fully appropriated the Aristotelian world view, did not hesitate to declare that sexuality in itself was good; evil could be only in its inordinate use. Hence, marriage itself was entirely good and the act of generation was not sinful, Augustine's authority notwithstanding. He saw the ends of the institution of marriage in strict hierarchical order: the propagation of the human race first, a remedy for concupiscence afterwards; with not much importance given to mutual love. He hesitated however to call marriage a contract; the new legal theories have not fully conquered the theological minds as yet.

But Thomas made one more lasting contribution: he explained the consent theory in terms of Aristotle's metaphysical psychology. The highly pragmatic and ill-defined concept of the Romans underwent a refinement. Consent was defined as an internal act of one of the spiritual faculties of the of the soul, namely of the will, under the guidance of another faculty, the intelligence. For Thomas, neither of the two faculties was autonomous; they mutually supported and completed each other; the mind led the will and the will prompted the mind.

This delicately structured theory of Aristotle and Aquinas, however, was less than well understood by some theologians and lawyers of later generations who were responsible for the subsequent development of the doctrine and law of matrimonial consent. They granted so much autonomy to the will that its dependence on the mind became minimal, if not nominal.

Nonetheless, Greek philosophy helped the Christian theologians to a much broader vision than they ever had before. They recovered a scriptural understanding of marriage: they saw it as a sacred alliance between a man and woman in a thoroughly good universe created by God. The articulation of their insights and discoveries was immensely helped by the abundance of philosophical categories found in the works of Aristotle.

The dialectics of the sixteenth century: The Council of Trent versus The Reformers

Martin Luther (1483-1546) and John Calvin (1509-1564) were the two leading theologians on the side of the Reformers. Their views concerning marriage flowed from their understanding of the original sin and its consequences. They saw human nature as God's creation but fallen into corruption by sin; human beings were saved not by any internal transformation but by the attribution of the merits of Christ. Sexuality, being part of this corrupt nature, was in constant need of being properly disciplined.

They taught that marriage was a human institution because it existed before the coming of Christianity, and it continued to exist among non-Christians. It followed, for them, that it could not be a sacrament of the New Covenant. The marriages of the patriarchs were no less holy than the marriages of the Christians.

The scholastic teaching that marriage signified and conferred grace had no foundation in the scriptures. Yet, a marital union lived with faith in God's justifying power could be indeed a "remedy of concupiscence" and a sign of God's favor.

Precisely because marriage was, in their view, a merely human institution, it had to be under civil jurisdiction. This principle was taken strictly by Calvin, less so by Luther, who admitted that when matters of conscience are involved civil and ecclesiastical "commissions" could act jointly.

Both stressed "in principle" the indissolubility of marriage, but both held that through adultery the bond could be dissolved. Luther went even further: the supreme judge in a case of dissolution was exclusively the conscience of the party involved. His followers however modified this rule by teaching that whenever a civil tribunal found grounds for the dissolution of a marriage, the parties were entitled to follow its decision.

The Reformers' position was certainly a radical change in horizon; marriage was viewed as a merely secular reality, and it was explained in humanistic categories. Behind this exposition, there was also a deeply pessimistic theory concerning our lapsed human nature.

The discussions at the Council of Trent on marriage started in Bologna in 1547, and were concluded at Trent in 1563, with a decree that substantially defended the positions established by theologians and canonists over so many centuries. Until Vatican Council II it was the only major document on the sacrament of marriage by an ecumenical council; its importance for the development of doctrine and discipline can hardly be exaggerated. It is also a complex document; behind the obvious meaning of its statements there are nuances that can be known from the circumstances of the debates only. The decree must be read as a dialectical response to the Reformers' assertions; to take it out of that context is to falsify it. While it contains much of the traditional Catholic doctrine concerning marriage, it includes also historically conditioned pronouncements and decisions. To separate the two is not an easy task; but enough work has already been done by scholars, such as Fransen and Lennerz, to make one cautious in interpreting the texts.

The decree on marriage states unequivocally that marriage belongs to the order of the sacred in the strictest sense, it is one of the seven sacraments; it signifies and confers grace (D-SCH 1801). It is a union between one man and one woman; polygamy is against divine law (1802). The church has the power to establish diriment impediments (1803, 1804).

Further, marriage cannot be dissolved by the partners for reasons of heresy, cruelty or separation (1806), although a sacramental marriage, provided it was not consummated, can be dissolved by solemn religious profession (1806, 1807).

The issue of indissolubility caused some peculiar difficulties. The fundamental assumption of the Fathers was that the Council was not called to condemn those Catholics and the "Greeks" who held that in some special circumstances even a consummated sacramental marriage could be dissolved, but it was called to uphold the truth of Catholic beliefs against the Reformers. To achieve that end, after long debates they agreed on a somewhat ambivalent "canon" on indissolubility; it is canon 7 on the sacrament of matrimony.

If anyone says that the church is in error for having taught and for currently teaching, according to the evangelical and apostolic doctrine (cf. Mk 10; 1 Cor 7),

that the bond of marriage cannot be dissolved because of the adultery of the other spouse;

and that neither of the two, not even the innocent one who has given no cause for adultery, can contract another marriage during the lifetime of the other;

and that the husband who dismisses an adulterous wife and marries again, and the wife who dismisses an adulterous husband and marries again are both guilty of adultery,

anathema sit. (1807)

For the correct interpretation of this text, the following factors must be taken into consideration:

(1) The declared intention of the Council Fathers, articulated in the course of the debates:

— the decree should be more than a mere disciplinary provision but less than a dogmatic definition;

— the decree should not say explicitly that indissolubility is revealed doctrine; but it should affirm that the origin of this doctrine is in divine revelation;

— the decree should not say that indissolubility was always taught by the church but it should state that the present understanding and practice of it is part of the living tradition of the church.

Thus, the Greeks were not condemned since they were not saying that the Latins were in error by being faithful to their own tradition; the Reformers were condemned because they did say that the church was in error concerning this matter.

(2) The dialectical nature of the document; it is an answer to the Reformers' claim that a marriage can be dissolved for reason of adultery, and, as Luther stressed it, by the parties themselves, following the dictate of their own conscience.

Thus, canon seven is not answering the more abstract question, whether or not the church has the radical power to dissolve such marriages. It does say however that the parties cannot dissolve the marriage.

(3) The meaning of the concluding anathema, which was not used in a uniform sense throughout the documents of the Council. At times the Council used it to condemn those who professed heretical doctrines, at other times, to condemn those who by their preaching and teaching disturbed the peace of the community.

Thus, from the use of the *anathema* it is illegitimate to conclude to a dogmatic definition, unless there is other evidence to prove that such is the case.

Further, in order to combat clandestinity, the Council, through its Decree *Tametsi* (D-SCH 1813-1816), imposed a compulsory "canonical form" on all marriages: for validity they had to be contracted in the presence of the parish priest, *parochus,* or of an otherwise authorized priest. The very idea of adding a "canonical form" to the theological structure of a sacrament was a new departure; it has never been done before — or after. It was the introduction of a new category in sacramental theology. In all probability, the new law appeared simple enough to the Council Fathers, its implementation, however, proved anything but simple.

The overall achievement of the Council of Trent was not so much in new insights as in the articulation and systematic exposition of the doctrine, and to some extent discipline, that developed in the Middle Ages and by and large was held and followed peacefully until the Reformation.

Disputes concerning the contract and the sacrament: from the sixteenth century onward.

Another clarification that took place from the sixteenth to the nineteenth centuries concerned the relationship of the contract to the sacrament. This process, too, was a dialectical one, partly initiated by some theologians, partly by some "political thinkers," both groups claiming, for very different reasons, that the marital contract could be separated from the sacrament.

Melchior Cano (1509-1560), who distinguished himself at the Council of Trent as well, was a representative figure for the theological theory. He held that the matter of the sacrament was the consent of the parties; the blessing of the priest was the form. If a couple contracted without the blessing, they were married but without the benefit of the sacrament. There was a valid marriage, but no valid sacrament.

Cano's opinion gained little support among the theologians. As they continued to debate the "causes" of the sacrament of marriage, they placed the role of the priest outside of its structure: his specific role was to witness the agrement, no more. The ministers were the parties themselves. Official documents, too, were careful to speak of the priest whose presence was required for validity after Trent, as a "qualified witness."

The so-called Royalists were politically interested thinkers in France; their movement began in the seventeenth century; their ranks included lawyers and theologians. Their real aim was to restrict the church's power over marriages. To achieve that, they invoked a seemingly clear and distinct principle: the church had jurisdiction in sacred matters, the state in secular matters. In marriage, the sacrament is sacred, hence it must remain under the power of the church; the contract is secular, hence must be brought under the jurisdiction of the state.

The church reacted by condemnations. *Pius VI (pope 1775-1799)* vindicated the exclusive jurisdiction of the church over the marriages of Christians (D-SCH 2598). *Pius IX (pope 1846-1878)* condemned the opinion that the contract could be separated from the sacrament (D-SCH 2966). This point of doctrine was later incorporated into the Code of Canon Law, old and new.

Problems, however, remain: the sacrament is clearly an added dimension to the contract, hence the two cannot be fully identical. Moreover, when a baptized person marries a non-baptized one, the official position of the church is that they truly contract without the benefit of the sacrament, hence, in that case at least, a Christian can contract without the benefit of the sacrament.

The first Code of Canon Law, 1917: emphasis on the institution

The main architect of the law of marriage in the first Code was *Pietro Gasparri (1852—1934)*. He inherited the qualities of the classical Roman lawyers; his legal works are marked with clarity, conciseness and balance. His theological horizon, however, was rather narrow. His main concern was to uphold and to protect the institution of marriage. Hence, the Code drafted under his direction paid little attention to the legitimate desires and needs of individual persons. It stressed throughout the propagation of children as the primary end of the institution; it made the acts apt for the generation of the offspring the principal object of the contract. As long as this institutional end could be achieved, it made virtually no concession to personal dispositions and mistakes, not even when they were induced by wilful deception. In mixed marriages the conscience of the non-Catholic could not be taken into account. This attitude extended into the field of judicial procedures: individual persons often had to wait for years before ecclesiastical courts were ready to pronounce a judgment.

Vatican Council II, 1962-65: return to the sources

Several documents are relevant for the theology and law of marriage. The foundations for a new approach were laid in the Dogmatic Constitution on the Church, *Lumen gentium*, which proclaimed the overriding dignity of the People of God due to God's mysterious election (Chapter 2), and stated that all were called to holiness (5). Married persons, therefore, have the same dignity as anyone else; they are called to the same degree of sanctity as everybody else.

The issue of marriage was taken up in the Pastoral Constitution on the Church in the Modern World, *Gaudium et spes*, which recovered the biblical pattern: first, God has given a mate to man to relieve his solitude, then procreation followed. This brought an end to the classical presentation of the ends of marriage. There was no word about a hierarchy of ends, but mutual love was mentioned in the first place; the Augustinian theory that haunted the church for so long had been put to rest officially and for good. The equality of man and woman was affirmed in unmistakable terms.

The Decree on Ecumenism, *Unitatis redintegratio*, acknowledged the work of the Spirit in non-Catholic Christian churches and ecclesial communities; it followed that the marriage of a Catholic to a Christian of another denomination need not be a dangerous source of "perversion"; it could be a marriage "in the Lord."

The Declaration on Religious Freedom, *Dignitatis humanae*, stressed the right of all human persons to follow the light of their own conscience and their right to profess publicly their religious convictions. It followed that the rules for the promises concerning the education of children born from a mixed marriage had to be revised.

The picture would not be complete, however, without mentioning another document: the Dogmatic Constitution on Divine Revelation, *Dei verbum*. It affirmed and explained the historical nature of God's revelation. It followed that marriage as a saving mystery can be understood only as embedded in human history, as a permanent gift from God, unfolding in our midst.

It took nearly twenty years for the church to translate some of the insights of the Council into practical norms.

The Second Code of Canon Law, 1983:
more emphasis on the persons

The new Code has retained the strongly institutional orientation of the old one but the insights of the Council concerning the dignity and rights of individual persons have made substantial inroads into the old structures. The result is a somewhat uneasy coexistence of two diverging trends, one upholding the primacy of the institution, the other the importance of human persons. Also, the understanding of marriage appears now in a broad religious context through the doctrine of the covenant, yet the highly juridical language of the contract is still present in many traditionally formulated canons. The difficulties that have surfaced in recent years reflect this conflict: the increased number of declarations of nullity shows a concern for the welfare of individual persons; the stricter control of the courts and the restrictions imposed on their operation display a preoccupation with the institution. As always, we shall have the correct solution when the two seemingly conflicting trends meet in peaceful harmony; when concordance is achieved between the apparently discordant purposes.

Be that as it may, through the theological insights of Vatican Council II, we are now in possession of a horizon that has all the breadth and length, all the height and depth that we can wish for. Within its parameters, however, the specific legal categories and concepts that we have inherited, and many of which served us well, ought to be looked at, examined, and evaluated for future use. To some extent this has already been done through the revision of the Code, but the process has not been concluded.

As the church lives, God's revelation will continue to unfold.

PRINCIPLES OF INTERPRETATION

There are many principles of interpretation and a good number of them are used in this book. Three major ones, however, play a dominant role in the explanation of the canons. They are:

(1) The principle of literary form: To find the meaning of a canon its literary form must be taken into account.

(2) The principle of value: To appreciate a law, the value that it intends to uphold must be known.

(3) The hermeneutical principle of pastoral orientation: it is best expressed in a symbol which is the biblical image of the good shepherd.

In these principles, we have important clues for the interpretation of the canons:
— the literary form is the clue for the understanding of the *meaning* of a norm;
— the value (or the lack of it) behind a norm is the clue for determining the vital strength (or internal weakness) of the law;
— the pastoral context of the law offers clues for judicious application of an abstract norm in concrete situations.
Let us explain these principles further, one by one.

(1) Literary forms.

The Code of Canon Law carries the message of the legislator to his subjects. To understand this message correctly, the subjects should be aware that they have in hand a document that contains a collection of small literary pieces of different types. To find the specific meaning of a canon, its literary form must be first determined.[1]

Here are the principal literary forms, found in the Code in general, and in the chapters on marriage in particular:

*Statements of Catholic belief. They are part of our creed, even if they are not inserted into it. To find their meaning, the interpreter must turn to theology and must use its sources and methodology. To handle them as if they were juridical norms could lead to incorrect conclusions. The assertion in canon 1055 § 1 that marriage is a sacrament is such a statement of belief.

*Theological opinions. They are theological affirmations but they do not have behind them the authority of the believing church, only that of a theological school. They must be critically evaluated according to ordinary theological criteria; they must not be taken for law. Some of them may be representing a high point in the development of doctrine, but as yet, they all fall short of being part of our profession of faith. The doctrine concerning the inseparability of the contract and the sacrament in canon 1055§ 2 belongs to this category.

*Metaphysical theories. They represent the conclusions of philosophers; their authority is as great as the weight of the reasoning behind them. While a legal system can use the insights of philosophers, it cannot canonize any philosophical principle because metaphysical truth exists independently from any law or custom. All such theories must be explained and judged by the usual philosophical criteria.

---

[1]It should not be surprising that the canons in the same Code can be of different literary forms. Fransen has shown that such differentiations exist among the canons of an ecumenical council; they exist even among the canons on the very same topics, such as the canons of Trent on marriage; and without taking them into account a false meaning can be (and has been!) imposed on them. If that happens with the documents of the great councils, how much more it is likely to happen with our collection of canons in a code! (*See* in Bibliography: Fransen.)

The theory that the Code is relying on to explain the nature and operation of the matrimonial consent is a theory taken from Aristotelian-Thomistic philosophy; cf. canon 1057§2 which asserts that consent is an act of the will; also, several other canons in Chapter Four on Consent.

*Findings of empirical sciences. The findings of scientific research are independent of any legislation. In order to understand and judge human behavior, the law must seek help from human sciences, especially from anthropology, sociology, psychology, and so forth. This means that the sense of some canons cannot be ascertained unless the findings of the relevant sciences are taken into account; in fact, some canons simply refer the interpreter to valid scientific conclusions. In canon 1095 the meaning of "lack of sufficient use of reason," "lack of discretion of judgment" and "incapacity to assume marital obligations" certainly cannot be determined by law alone; the interpretation of that canon must include the very best and most recent findings of the science of psychology and psychiatry.

*Exhortations. This category is more important than it looks. At times the legislator expresses a desire, or proposes an ideal, without wanting to create an enforceable legal duty. If such an intention is misunderstood, the interpreter will transform an encouragement into a binding, and possibly sanctioned, obligation. Several canons in Chapter One on Preparation for Marriage fall into this category, for instance canon 1065 on the reception of the sacraments of confirmation, penance and eucharist. The meaning of such canons is not that the issue is not important; it can be very important in the realm of values, but that the actions proposed should be left to pastoral care and personal generosity.

*Creation of right-and-duty situations. The canons which create rights and impose duties in the realm of the law are the true legislative pieces in the Code. Such canons must be understood in the context of the whole legal tradition of the church; their meaning must be determined through strict juridical methodology. An obvious example would be canon 1108 imposing the canonical form; or any of the canons defining an impediment in Chapter Three.

The objection has been raised against this theory of literary forms that it destroys the juridical character of the Code, which is a unified, integrated and indivisible document, promulgated with the same authority, having the same binding force throughout, even if at different degrees.

But the objection does not hold; if it is accepted it would lead to patently absurd consequences. Statements of belief incorporated in the Code could have different meanings in dogma and in law; theological opinions, philosophical theories and scientific findings would not have to be judged on the basis of the evidence and criteria proper to each but on the authoritative pronouncement of the legislator. Exhortations would swell the body of laws. There would be an overall tendency toward legalism.

The objection takes for its model and ideal a civil code, which is always a collection of strict legal norms. But as the Christian community differs from a civic society, so must our Code differ from a civil code.

(2) Values.

To understand the role of values in the life of the church, and in particular in the *legal* life of the church, it might be helpful to reflect on the role of values in the life of human persons.

Human persons are never perfect; for them to live is to grow and to develop. This process requires an on-going search for whatever can sustain life and enrich it, physically, emotionally, intellectually and spiritually. Of course, not everything that looks good contributes to the genuine welfare of human persons. They must seek out authentic values, and when they find them, they must transcend themselves by actively reaching out for them.

Values exist independently from the searcher; they must be discovered. They are embedded in the concrete universe. They can be appropriated only through a slow and exacting process of understanding them, deciding to reach out for them, and by taking active steps to obtain them. But once authentic values are appropriated, they enrich those who have accepted them, and thus human persons grow and develop.

Brief and summary as this description is, it can serve as an analogy to understand how the church grows and develops through the appropriation of values.

No human community is ever perfect; not even the community of faith, hope and love that is the Christian church. It must progress in the understanding of the evangelical message (cf. Jo 16:13); it must fulfill in deeds the evangelical mandate. The church, as it is, must continuously search for values that can enrich the community and can give growth to its members.

In the life of the church, too, there is an on-going movement, similar to the process of development in the life of an individual person. The church, too, needs to discover values that can enrich the community and its members; it must make decisions to appropriate those values, and must actively reach out for them.

The making of the laws is part of this process. First, the legislator comes to the discovery of a value that could benefit the community. Then, he formulates a "norm of action" for obtaining it. Finally, the community acts on the norm, and the value is appropriated. By way of example: the Council of Trent had come to appreciate the value of the ecclesial celebration of a marriage — more than any legislator ever did before. Out of this "knowledge" a decision was born, and a norm of action was formulated in the Decree *Tametsi.* Slowly and gradually (as it happened for historical reasons) the community began to act on the norm. Eventually, the value that a public ecclesiastical celebration represents, has been fully appropriated.

It is not always necessary to discover new values; a legislative decision and action may concern values which were known for a long time but were not legislated about. The value of life-long fidelity in marriage was well known before the first positive laws were enacted to enforce indissolubility.

The closer a legal system is bound up with the objective and authentic system of values, the healthier it is. Laws have no life in themselves; they are good, fitting and beneficial as far as they uphold a value, or to put it in a different way, as far as through them the community is able to learn about a value, reach out for it, and appropriate it through action.[2]

---

[2]Ideally, a legal system should be fully bound to, and united with, a value system. Equally ideally, both the legislator and subject should be aware of this connection.

Every legal rule is conceived in the mind; by its very nature it is an abstraction. Authentic values exist independently from our norms; we have to discover and respect them. When an abstract norm of action and a concrete value find each other, there is harmony; there is good and sensible legislation; there will be order, peace and prosperity. The reason why political utopias fail is because a regime tries to enforce a set of ideologically inspired norms which do not correspond to objective values.

When both the legislator and the subjects are aware of the values the laws intend

It follows that the science and art of interpretation must include the evaluation of the laws as well. It makes a great difference for the very meaning of the law, if it supports a much needed value for the community, or it covers none because the value for which originally it was enacted has lost its significance. Many rules of the old Code have been discarded precisely because they have become empty formalities, even if once they were in the service of true values.

Therefore, part of the task of the interpreter is to determine the values which the norms are upholding, protecting and promoting. Once a norm is detached from the world of values, it has really no right to exist; the church always rejected nominalism.

The clue to the sound development of the law is precisely in the good knowledge of the system of values behind it which can tell us what rules should be kept, what norms should be dropped, how some of the structures and procedures could be improved upon. In recent centuries, one reason why canon law was slow to develop and provide for the new needs of the church was certainly in the fact that its commentators rarely ventured into the realm of values. Outside of it, however, there are no criteria for evaluating the law. Part of the ministry of the interpreter is to provide the legislator with a critically correct and balanced report on the relationship of the abstract legal norms to the concrete world of values.

(3) Pastoral orientation.

Among the principles that governed the revision of the first Code, we find these two:

> While unique in its evangelical and pastoral purpose, the Code must retain its juridic quality...
>
> Pastoral care should be the hallmark of the Code...
> (Cf. COM-USA, p. 6)

to support, there is an easy communication between the two. The subjects can receive the law with intelligence and freedom; mere obedience is transformed into a pursuit of values.

In studying the connection between a system of laws and the values that it intends to promote, we should keep in mind also that some values are permanent, some are historically conditioned. A legal system may lose its effectiveness if it tries to uphold values that have lost their significance.

These two principles point to the complex character of the Code. It has an overall juridic character but its purpose and its hallmark throughout should be pastoral. No civil Code can ever be described in this way.

At this point we are not concerned with the juridic quality; attention to the right-and-duty situations created by the canons can take care of that. We are interested in the *pastoral character* which, if it is not to remain an empty slogan, must become a guiding principle in the interpretation and application of the norms. Therefore the question is, what is pastoral?

It would be a mistake to seek clarification through a conceptual definition. We are dealing with a term that evokes a symbolic image; its meaning, or its message should be sought through that image.

"Pastoral" speaks of the biblical image of the shepherd and the sheep. Yahweh was the shepherd of Israel. Jesus presented himself as the good shepherd. He commissioned Peter to be shepherd to his flock. Every time this image of the shepherd and his flock comes up in the Bible, it signifies a total dedication to the welfare of the flock, solicitude for every single sheep, especially for the ones which may have gone astray; an excess of love in the heart of the shepherd to the point that he is willing to lay down his life for the sake of those who have been entrusted to his care. A hireling, possibly faithful to his duties, would never do that. (Cf. Jo 10:7-15) There is the difference between the biblically pastoral and the strictly legal approach to the welfare of the flock. While the symbol speaks eloquently, concepts could not express it adequately.

To be "pastoral" means to be inspired by the image of the good shepherd. The whole Code has a pastoral orientation in the sense that it is a part of the overall care of the church for the faithful; it supports an operation that transcends the laws, an operation that ought to be dominated by tender love for all, solicitude for the lost ones, and unselfish dedication to an excess. This context is what imposes and imprints the pastoral character on the Code; outside this context the Code has no scope. In it, it plays a humble role. Its purpose is to promote justice in a community that ought to be ruled by charity. There is no contradiction in this requirement: authentic justice is nothing else than the minimum of charity.

For the Code to be pastoral means also to point to higher demands than the law can define. It is to give priority to charity in the care for the community. Whatever can be achieved without recurring to legal means, should be so achieved.

The hermeneutical principle of pastoral orientation points also toward the legitimate use of *epieikeia* (epikeia) and equity; also, as far as our Latin tradition presently permits it, of *oikonomia* (economy) — so well known to our brethren of the Eastern churches.[3] Further, it implies that when doubt exists whether a "pastoral" or legal approach is correct, the former one should be chosen. Through such practical applications the pastoral orientation of the Code, and of every canon in it, can become a living reality.

The objection can be raised that such a general principle is too vague and can confuse both the shepherds and the flock. The answer is that the church has learned well from its Founder how to live by symbols and images; there are not many precise definitions in the New Testament. We can safely continue with the same method — not excluding others whenever so warranted.

In the chapters that follow, before we comment on the canons, we shall explicitly refer to their literary forms and the values they intend to uphold. In the actual exegesis of the canons, we tried not to forget ever the hermeneutical principle of "pastoral orientation," even if we do not make frequent mention of it.

[3]At the root of *oikonomia* is the belief that the church possesses an intuitive capacity to discover what is right even if its theologians are unable to provide a fully satisfactory explanation for it. Probably for this reason, the Eastern church sees it as an exercise of the episcopal power; it comes from a sacrament. We, Latins, acknowledge that a similar intuitive power operates in an ecumenical council; the authority of a doctrinal decision comes from the *consensus* of the participants, not from the arguments they used in their debates. Vatican Council II speaks also of the universal people of God as having a "supernatural sense of faith" that has an "unerring quality," — clearly an intuitive capacity. In a broader sense, *oikonomia* is our common inheritance; if we, Latins, acknowledge its valid use in great issues (although not under that name), it should be possible to extend it to smaller ones.

INTRODUCTORY CANONS
ON MARRIAGE IN GENERAL
1055 — 1062

This introductory chapter lays a broad doctrinal and terminological foundation for the detailed norms that follow in the next ten distinct chapters.

Transitions from the old Code to the new Code: *From a strictly legal approach to a broadly theological presentation.* CIC/17 focused narrowly on the contractual aspect of marriage and defined the object of the contract as the mutual giving and accepting of rights and duties concerning the performance of potentially generative acts. CIC/83 begins with the much broader theological concept of covenant, without excluding the contractual aspect, and defines the object of the covenant as the marriage itself with all that such a state of life can comprehend.

The old law insisted on classifying the ends of *marriage as an institution* into a primary one: the procreation of children, and into a secondary one: mutual help and remedy of concupiscence, giving overwhelming importance to the former and much lesser significance to the latter. The new law retains the doctrine of the ends; it could not have done otherwise since the institution itself *must* have a purpose. But the mutual help and the procreation of children are presented as joint ends, neither of them enjoying a superiority over the other.[1]

This new approach is a shift to broader horizons; the whole body of the law of marriage has been placed into an expanded framework. The consequences of such "transposition" are far reaching and to a large extent still to be explored, but it is already clear that the new environment has its impact on old concepts; some ancient definitions do not fit well any more, and some new ones are emerging. The promulgation of the new Code is the conclusion of a stage in an evolutionary process, it is also the beginning of another.[2]

Because the church has now firmly placed the law into a theological context, the governing principles for the interpretation of the canons must be taken from appropriate theological sources, in particular from the chapter on "The Promotion of the Dignity of Marriage and the Family" in the Pastoral Constitution on the Church in the Modern World, *Gaudium et spes* (47-52).

Within the new theological framework, however, many traditional legal elements have been kept. Inevitably, there is a lack of harmony and cohesion; at times the new and the old coexist in an uneasy and precarious balance. For instance, after the initial emphasis on marriage as a covenant, the canons revert to the contractual terminology; no less than forty times they speak of the marital contract or of contracting marriage! Or, the canons display an extraordinary openness to modern psychological insights and discoveries (cf. canon

---

[1]The "remedy of concupiscence" does not appear in the new law at all.

In fairness to our traditions, it should be pointed out that this expression did not always signify "a legitimate outlet for sexuality" as it often appeared in canon law manuals; in the writings of the best of scholastic doctors it carried a deeper meaning: for them concupiscence was an internal drive that may carry a person away from God (not unlike *sarx* for Paul), and because marriage was a sacrament, it was also a "remedy of concupiscence"; it brought God's healing and strengthening grace — as did the other sacraments. *See* e.g. *Concupiscence*, DTC, 4:121.

[2]In Lonergan's philosophy of development we could speak of the opening up of new horizons; in Kuhn's explanation of progress of the discovery of new parameters. In either case the idea is a similar one: a radical change in the understanding of some known facts comes through a new and broader framework into which they are transposed. This is how the human mind is able to comprehend old realities anew, whether it operates in the field of natural sciences or in the field of humanities.

1095) but at the same time they use medieval metaphysical categories to evaluate the operation of the human spirit (cf. the canons on consent). The law still states with reasonable clarity whatever is required for the fulfillment of the old primary end, namely the procreation of children, but it remains reticent and rather unhelpful in determining what is necessary to fulfill the old secondary end, namely mutual help or *consortium*.[3]

Such a state of things, however, is a normal state whenever an institution is being shaped by evolutionary forces; it displays conflicting trends. When this happens, there is no other correct interpretation than the one that faithfully reports on such trends, explains their origins and describes their interplay in the body of laws.

Literary forms: *There is a great variety of literary forms in this chapter.* There are dogmatic affirmations (marriage is a sacrament: 1055 § 1, the church has power to regulate its administration: 1059), there are theological statements in need of further distinctions (the contract cannot exist without being a sacrament: 1055 § 2), there are philosophical statements in need of refinement (unity and indissolubility are the essential properties of every marriage: 1056); all, of course, have significant legal implications. There is a canon proclaiming a fundamental right (the right to marry: 1058), another stating an overriding procedural principle (marriage has the favor of the law: 1060), there are others defining the juridical meaning of certain terms (ratum, consummatum, etc. 1061). It cannot be stressed enough that the determination of the literary form of a canon, or of a clause in a canon, is of paramount importance, because the full and correct meaning of the text cannot be determined unless it is first restored into the environment in which it was conceived.

The values the canons in this chapter intend to uphold and to protect are the fundamental values of marriage, both natural and Christian. The two traditions, that of natural philosophy and that of Christian theology, are intertwined in the canons; at one point they

---

[3]On the difficulty of expressing the meaning of *consortium* in legal terms, *see* the study by David E. Fellhauer, "The *Consortium totius vitae* as a Juridical Element of Marriage," in *Studia Canonica*, 13 (1979), pp. 3-171.

speak of the naturally ordered ends of marriage and its essential properties, at another of its sacramental nature. The reader has to be attentive to such distinctions; the texts do not explicate them. As we shall see later, no matter how valuable a natural marriage may be, it can be sacrificed (or abandoned) for the sake of religion (e.g. privilege of the faith), while the bond of a sacramental marriage (once consummated) is so precious that it cannot be broken by any process of law. Clearly, there are values in a Christian marriage that cannot be found in a natural one. The Code is upholding them all: all marriages have the favor of the law; yet it acknowledges also that there is a special strength in the sacrament, and thus canon law favors a sacramental marriage even more.

Right from the beginning it is stated that there is no value in the marriage covenant unless it is the fruit of the responsible decision of the parties within an ecclesial context. Thus, the values of any marriage exist only as far as they are rooted in freedom; the values of Christian marriage can be created only within the Christian *communion.*

❦

What is the matrimonial covenant?
What is the matrimonial covenant between baptized persons?

Canon 1055 § 1.

Matrimoniale foedus,
quo vir et mulier inter se
totius vitae consortium constituunt,
indole sua naturali ad bonum coniugum
atque ad prolis generationem et educationem ordinatum,
a Christo Domino ad sacramenti dignitatem
inter baptizatos evectum est.

The matrimonial covenant,
by which a man and a woman
establish between themselves a *consortium* of the whole life,

[*and which*] by its very nature is ordered to the good of the spouses and
to the procreation and education of children,
has been raised by Christ the Lord
to the dignity of a sacrament between baptized persons.

The canon is a short narration of the history of marriage: a secular reality has become a saving mystery.

covenant is the translation of *foedus*. In Roman law *foedus* was used for agreements which transcended the ordinary categories of contract, e.g. treaties between nations or peoples, pacts with religious significance, promises among friends or the members of a family without creating strict right-and-duty situations.[4]

Vatican Council II, wishing to break away from the rigidly limited contractual conception of marriage, used the term *foedus* to describe the marital agreement. Since in the usual Latin translations of the Scriptures *foedus* is the term used to describe the relationship of Yahweh to his people, his covenant with Israel, the word was eminently suitable for bringing out the sacred dimensions of marriage. In English, covenant has become the standard translation of *foedus*.[5]

Covenant, however, was not used by the Council to exclude altogether the presence of contractual elements in the marital promises (the more can contain the less), but the Council wanted the strictly legal elements to be incorporated into a sacred context. Accordingly, contractual elements can be still recognized in the exchange of the promises, but that exchange can no longer, not even in canon law, be adequately defined as contract.

This new relationship between contract and covenant is best understood if the move from contract to covenant is considered as a move to a higher viewpoint. Nothing is lost, everything is enriched; contract is contained in the covenant but does not exhaust it.

Yet, in the Christian context, covenant itself must be given an even richer meaning than that of a religiously sanctioned agreement be-

---

[4]*See* OLD:719.

[5]Apart from the broad religious meaning, *covenant* has also a narrow legal meaning; cf. e.g. the doctrine of restrictive covenants in real property law.

tween two persons. When Christians marry there is a covenant between God and the couple, much in the same way as there was a
covenant between Yahweh and his people and there is one between
Christ and his church. God's covenant is one sided; it is a gift that
Christian theology explained through the doctrine of grace. The
source of the firmness of Christian marriage is precisely in God's own
promises and in his fidelity to his own word and to the couple whom
he calls and consecrates through the sacrament.

consortium is virtually impossible to translate correctly; it has no
equivalent in English. Literally, it means a close association of persons sharing the same fortune, fate and destiny.[6] It is less than *communio*, which is the closest of intimate relationships. Yet it is more
than *societas*, which can be a loose partnership for business purposes. In choosing the word *consortium*, canon law tries to strike a
middle course between the ideal of a perfect union of minds and
hearts, and the unsatisfactory state of a merely external association,
so that the legitimate marital customs and traditions of various peoples could be accommodated. This interpretation is supported by the
history of this canon. An earlier draft (SCH/80) defined marriage as
communio, but a later one (SCH/82) preferred the term *consortium*,
a broader term, more suitable for varied cultural situations (cf.
REL/81, ad can. 1008).

We have to be careful not to make an exaggerated version of
Western personalistic philosophy so absolute that the marriages of

---

[6]OLD:418 gives the following meaning of *consortium*: *1* The sharing of property,
community of life. *2* A sharing, partnership, possession in common...*3* A close
connection, company, association, conjunction (of stars).

The Romans did call marriage a *consortium* but they did not understand or
explain marriage in the categories of modern Western personalistic philosophy. The
definition of marriage attributed to Modestinus (D 23, 2:1) gives a clue as to what
consortium meant in the case of marriage: *nuptiae sunt coniunctio maris et feminae
et consortium omnis vitae, divini et humani iuris communicatio.* The *divini iuris
communicatio* probably meant to be under the protection of, and the common cult
of, the *Lar familiaris*, the tutelary god of the husband's family into which the new
wife has been incorporated; the *humani iuris communicatio* signified the set of legal
relationships that bound and kept the family together. Note that this definition
should not be considered as *the* exact legal definition of marriage but rather as the
description of a state of life. (Cf. Buckland, p. 106)

Christians living in another culture should be considered invalid.[7]
Because *consortium* is more a state of life than a given act, it will
not be easily given a legal definition. None the less, it will remain a
key concept in the law of marriage, steadily interpreted and refined,
but never quite defined. A not uncommon phenomenon in legal
history: life can be taken out of a foundational concept by a precise
definition. The ancient Romans were aware of this; they never defined the meaning of equity, natural justice, or of good faith —
concepts which were both legal and inspirational. Thus they succeeded in keeping their laws flexible and human.

by its very nature is ordered: the canon speaks of the nature of the
institution, not of the intended purpose of the parties. Here we find
the doctrine embraced by Vatican Council II expressed in legal
terms. The Council rejected a hierarchical classification of the ends
of marriage, as it is found in CIC/17 where the procreation and
education of children were named as the primary end, mutual help
and remedy of concupiscence as the secondary end. In CIC/83 the
doctrine of the ends has been retained, but it has been modified. The
good of the spouses is mentioned in the first place, the generation
and education of children in the second. The enumeration, however,
does not imply ranking: the two ends are joined into a unity; they are
of equal importance, together they make up the integral purpose of
marriage. The term "end," *finis,* is not used, but the verb "ordered,"
ordinatus, expresses the same thought: there is a built-in finality in
the institution of marriage.

---

[7]Let the following quotes from the autobiography of John C. H. Wu, the distinguished jurist and diplomat from China, a convert to Catholicism, illustrate the
cultural differences that exist among different nations:
    Although I was engaged not by my own will, I had absolutely no doubt that
    the one to whom my parents had matched me was predestined to be my wife. In
    one sense, such a betrothal had a greater dignity than the civil engagement by the
    free choice of the parties; because it was, as it were, registered in Heaven. If one
    has chosen one's own fiancee, one is liable to wonder at times if one has made the
    right choice. If, on the other hand, one believes, as we did, that every marriage is
    made in Heaven, there could be no room for regret....To the Western reader,
    the old Chinese marriage system must appear inconceivable. I remember that
    when I told my dear friend Dom Edouard Neut, the Belgian Benedictine, about

to the good of the spouses: that is, the institution of marriage is ordered for the good of the spouses: an all embracing expression. It includes the physical, emotional, intellectual, and spiritual welfare of the couple. To achieve this common good, each must be intent on promoting the good of the other. To enter marriage with the purpose of personal fulfillment only is to bring into it the seed of destruction; a person doing so would not be dedicated to the true values of the married state of life.

to the procreation and education of children: again, the institution is ordered to these purposes. The spouses must appropriate the same goals, otherwise they fail to enter the married state. While they "should regard as their proper mission the task of transmitting human life", they must "fulfill their task with human and Christian responsibility" (GS:50).

Education is a broad concept. It includes more than providing for the physical needs of the child; the parents must attend to his emotional and spiritual needs as well.

has been raised by Christ the Lord to the dignity of a sacrament: this clause is an affirmation of the traditional Catholic belief that marriage is one of the seven sacraments. If taken literally, the statement is anachronistic; there is no evidence in early apostolic literature that Christ would have made such a declaration; in fact the church did not become aware of the exact number and nature of the sacraments until the twelfth and thirteenth centuries, a typical example of the development of a dogma. But marriage was recognized as a sacred and sanctifying reality long before it was classified as one of the sacraments.

---

it, he simply could not believe it. All amazed and amused, he asked me, "Do you mean to say that you actually had not seen your wife before you were married?! How could that be?" On my part, I was amazed by his amazement and amused by his amusement. I said to him, "Father, did you choose your parents, your brothers and your sisters? And yet you love them all the same." John C. H. Wu, *Beyond East and West* (New York: Sheed and Ward, 1951), pp. 58, 61.

Of course much has changed in China in recent times, and there is no question of introducing a similar custom in the West! Differences, however, in conceiving marriage in general and *consortium* in particular continue to exist in varying degrees.

between baptized persons: marriage is a human reality; in one way or another it existed always. But in the community of the believers, it received a new dimension. It signifies and brings grace; it is part of the new creation. Theologically, however, the text is incomplete; for an adult to be Christian and to be able to receive the sacrament more is required than the fact of baptism: he must also believe in Christ. On this point the Code is still using a terminology that goes back to the times when all baptized could be rightly assumed to be believers. It is not so any more. Further, it is only in relatively recent times that we have come to the clear understanding that no grown-up person can be Christian in the full sense unless he or she has freely surrendered to God through an act of faith.

⌒⁎⌒

What is the relationship between the contract and the sacrament?

Canon 1055 § 2.

**Quare inter baptizatos
nequit matrimonialis contractus validus consistere,
quin sit eo ipso sacramentum.**

**Therefore, between baptized persons
no valid matrimonial contract can exist
that is not, by that fact, a sacrament.**

In a positive formulation the meaning of this paragraph is that "since Christ raised the matrimonial covenant to the dignity of a sacrament among baptized persons," whenever they choose to marry, they receive the sacrament of matrimony. They cannot have the secular reality without the saving mystery. Clearly, we have here a doctrinal statement, to be weighed and explained according to theological criteria.

The issue of the relationship between the contract and the sacrament arose more than once in the past in widely different historical circumstances.[8]

(1) Some theologians in the 16th century, using Aristotelian and Thomistic categories, saw the *matter* of the sacrament of marriage in the contract, the *form* in the blessing of the priest. Logically then, the contract could be concluded without having the blessing, that is, Christians could be married without having received the sacrament. Most others, however, were in agreement that the contract itself was the *form* of the sacrament; therefore, the two could not be separated. This view prevailed, and the canon echoes it.[9]

(2) Some French civil lawyers in the beginning of the 17th century (the so called Royalists) initiated another theory to support the claim of the secular power to have jurisdiction over the marriage of Christians. They claimed that the essence of marriage was in the contract, a secular reality. As such it had to be subject to secular jurisdiction. The church could have power over the sacrament only, a shadowy entity in their conception. In practice, they wanted all power over marriage, such as the right to determine impediments, to judge the validity of the contract, to grant separation, etc., to be transferred to civil jurisdictions. The official answer of the Catholic Church was in stressing the inseparability of the contract from the sacrament. Since the two were inseparable, those who had authority over the sacrament had also an exclusive power over the contract, except for its

---

[8]The most exhaustive study of the relationship between the contract and the sacrament is the work of John Baptist Sequeira, *Tout mariage entre baptisés est-il nécessairement sacramentel?* Etude historique, théologique et canonique sur le lien entre baptême et mariage (Paris: Cerf, 1985). Here is one of his conclusions:

In the concrete order, we wish, with numerous theologians, canonists and persons entrusted with pastoral ministries, that canon 1055 § 2 be suppressed. Also, that canon 1108, which imposes the canonical form for the validity on all marriages of baptized Catholics, be suppressed. It should be declared that all marriages concluded in a public form are true marriages although they do not have the perfection of a sacramental marriage. (*See* p. 680)

The author is aware that his proposals are not without difficulties, but he believes that to implement them would bring us closer to the ideal toward which the law of the church must strive all the time.

[9]For this dispute *see* DTC 9.2: 2231, and 2255-2261, also Caffarra in PCM: 130-137. Melchior Cano was the principal exponent of this opinion.

specifically civil effects. They had the right to determine the conditions for the legitimacy of the marital promises; they were the only judges of its validity.[10]

Pius IX repeatedly reaffirmed this doctrine and the condemnation of the separability of the contract and the sacrament has found its way into his Syllabus (D-SCH 2966, 2973). Thus, our canon is a response to the French Royalists as well.

In our times, however, a new problem surfaced: the world over, in the West and in the East, there are many persons who are baptized but have no faith at all in the Christian revelation. They are Christians in the sense of having been baptized, but not in the sense of believing in Christ. If they want to marry, what should the stance of the church be?

This canon is often quoted as the answer. After all, there is some similarity between the two old problems and the new one. Presumably, our modern unbelievers want the contract but not the sacrament, which doctrine has been declared impossible — in other circumstances.

But the answer to issues raised in the past may not be the one to solve our present difficulties. If this canon is taken literally, it would put before the church an absurd dilemma. Since the contract and the sacrament cannot be separated, if a baptized but professed unbeliever wants to marry, the church should either impose the sacrament on him, or should tell him not to marry at all because he cannot marry otherwise than by receiving the sacrament. There must be another solution.

Such persons have not lost their natural right to marry, and if they want to do so, they must marry as they can, that is not sacramentally. Certainly, the church cannot recognize such marriage as sacramental, but no theological reason exists why it could not be recognized for what it is, a non sacramental marriage. The response once given in order to settle a theological dispute, or to oppose a movement for the secularization of Christian marriages, is neither suitable nor satisfactory for resolving a contemporary pastoral problem. Baptized unbelievers, too, have a right to marry, and the church has no right to force the sacrament on them, especially if they never came to

---

[10]*See* DTC: 2261-2267, also Caffarra in PCM: 138-156.

believe in the church and its sacraments. Because they are human beings blessed with intelligence and freedom, they can enter into a marital agreement. Once they did, the church can do no less than to recognize that fact. In no way is such an attitude against the doctrine of our faith.

The correct method of handling the issue of baptized unbelievers is not by turning to the abstract principle that affirms the inseparability of the contract and the sacrament, but by considering their fundamental right to marry and the duty of the church to respect their conscience. This is no more than handling the issue according to the principles laid down by Vatican Council II in its Declaration on Religious Freedom, *Dignitatis humanae:* "In all his activity a man is bound to follow his conscience faithfully . . ." and "It follows that he is not to be forced to act in a manner contrary to his conscience" (DH:3). Once the correct point of departure is found, it is easy to arrive at the right solution.

It follows also that the statement, often invoked, "the contract cannot be separated from the sacrament" can be true or false, depending on who the parties to the marriage are, believers or unbelievers.

(1) When baptized believers intend to marry in the Christian way, they receive the sacrament; that is, their covenant cannot be anything less than the sacrament. In their case, the statement is true, the contract cannot be separated from the sacrament.

(2) When baptized unbelievers marry, for lack of faith, they cannot receive the sacrament. But like any human being, they retain the capacity to marry. In their case, there is a contract but there is no sacrament.

An important qualification: By unbelievers we understand those who never came to any act of faith in spite of their baptism, or explicitly rejected all belief in the Christian mysteries; a category apart. The case of those who are weak or hesitant in their faith is a different one; they are able to receive the sacrament.

A remark: The canon speaks of baptized persons; if, however, a baptized person marries legitimately another who is not baptized, the official position of the church is that the baptized one is bound by the contract but does not receive the sacrament. This is an officially acknowledged case of the separation of the contract and of the sacrament.

❧ ✳ ❧

What are the essential properties of marriage?

Canon 1056

Essentiales matrimonii proprietates sunt unitas et indissolubilitas, quae in matrimonio christiano ratione sacramenti peculiarem obtinent firmitatem.

The essential properties of marriage are unity and indissolubility, which in Christian marriage, by reason of the sacrament, obtain a particular firmness.

essential property: a quality of the "essence" of the marriage, so much part of the essence that without it there is no marriage. The canon is formulated in scholastic categories; it assumes that marriage has an "essence" and this essence includes in its very nature unity and indissolubility.

unity means one partner and no more, either simultaneously or successively; hence polygamy, polyandry, remarriage after divorce while the first party is still alive, are all excluded.

indissolubility: the issue of indissolubility is explained in greater detail in the comments on canon 1134. Suffice it here to say that the term "indissolubility" can be used and has been used historically to signify different things:
(1) it may refer to a *moral obligation,* to the duty to uphold the permanency of marriage; or
(2) it may refer to the *nature of the bond,* meaning that it is permanent and cannot be dissolved. When the bond is called indissoluble, it is usual to qualify the term further: *intrinsic* indissolubility is the capacity of the bond to resist any attempt to be dissolved from the inside, that is, by the partners; *extrinsic* indissolubility is

the immunity of the bond to any attempt to be dissolved from the outside, that is, by any external authority, civil or religious.

Christian marriage: the first clause refers to any marriage, the second one to a specifically Christian marriage, as distinct from a natural marriage.

In a Christian marriage the qualities of unity and indissolubility are said to acquire a *particular firmness*; by implication the same qualities must be less than specially firm in a natural marriage. A distinction difficult to explain because neither unity nor indissolubility admits degrees. But the subtle qualification is there to account for the dissolution of certain types of marriages.

Indeed the church regards only sacramental consummated marriages as absolutely indissoluble "by any human power" (cf. canon 1141).

Canon law offers various ways and means for dissolving the natural bond between two unbaptized persons whenever the Catholic cause would benefit from this dissolution, that is, "for the sake of the faith." Also, the bond between a baptized and a non-baptized person can be dissolved in similar circumstances. Further, the sacramental bond between two baptized believers can be dissolved if the marriage has not been consummated.

This canon should be taken as affirming that

(1) there is a moral obligation to uphold the unity and indissolubility of all marriages, natural or sacramental, consummated or not;

(2) the firmness (binding force) of this obligation has degrees; in some cases it may even allow the dissolution of the bond, but when it reaches a "particular firmness" (in a sacramental consummated marriage) the bond cannot be broken.

What brings marriage into existence?

Canon 1057 § 1.

**Matrimonium facit partium consensus
inter personas iure habiles legitime manifestatus,
qui nulla humana potestate suppleri valet.**

Marriage is brought into existence by the consent of the parties,
lawfully manifested between legally capable persons;
[*this consent*] cannot be supplied by any human power.

marriage in general, not just Christian marriage.

brought into existence: literally, it is "made"; this should not be
taken in an exclusive sense; the clause means that the consent is
absolutely necessary but it does not mean that other factors are not.
Since marriage is a sacrament, the Spirit of God is the primary agent
in "making" it.

consent will be defined in § 2 of this canon; comments will follow.

lawfully manifested between legally capable persons: the matrimonial contract is a juridical act, hence it must follow the pattern
(solemnities) prescribed by the law, and it must be enacted by persons duly qualified in law; otherwise in the world of law the act
simply does not exist.

it cannot be supplied by any human power: no human being of
whatever authority can consent for another; to marry is to establish a
union with another person and to create a new right-and-duty situation. No third person should ever attempt to impose such a relationship on someone who does not want it. The text excludes the possibility of a union being forced on a couple by anybody, for any
reason, such as reasons of family, tribe, state, and so forth.

ᠬᢌ᙮ᢏᠤ

What is consent?

Canon 1057 § 2.

Consensus matrimonialis est actus voluntatis,
quo vir et mulier
foedere irrevocabili
sese mutuo tradunt et accipiunt
ad constituendum matrimonium.

Matrimonial consent is an act of the will,
by which a man and a woman
with an irrevocable covenant
give and accept each other mutually,
in order to bring into existence a marriage.

consent is the indispensable internal element in the creation of the
bond (in ordinary circumstances the canonical form being the external element), and consequently a foundational concept in the canon
law of marriage. Without personal consent there is no marriage; "it
cannot be supplied by any human power"; there is no substitute for
it. It is a deep seated act in the spirit of a human person; the law can
only recognize through external signs its presence or absence. It
follows that canon law alone can never provide an adequate definition of consent; it must turn for help to all those sciences which can
enlighten us about the nature and qualities of the internal acts of a
human person.[11]

act of the will: our canon law finds the act of consent among the
acts of the will. To understand what the law means and to evaluate it
critically we must know its historical origins, its meaning in the
philosophy on which the canonical doctrine is built, and its value
(truth) in the light of modern psychology.

(1) Classical Roman law admitted "consensual contracts," that is,
agreements created without any specific formality (not with the
handing over of a thing, not with solemn words, not in writing); all
that the law required was some evidence that the parties consented to
the agreement. But the Romans never put any metaphysical theory
behind their practice; for them to say that consent was an "act of the

---

[11]As a matter of fact this is what has happened; canon law turned to scholastic
philosophy and theology for the explanation of the nature and the qualities of
consent. Its definitions and explanations, once satisfactory, have revealed themselves
as incomplete and deficient given recent developments not only in philosophy but
also in empirical human sciences. E.g. in the context of Lonergan's epistemological
reflections or Jung's analytical psychology our canonical statements concerning the
operations of the mind and the will appear naive and simplistic to a degree; these
two schools are quoted by way of examples only; others could be adduced. The
point is that canon law must turn somewhere for the understanding of consent but
must also keep looking for new developments.

will" would have carried no more than a simple common sense meaning.

Marriage in Roman law, however, was not one of the consensual contracts; it was a state of life, it belonged to the law of the persons. Its existence did not hinge on an initial agreement but on the fact whether or not the couple lived together as man and wife, with visible marital dedication to each other, with public display of *affectus maritalis*.[12]

(2) The revival of Roman law in the twelfth century brought the ancient system of contracts into focus again, and the parallel between the "consensual contracts" and the newly elaborated doctrine of marriage coming into existence through consent and not copula, was, no doubt, noted by the canonists. So, they classified marriage among the consensual contracts. It explained how someone could be fully married before the execution of the contract.

The twelfth and thirteenth centuries saw the data of faith explained, for the first time, in Aristotelian categories. Human persons were described as composed of matter and form, that is of body and soul; the soul as operating through its distinct faculties, the mind and the will, one able to perceive the truth, the other to pursue the good. Since the objects of those two faculties were different, they could act more or less independently from each other. Since marriage belonged to the category of "good," consent to marriage had to be an act of the will.

Because the goodness of marriage would attract and enrich any well disposed person, no more than some initial cooperation of the mind was required. Thus consent became *fully* defined as "an act of the will," of the faculty that even in the Aristotelian metaphysics had no full and autonomous existence, being only one of the faculties of the soul.

(3) One of the solid acquisitions of modern psychology is that the conscious self is deeply rooted in and steadily influenced and balanced by the self that is not in our awareness. Thus to speak of an isolated act of the will (as the consent to a marriage would be) does

---

[12] In many jurisdictions common law still recognizes *de facto* marriages as legally valid. In this, common law is indebted to canon law, which in its turn was inspired by Roman law.

not make much sense; an "act of the will" is really nothing else than a perceptible manifestation of the complex operations of the human psyche, of which a small portion only is open for our observation while the larger part of it remains hidden and active in influencing our decisions.

Modern canon law retains the medieval approach in holding that consent is an act of the will in the Aristotelian sense. Such a position is at best alien to modern empirical psychology, and is at worst is in open conflict with it. One can easily see that in a given case two tribunals could arrive at contradictory decisions, depending on which way the judges were leaning.

Be that as it may, every canon lawyer must know and use the old official terminology. Yet no canon lawyer can dispense himself from being aware of facts established by modern sciences; nor is he entitled to avoid their application. Matrimonial consent is in fact much more than a mere act of the will. Everything in a human psyche contributes to it in varying degrees.

by an irrevocable covenant: indissolubility is affirmed in the sense that the parties must have the intention to establish a permanent union, and they have no right, not even the capacity to revoke their commitment. The clause says nothing about the power of the church over the bond.

they give and accept each other for marriage: the purpose of the covenant, that is the object intended by it, is marriage with all of its specific rights and duties. CIC/17 defined the object of the consent as the right over the body for the procreation of children; it was clearly a partial view of what marriage was. This canon expresses a much more wholesome understanding of the object of the consent: the parties give themselves for marriage.

Who have the right to marry?

Canon 1058

Omnes possunt matrimonium contrahere, qui iure non prohibentur.

All who are not forbidden by law can contract marriage.

There are two affirmations in this canon, one explicit, another implicit.
The explicit statement is that every person is presumed to have the right to marry, unless the contrary can be established on legal grounds.
The implicit statement is that competent authorities have the right to forbid marriage, or to impose certain conditions, which, if not observed, invalidate it.

❧✳❧

Who has authority over the marriage of Catholics?

Canon 1059

Matrimonium catholicorum,
etsi una tantum pars sit catholica, regitur iure non solum divino, sed etiam canonico,
salva competentia civilis potestatis
circa mere civiles eiusdem matrimonii effectus.

The marriage of Catholics,
even if one only party is Catholic,
is governed not only by divine law but also by canon law,
save the competence of the civil authority
regarding the merely civil effects of the same marriage.

Canon 11 of CIC/83 states that only those who have been baptized in the Catholic church, or were received into it, are bound by the so called "merely ecclesiastical laws" (cf. COM-USA: 31). Here an exception is stated: the church claims jurisdiction over all marriages where one of the parties is Catholic. Thus, the non-Catholic person, baptized or not, is brought into the orbit of our canonical legislation.

There were times when the opposite was true. After the Council of Trent, for a long time, if one party was not bound by the decree of the Council concerning the canonical form, for lack of proper promulgation, he or she communicated his or her immunity to the other.

It cannot be excluded *a priori* that the presently valid two provisions converging on the same non-Catholic person could create a conflict of laws. If that happens, the presumption should be that the non-Catholic person is free from any obligation that has its origin in a merely ecclesiastical law, unless it can be shown that the law was made "for the marriage" to which the non-Catholic is party. The law reaches him, as it were, indirectly, through the marriage. He accepts the obligation to abide by canon law by agreeing to a marriage that falls under canonical legislation.

merely ecclesiastical law is man-made law in the church; it is less than an ecclesiastical law proclaiming divine law.

divine law is always a difficult concept, whether it means certain precepts of the natural law or the commandments of the gospel. In the first case there is the question how far we are able to establish with more than fallible human certainty that a given norm is divine law; in the second there is the question how far it can be proved from Christian tradition that a norm is indeed an integral part of the divine revelation.

Whenever we say a law is divine, the epistemological issue cannot be avoided. If we arrived at our conclusion through human reasoning, we have no more than a human conviction about a divine law. Such conviction is, of course, fallible and changeable. At best, we have a theological opinion. But if we learned through divine revelation that a law is divine, then we can speak of divine law in the strong and full sense of the term. We are then proclaiming a point of Catholic doctrine.

Caution therefore is indicated; unless we can show that the church believes, with the certainty of faith, that a norm is divine law, the most we can do is to make a human conjecture about the origin of that law.

the civil effects of marriage can concern citizenship, property rights and similar temporal matters.

✦

How to handle a marriage of doubtful validity?

Canon 1060

Matrimonium gaudet favore iuris;
quare in dubio standum est pro valore matrimonii,
donec contrarium probetur.

Marriage enjoys the favor of the law;
therefore in doubt
the validity of a marriage is to be upheld
until the contrary is proved.

Marriage enjoys the favor of the law: this norm comes into play whenever a doubt arises concerning the validity of a marriage. It is no more than a particular application of a general principle that brings stability to every legal system: once a juridical act has taken place, it is held for valid, unless the contrary is proved. In other terms, the effects of a juridical act cannot be extinguished by anything less than another juridical act. If a doubt (reasonable as it may be) could cancel out the certainty generated by a seemingly legitimate performance, the life of the community would be beset with uncertainties throughout, and the stability that the law is expected to provide would be undermined.

The law, however, favors truth even more than marriage. Therefore, if a serious doubt has arisen about the validity of a marriage, there is an equally serious obligation to investigate. If evidence emerges that proves beyond reasonable doubt that the marriage is invalid, there is a duty to honor the truth and take appropriate action. Precisely because the law favors truth above marriage, ecclesiastical tribunals are bound to examine the cases brought legitimately before them.

What is a merely ratified marriage?
What is a ratified and consummated marriage?

Canon 1061 § 1.

Matrimonium inter baptizatos validum dicitur
ratum tantum, si non est consummatum;
ratum et consummatum, si coniuges inter se humano
　modo posuerunt coniugalem actum
per se aptum ad prolis generationem,
ad quem natura sua ordinatur matrimonium,
et quo coniuges fiunt una caro.

A valid marriage between baptized persons is called
merely ratified, if it is not consummated;
ratified and consummated, if the spouses performed between
　themselves
　and in a human manner the conjugal act
　that is apt in itself for the generation of children;
to this [act] marriage is ordered by its nature,
and through it the spouses become one flesh.

We have here the definition of two terms used for Christian marriages, **ratum** and **consummatum.** Their origins go back to the Middle Ages when they were part of a triad: *matrimonium initiatum* (betrothals), *ratum* (solemnized), and *consummatum* (the conjugal act has taken place.)[13]

Each term signified a step in the slow process of concluding a marriage, according to the traditions and customs of the Germanic peoples of Europe.

The dispute as to "what makes marriage," mainly between the schools of Bologna (*copula* brings it into existence) and of Paris (*consensus* creates it), was resolved in the twelfth century in favor of the *consensus* theory, but not without some concession to the other

---

[13]*See* Jean Gaudemet, "Les étapes de la conclusion du lien matrimonial chez Gratien et ses commentateurs," *Société et mariage* (Strasbourg: Cerdic, 1980), pp. 379-391.

one. The position that has become the common doctrine, due principally to the decretal letters of Alexander III (1159-1181), held that
consent makes the marriage but consummation makes it indissoluble
(*see* D-SCH 754-756).[14] Ever since, canon law remained faithful to
this principle, and the church has not ceased to act on it. Yet the
same doctrine became a stumbling block for theology because, in a
subtle fashion, it separated the sacrament from its essential property,
that is, indissolubility. It meant that the bond could not be dissolved
as long as it remained "merely sacramental": indissolubility was the
effect of consummation, in itself not part of the sacrament.

in a human manner: the mere fact of physical consummation is not
enough to have the marriage consummated in the canonical and
theological sense; the act must be performed in a human manner,
that is, with that understanding and freedom which is necessary for a
morally responsible act. Consummation cannot take place if one of
the parties is so impaired mentally that he or she has no sufficient
knowledge of what is happening, or has no capacity to assent responsibly. Nor can it take place through force and fear.

❦

Is consummation ever presumed?

Canon 1061 § 2.

Celebrato matrimonio,
si coniuges cohabitaverint,
praesumitur consummatio, donec contrarium probetur.

If the spouses have lived together
after the celebration of the marriage,
consummation is presumed unless the contrary is proved.

---

[14]The complex process of the maturation of this doctrine is described in DTC, *see*
especially "Les premières synthèses, au milieu du XIIᵉ siècle." 9.2:2149-2154. For the
decisive role that Alexander III played in the final crystallization of the doctrine, *see*
ibid. 2158-2159.

A procedural rule. The fact of having lived together generates the presumption of consummation. It is, however, a simple presumption. Proof to the contrary are allowed.

❦

What is a putative marriage?

Canon 1061 § 3.

**Matrimonium invalidum dicitur putativum,
si bona fide ab una saltem parte celebratum fuerit,
donec utraque pars de eiusdem nullitate certa evadat.**

**An invalid marriage is called putative
if it was celebrated in good faith at least by one party,
until both become certain of its nullity.**

A special status is accorded to a union which was entered in good faith at least by one of the parties, but in fact was invalid. To such marriage the law accords many of the effects of a valid marriage. In particular, the children born from such a marriage are considered legitimate. It follows that when a marriage is declared null and void from the beginning, the children do not become illegitimate.

❦

How is engagement regulated?

Canon 1062 § 1.

**Matrimonii promissio sive unilateralis sive bilateralis,
quam sponsalia vocant,
regitur iure particulari,
quod ab Episcoporum conferentia,
habita ratione consuetudinum et legum civilium, si quae sint,
statutum fuit.**

A promise of marriage, whether unilateral or bilateral,
known as engagement,
is regulated by particular law
that the episcopal conference has enacted,
with regard to customs and civil laws that may exist.

The canon leaves it to the episcopal conference to judge whether
or not legislation is warranted.

⌦✳⌫

What are the consequences of a breach of promise to marry?

Canon 1062 § 2.

Ex matrimonii promissione
non datur actio ad petendam matrimonii celebrationem;
datur tamen ad reparationem damnorum, si qua debeatur.

From the promise of marriage
no right to an action arises to demand the celebration of marriage;
an action, however, is available for the reparation of damages if it
is due.

This paragraph speaks the language of Roman law. Its message is
that canon law will not compel anyone to marry a person even if
there have been promises to that effect. But if someone suffered
damage because of those promises, an ecclesiastical court is willing to
consider the issue of liability.

CHAPTER ONE
PASTORAL CARE AND
PREREQUISITES FOR THE
CELEBRATION OF MARRIAGE
1063 — 1072

This chapter, dealing with the issue of "preparation" for marriage, may not appear of great importance from a legal point of view. But in real life the acceptance of the demands of Christian marriage by the community and by its individual members depends on the firm belief in the mystery, on the appreciation of the values that it contains, and on the free and responsible dedication of each person (married or not) to those values. No amount of legislation can supplement for such internal dispositions in the minds and the hearts of the faithful. Therefore, the pastoral problem is how they can be helped to grow in such appreciation, and what the contribution of those who are entrusted with pastoral offices can be towards fostering such growth.

The New Testament conveys a high esteem for the married state in many diverse ways; it leaves no doubt about the mind of the early communities. Not surprisingly, there is no reference to annulments, although Paul acknowledges the possibility that a marriage between a Christian and a non-Christian may break down. Accordingly, he offers an appropriate remedy. Our times are different: ecclesiastical courts are judging an increasing number of marriages null and void from the beginning. In doing so, they convey a message to the community: the faith of the people ought to be strengthened; their sense of responsibility ought to be deepened. Only when they have achieved some understanding of the mystery can they be expected to make their marriage covenant in all seriousness and to commit themselves, in God's name, "for the better and for the worse." A certain intelligence of faith is necessary to surrender freely to God's saving mystery.

Transitions: *From legalities to pastoral care.* The old Code gave minute prescriptions concerning the formalities to be observed before the marriage; the new Code leaves their determination mostly to the episcopal conferences and focuses on the necessity of upholding and strengthening in the community the correct belief in the mystery of the Christian marriage, and on the need of offering proper help to those who intend to enter the married state.

Literary forms: *Exhortations predominate but they are not to be taken lightly.* Several canons recall the duties, moral and legal, of pastors and give directions for their fulfillment. Other canons create right-and-duty situations.

The values upheld, protected and promoted in this chapter are: the dignity of the married life and all that contributes to a conscious preparation for it.

Preliminary remarks

(1) *Today, by its practical attitude toward the laity, the church inevitably conveys a doctrinal message about marriage.* The correct understanding and appreciation of the sacrament of marriage has certainly suffered a great deal from the pessimism of the Augustinian theology (see below, our comments on canon 1063); it is therefore necessary to return to the scriptural sources and bring the "good news" concerning marriage to the awareness of the faithful. But a reformed theology of marriage is not enough; there must be also a renewed understanding of the place and role of the laity in the church. Apart from obvious doctrinal reasons, there is a pragmatic need to do so. Since lay persons mostly choose the married state as

their own, laity and marriage are closely associated in the mind of the people. It follows that unless they see that the laity is highly esteemed, and lay persons are given important responsibilities in the church, they will be tempted to devaluate the lay state — and the married state with it. In other terms, to make the preaching on the dignity of Christian marriage credible, it is necessary to proclaim the dignity of the lay state, more by deeds than by words.[1]

(2) *When a couple marries, a "domestic church" comes into existence.* The issue of marriage, whether in canon law or in theology, should be seen always within the broader issue of the Christian family. To let both doctrine and practice develop, the insight that the family is the smallest of Christian churches, a "domestic church," can be helpful. Such "churches" need also express themselves in home "liturgies." The devotional life of the Catholic community should not become centered so much on the parish that nothing is left to the family. It is good to recall that in the early church the homes of Christians were also places of common worship.

⸙＊⸙

How to proclaim and protect the dignity of Christian marriage?

Canon 1063

**Pastores animarum
obligatione tenentur curandi
ut propria ecclesiastica communitas christifidelibus assistentiam
　　praebeat,
qua status matrimonialis in spiritu christiano servetur
et in perfectione progrediatur.**

[1]There can be little doubt that the present system and policy of canonizations convey a powerful message: the examples of holiness are to be found among the clergy and religious. Hardly any father or mother of family who died in the married state, without being a martyr, has ever been honored as "confessor." Yet, one could ask who has instilled the love of God into the hearts of those holy clerics and religious in the first place? Further, we should not forget that in the existential order

Haec assistentia imprimis praebenda est:
1° praedicatione,
catechesi minoribus, iuvenibus et adultis aptata,
immo usu instrumentorum communicationis socialis,
quibus christifideles de significatione matrimonii christiani
deque munere coniugum ac parentum christianorum
instituantur;
2° praeparatione personali ad matrimonium ineundum,
qua sponsi ad novi sui status sanctitatem et officia disponantur;
3° fructuosa liturgica matrimonii celebratione,
qua eluceat coniuges mysterium unitatis
et fecundi amoris inter Christum et Ecclesiam
significare atque participare;
4° auxilio coniugatis praestito,
ut ipsi foedus coniugale fideliter servantes atque tuentes,
ad sanctiorem in dies plenioremque in familia vitam ducendam
perveniant.

Those entrusted with a pastoral office
have the duty to see that
their own ecclesiastical community provides assistance for the
faithful
to keep the matrimonial state of life imbued with Christian
spirit and
in constant progress toward perfection.
This assistance must be given principally
1° through preaching,
through catechesis adapted to children, young persons and
adults,
also through the use of the means of social communication,
so that the faithful are instructed
about the significance [dignity] of Christian marriage and
about the vocation [task, office] of Christian spouses and
parents;

Christian parents may well be called "the teaching church"; they are the first ones to proclaim the good news to each new generation. The procedures and policies of canonizations may be in need of critical revision so that they could contribute more effectively to the proclamation of the dignity and sanctity of married life among Christians. The Holy Scriptures present a better balance; both the Old Testament and the New Testament speak of married persons of exceptional holiness.

2° through personal preparation for entering marriage,
so that the spouses are well disposed toward the sanctity and
the offices of their new state;
3° through the fruitful liturgical celebration of marriage,
which brings to light
that the spouses [*together*] signify, and participate in,
the mystery of the unity and fruitful love between Christ and
the church;
4° through the help given to married persons, so that
by faithfully observing and safeguarding their conjugal
covenant
they may achieve each day a holier and fuller life in their
family.

This canon articulates a complex set of duties that is inherent to any pastoral office, in particular to the office of the parish priest and the bishop. It includes the steady duty to proclaim in its fullness the Christian doctrine concerning marriage. In such a proclamation primary importance should be given to what is best in our tradition; it should be based on scriptural sources, on other sources of dogma, on ancient and new liturgical texts, and on sound theological reflections. The explanation of the relevant rules of morality should follow afterwards. Informed and responsible moral choices can follow only from the correct perception and appreciation of the mystery.[2]

Such proclamation is all the more needed because the beauty and the richness of the scriptural doctrine has been obscured by the Augustinian tradition that has so closely identified "concupiscence" with original sin and explained the normal sexual instinct as an expression of this concupiscence, and therefore tainted with sin and leading into sin. Logically, marriage had to become an "inferior" state of life, the same marriage that Paul identified as the

---

[2]The market is flooded with books on the spirituality of marriage and on moral issues in marriage but it is very difficult to find a good systematic and scholarly exposition of the Catholic belief concerning the sacrament of marriage.

symbol of the love of Christ for his church. He could not have bestowed a higher praise on it.[3]

The Augustinian perception of marriage remained predominant until Aquinas corrected it on the basis of his own theology of grace and dissociated the sexual act in marriage from sin.[4] But his theoretical correction had little impact on everyday preaching and practice, marriage was still all too often thought of as an "inferior" state of life. The strong statements of Vatican Council II were needed to redress the balance.

A fair comment on the canon would be to say that the sanctity and dignity of Christian marriage should be preached *opportune et importune*, that is relentlessly, because we have so much to make up for.

The canon gives no detailed instructions on how this proclamation of the good news about marriage should take place; virtually everything is left to the initiative and creativity of those entrusted with pastoral offices. Rightly so, provided they will take advantage of the openness of the law.

❧✳❧

Whose task is it to direct the pastoral assistance?

Canon 1064

Ordinarii loci est curare
ut debite ordinetur eadem assistentia,
auditis etiam, si opportunum videatur, viris et mulieribus
experientia et peritia probatis.

---

[3]It is interesting to note that while many authors argue for indissolubility on the basis of Paul's text (a sacramental marriage is indissoluble because it represents the union of Christ with his church), they remain silent on the eminent sanctity of married life that has been described by the same Paul through comparing it to the relationship of Christ with his church.

[4]See the study by Josef Fuchs, *Die Sexualethik des Heiligen Thomas von Aquin* (Köln: Bachem, 1949).

**It is the responsibility of the local ordinary to ensure
that this assistance is properly organized,
after having taken the advice, if it seemed opportune,
of men and women qualified by their experience and expertise.**

Some ordinaries may well want to go beyond the letter of the law. They will do more than to take advice from qualified men and women; they shall invite them to take initiatives and be leaders in organizing and offering this assistance and help.

What sacraments should be received before the marriage?

Canon 1065 § 1.

**Catholici qui sacramentum confirmationis nondum receperint,
illud, antequam ad matrimonium admittantur, recipiant,
si id fieri possit sine gravi incommodo.**

**Catholics who have not yet received the sacrament of
confirmation
should receive it before being admitted to marriage,
if it can be done without grave inconvenience.**

Canon 1065 § 2.

**Ut fructuose sacramentum matrimonii recipiatur,
enixe sponsis commendatur,
ut ad sacramenta paenitentiae et sanctissimae Eucharistiae
accedant.**

**To receive the sacrament of marriage fruitfully,
the spouses are strongly advised
to receive the sacraments of penance and holy eucharist.**

This canon should not be interpreted as imposing strict legal duties; in reality it does more. It invites the spouses into a full participation in God's gifts.

~※~

Should there be an investigation before the marriage?

Canon 1066

Antequam matrimonium celebretur,
constare debet
nihil eius validae ac licitae celebrationi obsistere.

**Before the marriage is celebrated,
it must be established
that nothing stands in the way of its valid and lawful [*licit*]
celebration.**

This is normally the right and duty of the parish priest, or the one who is holding an equivalent office, or the person legitimately deputed by them.

~※~

Who is competent to enact norms for the investigation?

Canon 1067

Episcoporum conferentia statuat normas
de examine sponsorum,
necnon de publicationibus matrimonialibus
aliisve opportunis mediis ad investigationes peragendas,
quae ante matrimonium necessaria sunt,
quibus diligenter observatis,
parochus procedere possit ad matrimonio assistendum.

The episcopal conferences should enact norms
concerning the examination of the parties,
and the publication of the marriage banns,
and other suitable procedures for carrying out the
    investigations
which are necessary before the marriage.
After these norms have been complied with,
the parish priest may assist at the marriage.

Today in most dioceses the procedures are standardized.

⌾≈✳︎≈⌾

*How can the freedom of the parties be established
in danger of death?*

Canon 1068

In periculo mortis,
si aliae probationes haberi nequeant,
sufficit, nisi contraria adsint indicia, affirmatio contrahentium,
si casus ferat etiam iurata,
se baptizatos esse et nullo detineri impedimento.

In danger of death,
if no other proofs are available
and there is no evidence to the contrary,
the statement of the contracting parties
that they are baptized and free from any impediment,
even made under oath if the case warrants it,
is enough.

danger of death is less than the threat of imminent death. Such
emergency may arise even in ordinary settled circumstances, e.g.
when a person is so ill that he may die before the necessary investigations can be completed. If there is any doubt, the benefit should
be given to the person in dangerous condition.

Are the faithful bound to reveal the impediments known to them?

Canon 1069

Omnes fideles obligatione tenentur impedimenta,
si quae norint,
parocho aut loci Ordinario,
ante matrimonii celebrationem, revelandi.

**All the faithful are bound to reveal
before the celebration of the marriage
the impediments they may be aware of
to the parish priest or to the local ordinary.**

The number of impediments has been reduced so much that this obligation has become of much lesser consequence than it was in earlier times. Even so, problems may arise in case of professional persons who are in possession of confidential knowledge. They should not breach confidentiality, unless they are dispensed from it by their client. But they may, or must, professionally advise their client to be honest in these matters.

❧ ✳ ❧

Who is responsible for the investigations?

Canon 1070

Si alius quam parochus,
cuius est assistere matrimonio,
investigationes peregerit,
de harum exitu quam primum per authenticum documentum
eundem parochum certiorem reddat.

**If someone other than the parish priest,
whose responsibility is to assist at the marriage,
has conducted the investigations,
that person must, as soon as possible, inform the parish priest
by an authentic document of their outcome.**

The purpose is not only to keep the records in good order but to make sure that the parish priest who is ultimately responsible for ascertaining the freedom of the parties is properly informed.

~❈~

In what cases must the assistant request
the permission of the ordinary?

Canon 1071 § 1.

Excepto casu necessitatis,
sine licentia Ordinarii loci ne quis assistat:
   1° matrimonio vagorum;
   2° matrimonio quod ad normam legis civilis agnosci vel celebrari nequeat;
   3° matrimonio eius qui obligationibus teneatur naturalibus erga aliam partem filiosve ex praecedenti unione ortis;
   4° matrimonio eius qui notorie catholicam fidem abiecerit;
   5° matrimonio eius qui censura innodatus sit;
   6° matrimonio filii familias minoris, insciis aut rationabiliter invitis parentibus;
   7° matrimonio per procuratorem ineundo, de quo in can. 1105.

Except in a case of necessity,
without the permission of the local ordinary no one is to assist:
   1° at the marriage of homeless persons [*vagi*];
   2° at a marriage which according to the norm of civil law cannot be recognized or celebrated;
   3° at the marriage of a person who is bound by natural obligations originating in a previous union towards the former partner and the children;
   4° at the marriage of a person who has notoriously rejected the Catholic faith;
   5° at the marriage of a person who is under censure;
   6° at the marriage of a minor when the parents are unaware of it or are reasonably opposed to it;
   7° at a marriage to be entered through a proxy, as described in canon 1105.

The only common denominator in these cases is that the permission of the ordinary is needed before a person can "canonically" assist at the marriage, as described in canon 1108; otherwise they represent widely different problems.

1 - vagi are persons who have no domicile or quasi-domicile anywhere. The issue is usually in ascertaining that they are free to marry.

2 – marriage not recognized by civil law: there may be serious implications in civil law if an ecclesiastical marriage is performed. Since the welfare of the community, or the reputation or integrity of the couple or of the witnesses and of the assistant may be at stake, the case should be referred to the ordinary. In a given region, there should be a common policy agreed on by the local ordinaries.

3 – natural obligations: the purpose is to check more closely that someone is not using a marriage to evade natural obligations, and the church is not acting as an unwitting accomplice.

4 – notorious rejection of the Catholic faith: the rejection of the faith is of public knowledge, supported by reliable facts or witnesses; the proof may be in one formal act or in a certain amount of circumstantial evidence accumulated over a longer period.

5 – persons under censure: it should be a rare case. The problem would arise because a person is under some ecclesiastical penalty and at the same time wishes to receive a sacrament.

6 – minors in opposition to the wishes of their parents: the parents have important rights and duties, specified by canon and civil law, toward their children who are minors. The church wishes to respect such rights and duties when they are responsibly exercised.

7 – marriage by proxy: a rare and delicate event; the marital promises are made through an agent. Clearly, the church wishes to keep a stricter control over such a procedure.

What is the duty of the ordinary
in the case of those who abandoned the Catholic faith?

Canon 1071 § 2.

Ordinarius loci licentiam assistendi matrimonio eius
qui notorie catholicam fidem abiecerit ne concedat,
nisi servatis normis de quibus in can. 1125,
congrua congruis referendo.

The local ordinary must not grant the permission to assist
at the marriage of a person who has notoriously rejected the
catholic faith,
unless the norms stated in canon 1125 are observed,
as far as they are applicable.

has notoriously rejected the Catholic faith: see our comments on 4°
in § 1. Note that no "formal act" of rejection is necessary.

The canon is applicable if one of the parties is a believing Catholic
and the other is not any more. Then the canon directs the local
ordinary to handle the marriage as a mixed mariage: before permission is granted the promises and statements prescribed in canon 1125
must be made.

The canon is not applicable when both parties have notoriously
abandoned the Catholic faith. In that case the couple should not
marry as Catholics.

⸻ ❋ ⸻

What should be the policy
concerning the marriages of young persons?

Canon 1072

Curent animarum pastores a matrimonii celebratione avertere
iuvenes ante aetatem,
qua secundum regionis receptos mores
matrimonium iniri solet.

Those entrusted with a pastoral office
should do what they can to prevent the celebration of marriage
by young persons before the age
which, by the established traditions of that region,
is the customary age for marrying.

If the parish priest judges that the young persons intending to marry do not have the required maturity, he has the right, even the duty, to refuse them any assistance. In forming his judgment, he certainly should take into account the local customs, often born from the experience of many generations and rich in practical wisdom.

A note on diocesan policies. The local bishops or ordinaries are certainly entitled to issue policy guidelines concerning the preparation of the couples for the celebration of the sacrament; e.g. they can impose a waiting period, a certain number of instructions, etc., provided all such provisions remain within the limits of a general policy and in particular cases they are urged with due regard for individual circumstances. No bishop or ordinary has the right to infringe on the legitimate freedom of the persons who intend to marry.

CHAPTER TWO
IMPEDIMENTS IN GENERAL
1073 — 1082

Marriage impediments are found in every legal system; they protect the welfare of the spouses and of the community at large.

In canon law the same impediments have an ecclesiological significance. Through their use, the church determines (partially at least) to whom the sacrament of matrimony can be given. They set the conditions for the beginnings of a "domestic church." They convey also the message that the church is in possession of the sacrament; it has the power to regulate its administration. Even if in the Latin church the spouses are known as the ministers of the sacrament, they minister to each other in the name of the church.[1]

Any doubt concerning this radical power of the church has been resolved at the Council of Trent, which has solemnly decreed that the church had the right both to institute impediments and to require

---

[1]The Eastern church does not think of the sacraments and of their administration in the scholastic terminology developed in the West; in their tradition the blessing of the priest is what completes the sacrament of matrimony. While Western theologians and canonists continued to affirm ever since the Middle Ages that the spouses are the ministers of the sacrament, there has been an increasing importance attributed to the presence of a priest since the Council of Trent. Behind the two contrasting approaches there are two different perceptions of marriage: the Easterners understand it as the entering of a new state of life in the church; the Westerners regard it as an agreement between the spouses.

certain solemnities for the validity of a marriage (cf. D-SCH 1803, 1804, 1809 for impediments; 1813-1816 for solemnities).

In the beginning of its existence, the church simply followed local traditions: Jewish prescriptions in a few places, Roman customs and laws in many other places. In the Middle Ages a canonical system of impediments developed and it became prevalent through Christendom. With the rise of modern sovereign states, civil governments claimed the power to legislate over marriage, and the result is that today in most countries there is a system of impediments in civil law and another one in canon law. They usually operate independently of each other.

Transitions: *From complexity to simplicity.* The old Code distinguished two types of impediments, one called "impedient," forbidding the marriage but not invalidating it, the other called "diriment," forbidding it and invalidating it. Since they all originated in pontifical law, as a matter of principle, the Holy See alone had the power to dispense from any of them. The rigidity of the rule, however, was tempered by the frequent delegation of various faculties to the envoys of the Holy See and to the local ordinaries. In the new Code all impediments in the universal law are diriment. The local ordinaries have the power to dispense from them, unless a case is explicitly reserved to the Holy See.

Literary forms: Virtually all canons in this chapter are about *right-and-duty situations;* their content is legal. The norms for their interpretation must be taken from our canonical tradition.

The values the canons intend to uphold are: the power of the church over the sacrament of marriage, the dignity of the married state, also compassion for those who are in need of help in emergency situations.

What is a diriment impediment?

Canon 1073

Impedimentum dirimens personam inhabilem reddit ad matrimonium valide contrahendum.

A diriment impediment renders a person unable of contracting marriage validly.

A diriment impediment invalidates the marriage; it must be distinguished from a *merely impedient impediment* which forbids the marriage, that is, makes it unlawful, illicit, but does not interfere with its validity.

CIC/83 admits only diriment impediments in the universal law; it grants, however, the power to local ordinaries to forbid marriages in peculiar circumstances; *see* canon 1077.

All the twelve impediments listed in the CIC/83 render the marriage invalid by radically disqualifying a person from performing the necessary juridical act that brings marriage into existence.

The basic rules for the interpretation of such incapacitating laws are given in Book One of CIC/83.

— in doubt of law (the meaning of the law is not clear), they do not bind (canon 14);

— in doubt of fact (the meaning of the law is clear but the facts are not, hence there is doubt about the applicability of the law to this particular set of facts), they operate according to the true state of facts; therefore, dispensation is warranted, and usually easily given, for the sake of legal security, *ad cautelam* (canon 14);

— they produce their effect whether the parties are aware of them or not, unless the law provides otherwise (canon 15); it rarely does.

In this canon we have also a typical example of how the legal notion of contract returns after the initial insistence of the Code on marriage being a covenant. There are many more such "returns."

What is a public impediment?
What is an occult impediment?

Canon 1074

**Publicum censetur impedimentum, quod probari in foro externo potest;
secus est occultum.**

**An impediment is considered public if it can be proved in the external forum,
otherwise it is occult.**

public impediment *versus* **occult impediment:** they are distinguished on the basis of a pragmatic criterion, whether or not the existence of an impediment can be proved in the external forum, that is, either before a court of law or before a competent administrative authority, ecclesiastical or civil. Thus an impediment is public if there are witnesses who not only know the relevant facts but are also willing to testify, or there is documentary evidence to prove its existence; otherwise it is occult.

The distinction between public and occult impediment is important for procedural purposes only, not for determining the validity of the marriage, which depends on the objective existence of an impediment and not on the possibility of proving it.

❧ ✳ ❧

Who can authentically declare impediments of divine law?

Canon 1075 § 1.

**Supremae tantum Ecclesiae auctoritatis est authentice declarare
quandonam ius divinum matrimonium prohibeat vel dirimat.**

**The supreme authority of the church alone can declare authentically
when divine law forbids or invalidates marriage.**

The supreme authority in the practical order is the pope; in theory it could be, of course, an ecumenical council as well.

The intention of the legislator is to reserve to himself the right to proclaim that a given impediment is of divine law; no others, such as local ordinaries, should do so.

An authentic declaration of divine law could never be a merely legislative act; by its very nature it would be a dogmatic pronouncement. As such it should be interpreted and explained according to theological criteria.

divine law: as long as a final and solemn declaration "with full apostolic authority" has not taken place, one should be always careful in invoking divine law, since our human process of knowing is, and remains, fallible. It is not enough to say that a given norm is of divine law; it is necessary also to show that there is divine authority for saying that it is divine law. Few laws would qualify for that.

In other terms, even in the Code, when a law is said to be divine, it can mean two radically different things:

(1) the law is an integral part of the divine revelation and we know this through our faith; e.g. the law is that a believer must be baptized and we know about this law through the New Testament;

(2) the law is said to be divine on the basis of some human reasoning on the data of the revelation; e.g. when it is affirmed that by divine law the pope in person must grant the "privilege of the faith," we are in the presence of a theological opinion; the divine character of the law is humanly conjectured.

In the first case we have the "testimony of the Spirit" that a law is divine, and we must assent to it through an act of faith; in the second case we have the assertion of a human person that the law is divine; we should accept it only if the assertion stands up to a critical examination; even then our judgment remains subject to correction. Note, however, that in the complex process of developing doctrine a human assertion can be the first step toward a dogmatic declaration.

either forbids or invalidates marriage: it would be difficult to think of a divine law that forbids marriage but does not invalidate it.

Who can establish impediments of ecclesiastical law?

Canon 1075 § 2.

Uni quoque supremae auctoritati ius est alia impedimenta pro baptizatis constituere.

Also, the supreme authority alone has the right to establish other impediments for the baptized.

supreme authority: for all practical purposes it is the pope; theoretically it could be an ecumenical council.

for the baptized: CIC / 17 claimed jurisdiction over all the baptized, Catholics or not. CIC/83 applies to Catholics only. Although this expression was taken from the old law, it must be interpreted in its new context. Accordingly, baptized here means Catholic.

The significance of the canon is that no local ordinary should set up impediments unless this power is explicitly given to him, as it is in canon 1077.

~~~~~~❋~~~~~~

Can custom change the law of impediments?

Canon 1076

Consuetudo novum impedimentum inducens aut impedimentis exsistentibus contraria reprobatur.

A custom introducing a new impediment, or, a custom contrary to the existing impediments, is reprobated.

new impediment: any impediment that is not in the Code.

contrary custom: any custom that would infringe on the system of impediments as it is in the Code.

reprobated: indicates total rejection; should such customs arise, they must be suppressed and never allowed to return, cf. canon 5.

In ordinary language, CIC/83 has cleared the ground, established a new system of impediments and imposed it on the universal church. No future custom of any kind can add anything to it, or take anything away from it; it must be observed everywhere in its integrity.

❧ ✳ ❧

Can the local ordinary forbid anyone to marry?
Under what conditions?

Canon 1077 § 1.

**Ordinarius loci propriis subditis ubique commorantibus
et omnibus in proprio territorio actu degentibus
vetare potest matrimonium in casu peculiari,
sed ad tempus tantum,
gravi de causa eaque perdurante.**

**The local ordinary can forbid marriage to his subjects, no
    matter where they are,
and to all who are actually present in his territory,
in a peculiar case,
but for a time only,
for a grave cause and as long as it exists.**

The ordinary can forbid marriage: he has the power to impose an "impedient" impediment; if the subject disobeys and marries, the act is unlawful (illicit) but valid.

to his subjects: to those who have domicile in the diocese; not to those who have quasi domicile, since a law restricting a fundamental right must be strictly interpreted according to the letter and spirit of canon 18.

to all who are actually present in his territory: as regards strangers in the diocese, this is simply a positive ruling that they must obey.[2]

peculiar case: there is something special and unusual about the case; the use of this term restricts the power of the ordinary even more than the expression "particular case" would have done, which in canon law usually means an individual case, or an individual set of cases, but not necessarily different from what is of common occurrence.

for a time only: the decree of the bishop must determine how long the prohibition is to last.

grave cause: there should be a proportion between the cause and the effect. Without a grave cause the ordinary should not issue a grave prohibition. To forbid marriage is a grave interference with the fundamental freedoms of a person.

Canon 1077 § 2.

Vetito clausulam dirimentem una suprema Ecclesiae auctoritas addere potest.

The supreme authority of the church alone can add an invalidating clause to the prohibition.

The supreme authority can be the pope only or someone delegated by him.

---

[2]Canon 13 says that strangers or travelers, *peregrini*, are not bound by the particular laws of the territory where they find themselves unless those laws concern the *public order* or determine the *formalities of a juridical act* or refer to local *real property*; canon 1077 adds: unless the laws establish a marriage impediment for that territory.

Whom can the local ordinary dispense?
From what impediments?

Canon 1078 § 1.

Ordinarius loci proprios subditos ubique commorantes
et omnes in proprio territorio actu degentes
ab omnibus impedimentis iuris ecclesiastici dispensare potest,
exceptis iis, quorum dispensatio Sedi Apostolicae reservatur.

The local ordinary can dispense his subjects, no matter where
they are,
and all who are actually present in his territory,
from all impediments of ecclesiastical law,
with the exception of those from which the dispensation is
reserved to the Apostolic See.

The paragraph is self explanatory. A list of the impediments of
ecclesiastical law is given at the end of this chapter.

❧❀❧

What dispensations are reserved to the Apostolic See?

Canon 1078 § 2.

Impedimenta quorum dispensatio Sedi Apostolicae reservatur
sunt:
1° impedimentum ortum ex sacris ordinibus
aut ex voto publico perpetuo castitatis in instituto religioso iuris
pontificii;
2° impedimentum criminis de quo in can. 1090.

The impediments from which the dispensation is reserved to the
Apostolic See are:
1° the impediment arising from sacred orders, or,
from a public perpetual vow of chastity in a religious institute of
pontifical right;
2° the impediment of crime as mentioned in canon 1090.

sacred orders: diaconate, presbyterate and episcopate; cf. canon 1087.

public perpetual vow: as opposed to a mere private or temporary vow; cf. canon 1088.

in a religious institute of pontifical right: a direct dispensation from the impediments would be an unusual occurrence; the correct procedure in ordinary circumstances is to obtain a dispensation from the vow, which brings with it the freedom to marry. Note that the local ordinary can dispense from a vow taken in a religious institute of *diocesan* right.

What impediments are never dispensed from?

Canon 1078 § 3.

Numquam datur dispensatio
ab impedimento consanguinitatis in linea recta
aut in secundo gradu lineae collateralis.

No dispensation is ever given
from the impediment of consanguinity in the direct line,
or in the second degree of the collateral line.

direct line: it links the parents and their children, the grandparents and their grandchildren.

of the collateral line in the second degree: it exists between brothers and sisters, including half brothers and half sisters.

In addition, no dispensation is ever granted from any impediment that is considered to be of divine law.

In danger of death,
whom can the local ordinary dispense and from what?

Canon 1079 § 1.

Urgente mortis periculo,
loci Ordinarius potest tum super forma in matrimonii
　celebratione servanda,
tum super omnibus et singulis impedimentis iuris ecclesiastici
sive publicis sive occultis,
dispensare proprios subditos ubique commorantes
et omnes in proprio territorio actu degentes,
excepto impedimento orto ex sacro ordine presbyteratus.

In danger of death,
the local ordinary can dispense his own subjects no matter where
　they are,
and all who are actually in his territory,
both from the form to be observed in the celebration of
　marriage
and from each and every impediment of ecclesiastical law,
whether public or occult,
with the exception of the impediment arising from the sacred
　order of presbyterate.

danger of death: there is a threat to life but not necessarily an imminent threat; it should not be confused with the situation where death appears inevitable.

his own subjects: personal jurisdiction based on domicile or quasi-domicile; the bond with the ordinary remains no matter where the subject goes.

all in his territory: any person physically present in the territory.

dispensation from the form means that they are not bound to observe the canonical form. Any external sign of consent is enough. No witnesses are required.

presbyterate: the only reserved impediment in danger of death.

⌔ ⁕ ⌕

In danger of death,
if the local ordinary cannot be reached,
who can dispense and from what?

Canon 1079 § 2.

In eisdem rerum adiunctis, de quibus in § 1,
sed solum pro casibus in quibus ne loci quidem Ordinarius adiri
  possit,
eadem dispensandi potestate pollet
tum parochus,
tum minister sacer rite delegatus,
tum sacerdos vel diaconus qui matrimonio, ad normam can.
  1116, § 2, assistit.

In the same circumstances that are mentioned in § 1,
but in those cases only when not even the local ordinary can be
  reached,
[*the following persons*] have the same power to dispense:
the parish priest,
the sacred minister duly delegated,
the priest or deacon who assists at the marriage according to the
  norm of canon 1116 § 2.

In danger of death the dispensing power of the ordinary is extended
— to the parish priest,
— to the person duly delegated to be assistant, provided he is in sacred orders,
— to the person in sacred orders, invited to be present at the exchange of the promises but not receiving them in the name of the church, according to canon 1116 § 2.

In danger of death,
what can the confessor do?

Canon 1079 § 3.

In periculo mortis confessarius gaudet potestate dispensandi
ab impedimentis occultis pro foro interno
sive intra sive extra actum sacramentalis confessionis.

In danger of death the confessor enjoys the power to dispense
from occult impediments in the internal forum
both inside and outside the act of a sacramental confession.

The confessor's dispensing power is restricted to occult impediments and to the internal forum. He can use it immediately; he is not under duty to inquire if the ordinary can be reached.

If he is present at the exchange of the promises, by law he becomes a special witness in the sense of canon 1116 § 2; if so, in virtue of § 2 of this canon, he has the same power as the ordinary, provided the ordinary cannot be reached in time.

❦

When is access to the local ordinary impossible?

Canon 1079 § 4.

In casu de quo in § 2,
loci Ordinarius censetur adiri non posse,
si tantum per telegraphum vel telephonum id fieri possit.

In the case mentioned in § 2,
access to the local ordinary is considered impossible
if it can be done by telegraph or telephone only.

The law is made for the church universal. There are many places where communication by telegraph or telephone is difficult, and, even when possible, there is no assurance that confidentiality can be preserved.

The person authorized to grant the dispensation in an emergency may safely do so if he estimates that a response from the ordinary to a request sent by mail would not arrive in good time. If in doubt, he has the power to dispense.

✎ ✳ ✎

When an impediment is discovered before the wedding and there is no time for the ordinary process, who can dispense and from what impediments?

Canon 1080 § 1.

Quoties impedimentum detegatur
cum iam omnia sunt parata ad nuptias,
nec matrimonium sine probabili gravis mali periculo differri
possit
usquedum a competenti auctoritate dispensatio obtineatur,
potestate gaudent dispensandi ab omnibus impedimentis,
iis exceptis de quibus in can. 1078, § 2, n. 1,
loci Ordinarius
et, dummodo casus sit occultus, omnes de quibus in can. 1079,
§§ 2-3,
servatis condicionibus ibidem praescriptis.

Whenever an impediment is discovered
after all the preparations for the wedding have been completed
and
the marriage cannot be postponed without the probable danger
of serious damage
until dispensation is obtained from the competent authority,
the local ordinary,
and, provided the case is an occult one, all persons mentioned in
canon 1079 §§ 2-3,
enjoy the power to dispense from all impediments,
with the exception of those mentioned in canon 1078, § 2, n. 1;
provided all conditions there prescribed are observed.

No precise indication can be given as to the exact moment when the preparations must be considered advanced enough to warrant the application of this canon. Nor is it possible to determine with precision what the expression probable danger of serious damage implies. The person authorized to grant this dispensation should form a prudential judgment that takes into account all the circumstances.

The gist of the rule is:

— dispensation from the impediments of sacred orders and of public vow in a religious institute of pontifical right remains reserved to the Holy See;

— the local ordinary can dispense from all other impediments of ecclesiastical law, whether public or occult;

— the parish priest, the assistant, or the confessor can dispense from the same impediments provided they are occult.

⌒※⌒

When a validation is urgent,
who can dispense and from what impediments?

Canon 1080 § 2.

Haec potestas valet etiam ad matrimonium convalidandum,
si idem periculum sit in mora
nec tempus suppetat recurrendi ad Sedem Apostolicam
vel ad loci Ordinarium, quod attinet ad impedimenta a quibus
dispensare valet.

This power is granted also for the validation of a marriage
if the same danger exists in delay and
there is no time to approach the Apostolic See, or
the local ordinary in the case of impediments from which he
can dispense.

In the case of a validation the pressure is likely to come from other circumstances than the completed preparations; again, the person authorized by law to dispense should take on himself the responsibility of forming a prudential judgment about the course to follow.

*Who are responsible for the recording of a dispensation
granted in an emergency situation?*

Canon 1081

Parochus aut sacerdos vel diaconus, de quibus in can. 1079, § 2,
de concessa dispensatione pro foro externo
Ordinarium loci statim certiorem faciat;
eaque adnotetur in libro matrimoniorum.

The parish priest or the priest or the deacon, mentioned in
  canon 1079 § 2,
must immediately inform the local ordinary
of a dispensation granted in the external forum;
it must be recorded also in the book of marriages.

⤞ ❋ ⤝

How to record a dispensation granted by the Penitentiary?

Canon 1082

Nisi aliud ferat Paenitentiariae rescriptum,
dispensatio in foro interno non sacramentali concessa super
  impedimento occulto,
adnotetur in libro, qui in secreto curiae archivo asservandus est,
nec alia dispensatio pro foro externo est necessaria,
si postea occultum impedimentum publicum evaserit.

Unless the rescript of the Penitentiary directs otherwise.
a dispensation from an occult impediment granted in the
  internal non sacramental forum
must be recorded in the book which is to be kept in the secret
  archives of the curia;
no other dispensation is necessary in the external forum
if afterwards the occult impediment becomes public.

If the occult impediment becomes public, the dispensation can be
publicized, too.

Concerning the secret archives of the diocesan curia *see* canons 489 and 490.

Summary of the rules for dispensation

In ordinary circumstances:
The local ordinary can dispense from the following impediments of ecclesiastical law (not reserved):
age,
disparity of cult,
public vow in a religious institute of diocesan right,
abduction,
consanguinity, 3d and 4th degree collateral,
affinity,
public honesty,
adoption;

he cannot dispense from the following impediments of ecclesiastical law (reserved):
sacred orders,
public vow in a religious institute of pontifical right,
crime;

he cannot dispense from the following impediments of natural (not necessarily divine) law:
impotence,
previous bond (privilege of faith may be applicable by law),
consanguinity, direct and 2d degree collateral.

In danger of death:
The local ordinary can dispense from
the canonical form and
all impediments of ecclesiatical law;

he cannot dispense from
presbyterate.

The parish priest (parochus),
the delegated assistant (in sacred orders),
the invited priest or deacon,
the confessor (in the internal forum only):

all have the same power as the ordinary, whenever he cannot be reached (by mail).

The confessor can dispense from occult impediments in the internal forum only.

Completed preparations:
The local ordinary can dispense from all impediments of ecclesiastical law whether public or occult;

he cannot dispense from
sacred orders,
public vow in a religious institute of pontifical right.

The parish priest,
the delegated assistant,
the invited priest or deacon,
the confessor,
all have the same power as the ordinary but for occult cases only.

Validation: *see* the case of **completed preparations:**
The ordinary has the same power, provided he cannot reach the Holy See;

the others have the same power, provided they cannot reach the Holy See or the ordinary for cases within his competence.

CHAPTER THREE
DIRIMENT IMPEDIMENTS
IN PARTICULAR
1083 — 1094

Transitions: *From complexity to simplicity.* The old Code listed five "impedient" and thirteen "diriment" impediments, some of them (crime, consanguinity, affinity) quite far reaching and complicated. The new Code is restrained; it lists twelve diriment impediments. On the whole they are simple and impose a minimum of restrictions.

This chapter presents the new law only. The old law of impediments can be easily found in a commentary of CIC/17; to present it here would inevitably overload this chapter with historical data and obscure the clarity and simplicity of the present system. But it should be recalled that marriages contracted before CIC/83 entered into force should be judged on the basis of the old law.

Literary form: *Every single canon in this chapter is a legal norm concerned with rights and duties.*

A remark: Although the law distinguishes clearly between impediments and requirements, in some cases such differentiation may be due more to historical developments than to strict logic; e.g. sexual impotence is an impediment (canon 1084) but the capacity to fulfill the essential obligations of marriage is presented as a requirement in the chapter on consent (canon 1095). Laws develop pragmatically.

Preliminary survey of the impediments

The impediments can be grouped in various ways.

A person does not have the minimal requirements for marriage:
too young: *age*;
not able to have proper sexual relations: *impotence*;
historically these impediments were understood as particular applications of the natural law.

A fact with a religious significance can give rise to an impediment:
the intended partner is not baptized: *disparity of cult*;
a man has received the order of diaconate, presbyterate or
episcopate: *sacred orders*;
a person has taken the public perpetual vow of chastity in a
religious institute: *religious vow*;
these impediments have been established by ecclesiastical legislation.

An unlawful or criminal act can be at the origin of an impediment:
kidnapping or holding a person in captivity: *abduction*;
murdering a spouse, alone or in conspiracy: *crime*;
these impediments, too, have been instituted by ecclesiastical
legislation.

An existing relationship between two persons may exclude marriage:
close blood relationship: *consanguinity*;
close "in law" relationship: *affinity*;
cohabitation: *public honesty*;
legal relationship: *adoption*;
apart from consanguinity, which in direct line and in the closest of
collateral lines was often called of natural law, these impediments
have their origin in ecclesiastical legislation;
also, an existing marital relationship excludes any other one: *bond*;
bond is traditionally classified as an impediment of natural or divine
law.

The values the impediments intend to uphold are *varied and multiple*; the protection of one specific value cannot be always attributed to one specific impediment only. The whole system of impediments, however, is intimately related to a system of values. By way of examples, the following values can be mentioned as protected by the impediments:

the physical and spiritual maturity of the partners (age),
the preservation of Christian cult in the family (disparity of cult),
religious values in the community (sacred orders, religious vow),
personal freedom (abduction),
a certain integrity that should mark conjugal and family relations, also the welfare of the offspring (bond, impotence, consanguinity, affinity, public honesty, adoption),
the protection of human life, the integrity of the *consortium* (crime).

What is the legal age for marriage?

Canon 1083 § 1.

**Vir ante decimum sextum aetatis annum completum,
mulier ante decimum quartum item completum,
matrimonium validum inire non possunt.**

**A man before the completion of the age of sixteen,
a woman before the completion of fourteen,
cannot enter marriage validly.**

The minimum age for marriage is set in view of the universal church. The canon is based on an overall presumption: before the age indicated a person is not likely to be mature enough to understand the meaning of the marriage covenant and to commit himself or herself for life.

Canon 1083 § 2.

Integrum est Episcoporum conferentiae aetatem superiorem ad licitam matrimonii celebrationem statuere.

The episcopal conference can determine a higher age for the lawful [*licit*] celebration of marriage.

If the episcopal conference of a nation or of a region takes advantage of this canon, a good balance between the universal norm and the local needs can be established. True, the conference cannot impose an incapacitating impediment, but in practice its ruling would make marriage impossible, at least within its territory, because no ecclesiastical assistance would be available to those who are younger than the age required.

⌒⁂⌒

What kind of impotence constitutes an impediment?

Canon 1084 § 1.

Impotentia coeundi antecedens et perpetua, sive ex parte viri sive ex parte mulieris, sive absoluta sive relativa, matrimonium ex ipsa eius natura dirimit.

Antecedent and perpetual impotence to have sexual intercourse, whether on the part of the man or on the part of the woman, whether absolute or relative, by its nature invalidates marriage.

impotence is a negative term; its correct understanding must come from its positive counterpart, potency.

Potency in the canonical sense means the capacity to perform an act which by its very nature is apt for the generation of children.[1] In the case of the man this includes (1) the erection of the penis, (2) its penetration into the vagina, and (3) ejaculation. In the case of the woman it includes (1) the possession of the vagina and (2) the capacity to receive the penis into the vagina. Theoretically it may be disputable whether or not the vagina should be open towards the other internal organs to which the semen must be transmitted for fertilization; practically the jurisprudence of the Rota resolved the issue: potency means that the vagina is open to the uterus, cf. the decision *coram* Sabattani in 1965: "If the vagina itself. . .is closed by a natural defect or by surgery, the case is one of impotence," and "If the vagina leads not to the uterus but to some other organ, the case is one of impotence" (*see* CLD 6:615; the decision is an extensive explanation of female impotence; it may even be going too far in casuistry).

Canonical impotence then means the absence of any of the above described positive requirements; it is an incapacity to perform sexual intercourse in a natural way. This "canonical impotence" must not be confused with the meaning of the term in modern medical literature where impotence can mean infertility.

There has been a controversy whether or not the semen had to be "true," that is secreted by the testicles, irrespective of its fertility. The issue has been resolved by a Decree of the CDF in 1977: as long as there is ejaculation, there is potency; no biological examination is necessary to determine the precise nature or origin of the secretion. This development represents a return from an excessively scientific way of determining canonical requirements to an older and a more traditional approach based on common sense.[2]

[1]In the biological order two types of causation must be distinguished:

(1) once the cause is there, the effect necessarily follows; as the heart beats, the blood unfailingly circulates; there is a biological necessity from cause to effect;

(2) once the cause is there, there is a statistically demonstrable degree of probability that the effect will follow; if the semen has been deposited into the vagina, there is a degree of probability that conception may follow; the effect is due to the cause, but the cause does not always produce the effect.

Nature itself indicates that the purpose of an act "apt for the procreation of children" is not exclusively and necessarily the procreation of children.

[2]Cf. CLD 8:676-677. In this decree there are three affirmations:

(1) persons who have undergone vasectomy must be given the benefit of doubt, hence they have the right to marry,

Impotence can be either of physical or of psychological origin; canon law recognizes both.

antecedent: it must have existed before the marriage.

perpetual: the condition is such that it cannot be cured by ordinary means. There is no way of giving a precise definition of what is ordinary or extraordinary because there is an element of relativity in the concepts; they change not only with the progress of medical science, but also with the availability of medical help in a given place.

either on the part of the man, or on the part of the woman: if one of the parties is impotent, the marriage is invalid.

absolute: the person is incapable of sexual intercourse with anyone of the opposite sex.

relative: the person is incapable of sexual intercourse with a determined individual person of the other sex.

by its nature: if one of the ends of the marriage is the procreation of children, it is naturally required that the capacity to do what is necessary for their generation should be there.

꒒꒷꒫

How to proceed if the impotence is doubtful?

Canon 1084 § 2.

**Si impedimentum impotentiae dubium sit,
sive dubio iuris sive dubio facti,
matrimonium non est impediendum
nec, stante dubio, nullum declarandum.**

(2) the impediment of impotence consists in the incapacity to perform the sexual intercourse in a normal way, and,

(3) ejaculation is necessary but no semen elaborated in the testicles is required.

If the impediment of impotence is doubtful,
either for doubt of law or doubt of fact,
the marriage is not to be impeded,
nor to be declared null while the doubt persists.

This paragraph contains practical directions for procedure: what to do in the case of doubt, either before or after the marriage.

Before the marriage the benefit of doubt should be given to the person who intends to marry; to cancel out the fundamental right to marry, the impediment should be certain beyond any shadow of doubt. In recent times there has been a trend to interpret this norm with increasing generosity; couples were allowed to marry even if the likelihood that they would be able to have sexual intercourse was minimal.[3]

After the marriage has been contracted, the law favors the stability of the union; hence proofs must be produced, enough to establish "moral certainty" that impotence was there in the first place. In practice it might be easier to handle such cases by establishing "non consummation" than by attempting to demonstrate impotence.

A query often raised today is whether or not canonically impotent persons should (or could) be permitted to marry on the ground that they are able to achieve one of the joint ends of the marriage, which is companionship. After all, so the argument goes, canon law never held for invalid a marriage where the partners intended to transfer the "right to the body" but agreed not to make use of it; there is a marriage for companionship only. Besides, canon law always allowed old people to marry and refused to raise questions about their sexual potency, although it is a well known medical fact that many

---

[3]This trend appears to be present in some official Roman documents. Examples:
- Private reply, 16 February 1935, HO, reported in CLD 3:410-411:
  Question: If a man has undergone bilateral vasectomy which is total and irreparable, can he be allowed to contract marriage?
  Answer: Marriage must not be impeded.
- Private reply, 28 September 1957, HO, reported in CLD 5:506-507:
  The same question, the same answer.
- Private reply, 28 January 1964, HO, reported in CLD 6:616-618:
  Question: If a man subjected himself to an operation of bilateral vasectomy prior to his marriage, is his marriage valid?

old persons are impotent. There again, no matter what subtle distinctions we find in the books, as a matter of fact, the church lets marriages take place for the sake of companionship only. — The traditional answer is clearly stated in the Code, old and new: impotence is a diriment impediment. Still, the problem is not fully solved; the questioning continues. If nature has deprived some persons from pursuing both ends of the marriage, must our law deprive them from pursuing the one they can? Is there no room for doctrinal development? Is there not already a development in the attitude of the church towards those who have undergone vasectomy or towards old people? — Such are the questions raised. They are legitimate and they show that the problem is not fully solved; it deserves serious study. Ultimately the answer should come rather from the field of theology than from that of canon law.

꒰⊱✳⊰꒱

Is sterility an impediment?

Canon 1084 § 3.

**Sterilitas matrimonium nec prohibet nec dirimit,
firmo praescripto can. 1098.**

**Sterility neither forbids nor invalidates marriage;
the prescription of canon 1098, however, remains effective.**

This canon is easier to understand if its historical origins are recalled. Before the emergence of modern biological science, little was

---

Answer: The marriage cannot be declared null on the basis of impotence.
• Private reply, 11 June 1965, HO, reported in CLD 6:618-619:
Question: If a man underwent orchiectomy (removal of both testicles) and partial prostatectomy, can his marriage be validated?
Answer: His marriage can be validated.
• Decree, 13 May 1977, CDF, cf. CLD 8:676-677:
"...persons who have undergone vasectomy and other persons in similar conditions must not be prohibited from marriage..."

known about the laws of human generation. Two aspects of it were clear though: (1) conception was the effect of sexual intercourse, (2) not every intercourse produced conception. Fertilization was the mysterious work of nature, *opus naturae,* hence it could not be included in the marriage contract. But to provide the conditions for it through intercourse was the work of human persons, *opus hominum,* that could be included in the contract. Fertility or sterility was simply beyond the understanding of any human being; there nature acted in its own sovereign way.

The reference to canon 1098 is a reference to consent obtained through fraud; the law wants to make clear that a fraudulent misrepresentation concerning the fertility of the future partner may well cause the marriage to be invalid. Still, the cause of invalidity will be in the fraud perpetrated, not in the infertility itself.

༄ ✻ ༄

When is a previous marriage an impediment?

Canon 1085 § 1.

**Invalide matrimonium attentat
qui vinculo tenetur prioris matrimonii,
quamquam non consummati.**

**A person bound by the bond of a previous marriage,
even if it has not been consummated,
attempts marriage invalidly.**

Marriage here means a valid marriage, sacramental or not, consummated or not. An invalid bond can never create an impediment.

Canon 1085 § 2.

**Quamvis prius matrimonium sit irritum aut solutum qualibet ex causa,
non ideo licet aliud contrahere,**

antequam de prioris nullitate aut solutione
legitime et certo constiterit.

**Even if the previous marriage is invalid or dissolved for any
reason,
it is not therefore lawful [*licit*] to contract another one
before the nullity or the dissolution of the previous one
has been established legitimately and with certainty.**

This paragraph is concerned with the celebration of a second marriage. It is not permitted until the freedom of the person to marry has been established by a due process of law.

The second marriage, however, would not be invalid if the first was indeed null and void but as yet no official document has been issued to the effect. The impediment is in the existence of a previous bond, not in the lack of a document. The wording of the paragraph is consistent with this interpretation, since it speaks of "not permitted," *non licet*, a technical term that is not used lightly, and when it is used, it never implies invalidity.

❦

What is the impediment of disparity of cult?

Canon 1086 § 1.

**Matrimonium inter duas personas,
quarum altera sit baptizata in Ecclesia catholica vel in eandem
recepta nec actu formali ab ea defecerit,
et altera non baptizata,
invalidum est.**

**Marriage between two persons,
one of whom was baptized in the Catholic church or received
into it and has not defected from it through a formal act, and
the other of whom was not baptized,
is invalid.**

This impediment is known traditionally as "disparity of cult." If dispensation is granted, canon law handles the resulting marriage as a natural, that is, non sacramental union, with all the consequences that such a status entails. Since it does not have the "particular firmness" that the sacrament brings, it can be dissolved through the grant of the privilege of the faith.

A question for investigation: This attitude of the law is a pragmatic one; it should not be taken as settling a more subtle theological issue, whether or not the marriage covenant can play the role of sacramental sign for the Christian party. The traditional approach of the law has been and remains the denial of any such possibility. The justification for this negative response is usually summed up in the principle: *sacramenta non possunt claudicare*, "sacraments cannot limp," meaning that there must be an evenness in the reception of the sacrament; if one party cannot receive it, the other cannot have it either. The correctness of this principle, however, is far from having been critically established; the issue requires more study. The point of departure of such inquiry may well be the doctrine of Paul in 1 Co 7:14:

> For the unbelieving husband is consecrated through his wife,
> and the unbelieving wife is consecrated through her husband.
> Otherwise, your children would be unclean, but as it is, they are
> holy.

Clearly for Paul a marriage between a believer and an unbeliever is radically different from a marriage between two unbelievers. Canon law has not taken any notice of this forceful passage; nor have systematic theologians paid much attention to it. Paul leaves no doubt that there is a new sanctifying power in a union where one of the spouses is "holy." This sanctifying power is very close to what we call today the "effect" of a sacrament.

Note, however, that even if the exchange of promises could be interpreted as a sign that signifies and confers grace to the Christian party, such marriage itself could never be as fully sacramental as marriages between Christians are.

formal act: this expression causes a special difficulty in the North American continent where people do not change their religion through a "formal act," such as through a notarized statement recognized by secular authorities, as it can happen in other places where a person's religion is part of his civic identity. Therefore, to construe a universally applicable theoretical definition of "formal act" is virtually impossible.

The significance of an act must be determined on the ground of both its content and its context; identical acts can carry different meanings in different circumstances. For practical purposes, however, someone can be legitimately presumed to have left the Catholic church if he either performed certain acts or put himself into a situation that leaves no doubt that he intended to terminate his allegiance to the Catholic community, e.g. he received confirmation or ordination in another Christian church, or, he publicly declared himself to be an atheist. If the evidence for leaving the church is so strong that it could stand up to examination by a court, a "formal act" must be assumed.

❧ ✳ ☙

Under what conditions can dispensation be granted?

Canon 1086 § 2.

**Ab hoc impedimento ne dispensetur,
nisi impletis condicionibus de quibus in cann. 1125 et 1126.**

**From this impediment no dispensation is to be granted
unless the conditions stated in canons 1125 and 1126 are fulfilled.**

Those are the conditions to be fulfilled in the case of a mixed marriage; see our comments on the canons quoted.

❧ ✳ ☙

*What is to be done if after the wedding
doubts arise about the baptism of one of the parties?*

Canon 1086 § 3.

**Si pars tempore contracti matrimonii
tamquam baptizata communiter habebatur aut eius baptismus
erat dubius,**

praesumenda est, ad normam can. 1060, validitas matrimonii, donec certo probetur
alteram partem baptizatam esse, alteram vero non baptizatam.

If at the time when the marriage was contracted
one party was commonly held for baptized or his baptism was doubted,
the marriage must be presumed valid in accordance with the norm of canon 1060
until it is proved with certainty
that one party is baptized, the other is not.

This paragraph is concerned with a procedural problem and solves it through invoking the principle contained in canon 1060: "Marriage enjoys the favor of the law." A marriage should be declared invalid on the ground of this impediment when no doubt exists that at the time of the wedding one of the parties was baptized, the other was not, and of course no dispensation was granted.

❦

Can persons in sacred orders marry validly?

Canon 1087

Invalide matrimonium attentant,
qui in sacris ordinibus sunt constituti.

Those who are in sacred orders
attempt marriage invalidly.

sacred orders are the diaconate, the presbyterate and the episcopate.

Permanent deacons who wish to marry or who wish to remarry after the death of their spouse, may request a dispensation from the Holy See. All others must obtain a decree of laicization, which usually includes the dispensation from the law of celibacy, although it can be granted without it.[4]

---

[4]Cf. CLD 9:92-101 for the norms of laicization.

What vow constitutes an impediment?

Canon 1088

Invalide matrimonium attentant,
qui voto publico perpetuo castitatis in instituto religioso adstricti
sunt.

Those who are bound by a public perpetual vow of chastity in a
religious institute
attempt marriage invalidly.

religious institute: the institutes of consecrated life are divided into two categories: religious institutes and secular institutes; the impediment affects only the members of a religious institute, provided they have taken perpetual vows, simple or solemn.

It makes no difference if the religious institute is of pontifical or of diocesan right; the impediment is there in both cases.

The impediment does not extend to the members of a society of apostolic life, nor to canonically recognized hermits or liturgically consecrated virgins.

A simple perpetual vow of chastity taken in a religious order or congregation before CIC/83 entered into force was not a diriment impediment according to the common law of the church. It was, however, a public vow. It follows that the same vow must be regarded now as a diriment impediment.

How does the impediment of abduction arise?
How does it cease?

Canon 1089

Inter virum et mulierem abductam vel saltem retentam
intuitu matrimonii cum ea contrahendi,
nullum matrimonium consistere potest,
nisi postea mulier a raptore separata et in loco tuto ac libero
constituta,
matrimonium sponte eligat.

No marriage can exist
between a man and a woman who has been abducted or is at
**   least detained,**
for the purpose of a marriage to be contracted with her,
unless the woman, after she has been separated from the
**   abductor and established in a safe and free place,**
chooses marriage of her own accord.

Force and fear in this case is irrelevant; the physical fact of having abducted or holding a person captive is what counts. As long as she does not enjoy freedom from all such constraints, there is an impediment between her and the man for whose sake the mischief was perpetrated, even if he had nothing to do with the abduction. Indeed, the loss of freedom may have been brought about by others, e.g. by her family or by the friends of the would-be bridegroom.

There is no impediment if a man has been abducted or is detained in view of a marriage.

＊

What crimes give rise to an impediment?

Canon 1090 § 1.

Qui intuitu matrimonii cum certa persona ineundi,
huius coniugi vel proprio coniugi mortem intulerit,
invalide hoc matrimonium attentat.

One who for the purpose of entering marriage with a particular
**   person,**
brought about the death of that person's spouse, or of one's own
**   spouse,**
attempts that marriage invalidly.

brought about the death: murder is the cause of the impediment; the crime of homicide must have been consummated; if the victim survives, there is no impediment.

brought about: in any way, physically or morally; personally or by the agency of others.

for the purpose of contracting marriage: it refers to the intention of the murderer; if he or she was motivated by any other reason, good or bad, such as legitimate self defense, or illegitimate financial gains, the impediment does not arise. Not an 'entirely satisfactory rule; it allows a criminal to benefit from an otherwise evil action.

the other's spouse or of one's own spouse, or of both, of course. The impediment is relative; it bars marriage between the murderer and the person who was the intended spouse throughout the crime, provided the crime was committed to make that marriage possible. The criminal is free to marry anyone else.

Canon 1090 § 2.

Invalide quoque matrimonium inter se attentant
qui mutua opera physica vel morali
mortem coniugi intulerunt.

Also those who through mutual physical or moral cooperation
brought about the death of either of their spouses
attempt marriage between themselves invalidly.

persons: in this case a man and a woman must be guilty of both murder and conspiracy; they need not be the actual executors of the crime.

brought about the death: again, for the impediment to arise the crime must have been consummated; the physical fact of death must be there.

There is no mention of any specific intention or motivation in view of a marriage; the impediment arises even if the death was not inflicted for the purpose of marriage, provided there is criminal intention in the general sense.

To see clearly the difference between the two types of crime it may be helpful to illustrate them by cases, each case representing the simplest of many possible variations:

Case one: James is married to Jane but he wishes to marry Rose who is single. In order to be free, he brings about the death of Jane. The moment Jane dies, the impediment between James and Rose arises, although Rose knows nothing about his desire or about his crime.

Case two: Roger is married to Ruth. He is also the business partner of Clare who is single. The partners conspire to kill Ruth for the sake of financial gain. The moment the victim expires, the impediment between Roger and Clare arises, even if they never thought of marrying each other and the crime was not for the sake of any marriage.

In case one the criminal acts alone, the motivation for the crime is marriage with a particular person, the victim is one or both of the spouses, the intended partner may not be involved at all in the crime. The criminal cannot marry the intended partner.

In case two a man and a woman conspire to kill, their motivation for the crime need not be marriage, the victim is one or both of the spouses. The criminals cannot marry each other.

The reasons for this impediment could be summed up in two principles:

— a murderer for the sake of a marriage should not be rewarded by that marriage;

— partners in murder should not be partners in marriage.

⟲ ✳ ⟳

How far does the impediment of consanguinity extend?

Canon 1091 § 1.

**In linea recta consanguinitatis matrimonium irritum est
inter omnes ascendentes et descendentes
tum legitimos tum naturales.**

**In the direct line of consanguinity marriage is invalid
between all the ancestors and their descendants,
legitimate or natural.**

Consanguinity means blood relationship, nothing else. It arises through human generation, either in marriage (then the offspring is legitimate) or out of wedlock (then the offspring is natural). The rules for determining the degrees of consanguinity are given in canon 108; the following is a recapitulation of it:

The degrees of consanguinity signify the proximity of relationship. A simple way of counting them comes to us from Roman law: *tot sunt gradus quot generationes*, there are as many degrees as generations. Or, *tot sunt gradus quot personae stipite dempto*, there are as many degrees as persons involved, not counting the common ancestor.

The lines of consanguinity can be direct or collateral. Direct lines run "vertically," from the ancestors to their descendants; collateral lines are drawn "horizontally" among those who descended from a common ancestor.

To determine the degree of relationship merely numerically, the nature of the line is irrevelant. Thus, both the granddaughter and the sister of a man are related to him in the second degree of consanguinity; in each case two acts of generation have taken place, or in each case there are two persons related to each other, not counting the common ancestor.[5]

But when a marriage is contemplated, the nature of the line is of paramount importance; therefore in determining the extent of forbidden degrees, the law distinguishes the direct line from the collateral line.

---

[5]The new Code has returned fully to the ancient Roman method of determining the degrees of consanguinity. The old Code used another method, partly of Germanic origin. In the direct line it counted the generations as the Romans did. In the collateral line it counted the generations in one branch only if the branches were equal, in the longer branch if they were unequal. Thus, after the numerical determination of the degree, it was always essential to add "of the diret line" or "of the collateral line." By way of illustration: according to CIC/17 brothers and sisters are related in the first degree *of the collateral line*; in CIC/83 they are related in the second degree (of the collateral line). For more information *see* e.g. T. Lincoln Bouscaren and Adam C. Ellis, *Canon Law: A Text and Commentary* (Milwaukee: Bruce, 1953), pp. 82-83.

This canon tells us that among those who are related in *direct line* no marriage is permitted; understandably so.

Canon 1091 § 2.

**In linea collaterali irritum est
usque ad quartum gradum inclusive.**

**In collateral line it is invalid
up to the fourth degree inclusive.**

Further, among those who are related in the collateral line no marriage is permitted up to the fourth degree inclusive, which in common parlance means "no marriage between first cousins." Note that in each line there have been two acts of generation, or that there are four persons involved, not counting the common grandparent.

Canon 1091 § 3.

Impedimentum consanguinitatis non multiplicatur.

The impediment of consanguinity does not multiply.

When two persons have more than one proximate common ancestor, in the biological order there is a multiplication of the relationship of consanguinity. E.g. if a man and a woman have two common grandfathers or grandmothers, biologically they are more closely related than if they had just one. CIC/17 following a long standing tradition has taken into account such multiplication of the relationships and multiplied the impediments accordingly. Not so CIC/83: it takes no juridical notice of the multiplication of the biological relationship. Even when the spouses-to-be have more than one common ancestor, there is not more than one impediment.

Canon 1091 § 4.

**Numquam matrimonium permittatur,
si quod subest dubium
num partes sint consanguineae
in aliquo gradu lineae rectae
aut in secundo gradu lineae collateralis.**

**Marriage is never to be permitted
if a doubt exists that
the parties may be related by consanguinity
in any degree of the direct line, or
in the second degree of the collateral line.**

The doubt must be reasonable; it must be supported by some ascertainable fact. Mere suspicion would not be enough.

In the practical order a case may present itself where there is a serious probability, but no certainty, that a man and a woman have one parent in common. If the doubt cannot be resolved, the couple cannot marry.

How far does the impediment of affinity extend?

Canon 1092

Affinitas in linea recta dirimit matrimonium in quolibet gradu.

Affinity in any degree of the direct line invalidates marriage.

Affinity arises from the bond of a valid marriage, sacramental or not, consummated or not. It is a legal, "in law," relationship between one spouse and the blood relations of the other spouse; cf. canon 109.

The degree and the line of a relationship by consanguinity for the one is the degree and the line by affinity for the other. E.g. the wife's relationship to her own daughter from a previous marriage is that of consanguinity in the first degree of the direct line, consequently her present husband's relationship to the same daughter is that of affinity in the first degree of the direct line.

CIC/83 has broken with an old tradition that tended to spread the impediment of affinity far and wide. It invalidates marriage between those only who are related by affinity in any degree of the direct line; e.g. a man whose wife died cannot marry her mother or her daughter. He can, of course, marry her sister.

✿

How does the impediment of public honesty arise?
How far does it extend?

Canon 1093

Impedimentum publicae honestatis oritur ex matrimonio invalido
post instauratam vitam communem
aut ex notorio vel publico concubinatu;
et nuptias dirimit in primo gradu lineae rectae
inter virum et consanguineas mulieris,
ac vice versa.

The impediment of public honesty arises from an invalid marriage
after the common life has been initiated, or
from notorious or public concubinage;
it invalidates a marriage in the first degree of the direct line
between the man and the blood relations of the woman,
and *vice versa.*

The impediment of **public honesty** arises from a fact; a couple lived together, either as parties to an invalid marriage, or as partners in a notorious or public concubinage.

notorious or public concubinage: it is widely known; the evidence is so strong that the fact could be proven before a court, even if no one attempted to do so.

in the first degree of the direct line, that is between the man and the mother and the daughter of the woman, and between the woman and the father and the son of the man.

The impediment of public honesty is partly similar to, partly different from, the impediment of affinity. It is similar to affinity because it invalidates marriage with the blood relations of the partner; it is different from affinity because it arises from a factual situation (cohabitation) while affinity arises from a legal relationship (valid marriage).

⌒≈ ✳ ⌒≈

How far does the impediment of adoption extend?

Canon 1094

**Matrimonium inter se valide contrahere nequeunt
qui cognatione legali ex adoptione orta,
in linea recta aut in secundo gradu lineae collateralis, coniuncti
sunt.**

**Those who are legally related by adoption
in the direct line or in the second degree of the collateral line
cannot validly marry between themselves.**

The impediment of adoption is the logical application of the general rule of canon law concerning adoption: "The children who have been adopted according to the norm of civil law are considered as the children of the adoptive parent or parents" (canon 110).

The degrees and the lines are counted in the same way as for consanguinity. Marriage is barred in all degrees of the direct line (e.g. between a man and his adopted daughter) and in the second degree of the collateral line (between brothers and sisters by adoption).

CHAPTER FOUR
CONSENT
1095 — 1107

Transitions: *From conceptual rigidity toward pragmatic justice and equity.*

The norms of the old Code were conceived on the basis of a few philosophical assumptions, not explicitly stated in the law:

— consent was an act of the will;

— the will could operate, to a high degree, independently from the mind;

— the essence of marriage was always the same, eternal and unchangeable;

— even if a person was ignorant or in error concerning the properties of marriage, if he desired to marry he was bound by the eternal laws flowing from its nature;

— the substance of the marriage contract was the giving and the receiving of the right concerning the procreative act.

The laws born from these assumptions displayed the characteristics of an ideology: logically they were clear and consistent but often in conflict with the concrete demands of justice and equity.

The new Code retained some of the philosophical assumptions but introduced a few pragmatic rules to mitigate their harshest consequences; by doing that it opened the door to the world of empirical psychology. The result is a less cohesive system where the traditional abstract principles coexist uneasily with recent developments in human sciences.

Literary forms: *there are many* in this chapter. It contains *theological and philosophical assertions*, it permits *empirical psychology* to play a role in canonical practice, and it gives norms for both *substantive law and procedure.*

What is consent in itself, independently of the law? What is consent in canon law?

The issue of consent occupies a central position in the canonical doctrine of marriage. There the law meets theology, philosophy and empirical psychology. The result of these encounters is an extremely complex body of rules, feeding from different sources. To understand this complexity it is necessary to subject it to an analysis and to identify each of its components. Once its constitutive parts are known, critical questions can be raised about their respective roles and the internal balance of the whole can be evaluated.

Marriage is a sacrament in which two human persons mutually commit themselves for a new state of life. Such commitment is a theological and moral act; it has no value unless it springs from faith and charity, unless it is done intelligently and responsibly. By its very nature it is internal; it must be created in the very depth of the human spirit before it can be manifested externally. Its existence, or the lack of it, cannot be ascertained by any kind of empirical observation; it can be conjectured only from the presence of some appropriate external signs. The spiritual act of consent therefore cannot be the direct object of any legislation, since no law can see beyond the externals; its manifestations however are well within the realm of law.

Because of its incapacity to penetrate into the internal world of human persons, and its capacity to regulate and judge external actions, the law stands partly impotent, partly competent before the issue of consent. It stands impotent because it has no means of knowing how the human spirit works in general, or what it has done in a particular case; for such information the law must turn to other sciences. It stands competent because the manifestation of consent is an external act with far reaching social consequences. Indeed, if the law wants to bring marriages into its own orbit, as it does, it must have criteria for the recognition of an act of consent; it must also provide a procedure for judging its validity.

The law resolves this dilemma between its inability to penetrate the internal world of the human spirit and to regulate its external manifestations by calling on other sciences for help.

Theology provides the overall framework for the legal norms on matrimonial consent. More specifically, this framework comes from sacramental theology; there the principles for a valid intent and for the structure of a sacramental sign are laid down; canon law cannot but accept them. In matters of sacramental intentionality, to which consent belongs, the canonical norms are subject to and must be evaluated by theological criteria.

Philosophy provides a theory concerning the structure and the operations of the human spirit. The theory is a hypothesis, not the description of proven facts. It cannot be anything else, since not even philosophy has direct access to the internal world of human persons; its task is to speculate about it. The theory comes from Aristotle's metaphysics; Aquinas made it his own. Eventually, in a modified but not improved form, canon law adopted it.

The gist of this theory is that in a human person the soul is the operational principle of every intelligent and responsible act. The soul, however, needs faculties to act. Those faculties must be specifically adjusted to their objects. Since there are two distinct objects for their operation, truth to be known and good to be acquired, there must be two faculties as well, one to perceive the truth, the other to reach out for the good. They are the mind and the will.

For Aristotle, and especially for Aquinas, the soul, the mind and the will together were the human spirit, one and indivisible.

Whenever such philosophers spoke of a "real distinction" between the faculties, they did not mean that they could be separated and operate indepedently from each other, they meant only that there was a real structural complexity in the human spirit. In their language, the faculties, mind and will were not *beings, entia,* in the full sense but mere *constitutive elements* in a being, *principia entis.*

But such a subtle approach was lost on later generations of scholastic doctors. They interpreted the real distinction as allowing the faculties to operate independently from each other. Canon lawyers, mainly in matters concerning marriage consent, have taken the theory in this later form. Once accepted, it became a logical necessity to determine the specific roles of each of the faculties, the mind and the will. The Decretalists and the drafters of the old Code did it with clarity and consistency, but since their starting point was vitiated, their conclusions were bound to conflict with the demands of natural justice. For concrete examples see our comments on canons 1097 and 1098.[1]

The drafters of the new Code have certainly taken cognizance of the problem and tried to bring some relief. But they failed to break with the old theory, hence they could bring partial relief only. As it is now, the new Code presents a logically less consistent picture. It wants to remain faithful to the traditional theory, but it wants to embrace a more empirical approach as well. So, there is less clarity but there is more compassion for persons who, often without any fault on their part, were mistaken, misguided, or just plainly deceived.

Empirical psychology and medical psychiatry are newcomers in the field of sciences, but once they arrived, they developed by leaps and bounds and established themselves firmly, even if they still have immense territories to explore. Through their discoveries they have changed significantly our understanding of the internal world of a human being. We know that what is in our consciousness is only a small part of our whole self and that the unconscious can shape our convictions and motivate our actions without ourselves being aware of it. Also, we have learned that every human being must go through a developmental process before reaching maturity and that the stages of this "growing" process do not necessarily coincide with physical ages.

[1]There is a striking illustration and confirmation of Aquinas' famous statement in the Prologue of *De esse et essentia*: a small error in the beginning grows into a great one by the end, *parvus error in principio magnus est in fine*. One can qualify this saying further: a small error hiding in an abstract principle may lead to grave injustices in the concrete order. This is exactly what happened when, in the matter of consent, canon law began to use abstract hypotheses to solve concrete cases.

No human science escaped the impact of such new insights. Canon law did not remain immune to it either; canon 1095 in the new Code bears witness to the fact. Simply, it has opened the door to the findings of contemporary psychology and psychiatry.

Thus, the canons on matrimonial consent reflect in manifold ways the impact of several diverse sciences on canon law. Rightly so since canon law must turn to other sciences to learn what consent is in its ontological reality. The "canonical" idea of consent, therefore, is a special construct, composed by informed lawyers. It may be close to its ontological counterpart but it cannot be fully identical with it. Precisely because of this difference, the canonical idea is subject to corrections as we advance in the knowledge of the operations of the human spirit. Some such corrections are found in the new Code.

The value this chapter intends to uphold and safeguard is *the integrity of human persons in the act of choosing marriage.* They must be reasonably well informed; and above all, they must be free from serious constraint and deceit in dedicating themselves to a new state of life and to the extreme demands of marital love (cf. St. Paul, Eph 5). In other terms, the law intends to uphold the sanctity of the covenant.

❧ ✳ ☙

Who are incapable of contracting marriage?

Canon 1095

Sunt incapaces matrimonii contrahendi:
1° qui sufficienti rationis usu carent;
2° qui laborant gravi defectu discretionis iudicii
circa iura et officia matrimonialia essentialia
mutuo tradenda et acceptanda;
3° qui ob causas naturae psychicae
obligationes matrimonii essentiales assumere non valent.

They are incapable of contracting marriage:
1° who lack sufficient use of reason;
2° who suffer from a grave defect of discretion of judgment
concerning the essential matrimonial rights and duties,
to be given and accepted mutually;

3° who for causes of psychological nature
are unable to assume the essential obligations of marriage.

The canon approaches the issue of capability from a negative angle; it lists those who are incapable. Its meaning does not change, rather, it becomes clearer if we present the same norm in positive terms:

The following persons are capable of contracting marriage:
1° those who have sufficient use of reason,
2° those who are endowed with substantially correct discretion of judgment concerning the essential matrimonial rights and duties to be given and accepted mutually,
3° those who are psychologically able to assume the essential obligations of marriage.

Briefly, the overall meaning of the canon is that a person intending to marry must have the capacity to think rationally, to decide responsibly, and to carry out the decision by action. This capacity must be present *at the moment of the exchange of the promises.* If the validity of the promises is ever doubted, all that has happened before and all that has followed later can serve only as signs to determine the precise state of the spirit of the person at the moment of the exchange of the promises.

Since canon law as such has no competency in defining in what exactly the sufficient use of reason consists, what exactly the discretion of judgment is, and how much strength is enough to assume the obligations, this canon is an open invitation to the science of empirical psychology and medical psychiatry to fill the gap and provide the necessary information. It follows that the canonical comments on these norms must be restrained; the issues are not canonical. Further, because the criteria do not come from the field of law but from the field of the perpetually developing sciences of psychology and psychiatry, the meaning of this canon cannot be fixed; it will keep developing.[2]

---

[2] An interesting example of an openness that can be found in the Code. While the legal norms have been promulgated at a given date, and thus are historically conditioned, by their disposition they make it possible to take into account new developments in the field of other sciences, and thus they make the law into an instrument of

The first point of the canon is concerned with the use of reason; if that use is lacking there cannot be any commitment. The adjective sufficient indicates that the law recognizes degrees in the use of reason; for a valid commitment to marriage a proportionally developed capacity is necessary. The law does not use the expression "mental disease," which is a rather extreme condition. Nor does it speak of "lucid intervals," which in earlier ages meant a period of temporary sanity and, for that period at least, perfect self expression. We know that mental disabilities can influence the judgments and decisions of a person even if their symptoms may not be immediately manifest.

The second point of the canon is concerned with discretion of judgment about the essential rights and duties that must be mutually given and accepted. The assumption of the law is that there might be persons who are in possession of their mental ability but for some reason they cannot use it properly; they cannot form a judgment either about marriage in general or about the union they intend in particular. The defect must be grave; that is, the deviation of judgment from what is considered normal must be significant.

The third point concerns the psychological capacity to assume the essential duties of marriage. Such duties certainly include whatever belongs to the substantial fulfillment of the *consortium* and of the procreation and education of children. This psychological strength must be there at the moment of the promises. Should its absence be revealed later (as it is likely to happen), the evidence can serve to prove that it was not there in the first place. The expression, "cannot assume the duties for causes of a psychological nature," is very broad. It defies any precise definition, all the more since the psychological causes can be of an infinite variety.

The history of the drafting of this canon does not leave any doubt that the legislator intended, indeed, to broaden the rule. A strict and narrow norm was proposed first:

steady progress and evolution. This has important consequences for jurisprudence; e.g. in the case of a psychological incapacity it may be more important for the judges to study the findings of the contemporary medicine than the past decisions of the ecclesiastical tribunals based on dated medical knowledge.

Those who cannot assume the essential obligations of marriage because of a grave psycho-sexual anomaly [*ob gravem anomaliam psychosexualem*] are unable to contract mariage (cf. SCH/1975, canon 297, a new canon, *novus*);

then a broader one followed:

...because of a grave psychological anomaly [*ob gravem anomaliam psychicam*]...(cf. SCH/1980, canon 1049);

then the same wording was retained in the text submitted to the pope (cf. SCH/1982, canon 1095, 3°);

finally, a new version was promulgated:

because of causes of a psychological nature [*ob causas naturae psychicae*].

So the progress was from psycho-sexual to psychological anomaly, then the term anomaly was altogether eliminated. It would be, however, incorrect to draw the conclusion that the cause of the incapacity need not be some kind of psychological disorder; after all, normal and healthy person should be able to assume the ordinary obligations of marriage.

༄ ✻ ༅

What is the degree of knowledge required for valid consent?

Canon 1096 § 1.

Ut consensus matrimonialis haberi possit,
necesse est ut contrahentes saltem non ignorent
matrimonium esse consortium permanens inter virum et mulierem
ordinatum ad prolem, cooperatione aliqua sexuali, procreandam.

For matrimonial consent to exist,
it is necessary that the contracting parties be at least not ignorant
that marriage is a permanent *consortium* between a man and a
  woman
ordered to the procreation of children through some form of
  sexual cooperation.

Although the matrimonial consent is an act of the will, some knowledge about marriage is certainly required to set the will into motion. This paragraph determines the minimum knowledge demanded by the law. In positive terms:

> ...the contracting parties should know that
> marriage is a permanent union between a man and a woman
> naturally ordered to the procreation of children
> through some form of sexual cooperation.

should not be ignorant: it could be translated simply and positively as "they must know."

permanent *consortium*: a more than temporary association; something more than ordinary friendship.

There may be a problem here about the required awareness of a "permanent *consortium*." Permanency certainly means stability; but does it include lifelong commitment, that is, indissolubility? The question is not an idle one; there are many persons in the world who marry without ever having heard of the doctrine of indissolubility. Now, if permanency here means indissolubility, then the ignorance of it invalidates the matrimonial consent. Yet, canon 1099 clearly states that error concerning indissolubility does not necessarily invalidate the consent. Hence, the only possible conclusion is that while all should be aware of some kind of permanency required for true marital state, there is no need to know about indissolubility.

some form of sexual cooperation: indicates that some generic knowledge of the biological process of procreation is required; a meticulously precise rendering of the Latin *sexualis* in this context should be "genital."

⚘

What is the age limit for the presumption of ignorance?

Canon 1096 § 2.

Haec ignorantia post pubertatem non praesumitur.

Such ignorance is not presumed after puberty.

The age of puberty is not defined in the Code; the canon can be interpreted as meaning "such ignorance is not presumed after the person reached the legal age for marriage," that is 14 for a woman, 16 for a man.

༄༅ ❀ ༄༅

What is the effect of error
concerning the identity of the intended spouse?

Canon 1097 § 1.

Error in persona invalidum reddit matrimonium.

Error of person renders the marriage invalid.

error: a seemingly simple concept, in reality a very complex one. Error is not ignorance. In the case of error there is a judgment, in the case of ignorance there is not. In the case of an error the process of knowing started and went astray, in the case of ignorance it has not even started.

The process of knowing can go astray at various points. The information gathered in the beginning may have been incomplete; all conclusions after that will be deficient. Or, the data otherwise correct may have been misunderstood; a false judgment will follow. In either case the final result is an error.

error of person: there is no doubt that the traditional understanding of an "error of person" was that a mistake occurred about the identity of the spouse. Gratian stated it clearly in his *Decretum* (1140): "There is an error of person when someone is believed to be Virgil and he is Plato" (C.29,q.1.; Friedberg c.1091).

In recent times but before the new Code efforts have been made to extend the meaning of this rule to cases where technically the error was not in the identity of the person but in some highly important qualities, cf. the cases *Aosta* (1977) and *Cambrai* (1978), *coram Di Felice*, CLD 9:634-658.

The new Code, in an effort to remove such ambiguity, broadened the doctrine of the "error concerning a quality," as our comments on the second paragraph of this canon will show. The meaning of this first paragraph remains the classical one: no one can marry a person who is not the one intended.

❦

What is the effect of error
concerning a quality of the intended spouse?

Canon 1097 § 2.

**Error in qualitate personae,
etsi det causam contractui,
matrimonium irritum non reddit,
nisi haec qualitas directe et principaliter intendatur.**

**Error concerning a quality of the person,
even if it causes the contract,
does not render the marriage invalid,
unless that quality is directly and principally intended.**

The canon paraphrased:

An error concerning a personal quality of the intended spouse
does not render the marriage invalid,
not even if the act of consenting was "caused"
[*motivated, prompted*]
by that erroneous perception.

There is one exception, however:
an error concering a personal quality
directly and principally intended,
renders the marriage invalid.

error concerning a quality: an expression that has been the source of many difficulties, and continues to be so. We are in a problem area.

To understand the difficulties some historical information is necessary.

The Decretalists developed the theory that the principal object of the marriage contract was the right over the body of the spouse for acts naturally ordered to the procreation of children. This object was of the very substance of the contract. With impeccable logic they then concluded that as long as the object was there, the consent was valid. The qualities of the spouse were irrelevant. If someone was attracted to the marriage by a given quality of the intended spouse, or married for the sake of that quality, and later discovered that no such quality existed, nothing could be done, not even if the mistake was brought about by deliberate lies. As long as the right to the body of the other could be exercised, the consent was good and valid.

It is easy to see how on the strength of such theory innocent persons could find themselves in a radically unjust situation and without any remedy, because not even in the case of a calculated fraud could canon law provide relief by declaring the marriage invalid; the most it could do was to allow the separation of the spouses. An example may be helpful: if a fugitive from justice addicted to black magic and suffering from leprosy succeeded in passing himself off as an honest citizen and devout Christian in good health, the courts had to stand for the validity of the marriage, provided the "acts apt for the procreation of children" could be performed. The substance of the contract was there. If ever there was a case of *summum ius summa iniuria*, perfectly observed law leading to consummate injustice, this was it.[3]

---

[3]From a commentary on the old Code:

Unde si quis ducere velit virginem, sanam, nobilem, honestam, divitem, ducat vero leprosam, defloratam, infirmam, pauperem, matrimonium valet, licet a tali matrimonio toto animo abhorruerit, horroremque ante nuptias manifestaverit, matrimonium valet...

Therefore, if someone intends to marry a virgin, in good health, of noble birth, honest, wealthy, marries however one who is infected with leprosy, sexually used, infirm, poor, the marriage is valid, even if he held such marriage in horror with his whole heart, and made his horror public before the wedding, the marriage is valid...

See Felix M. Cappello, *De matrimonio* (Torino: Marietti, 1961), p. 513. — The commentator should not be blamed; he was faithfully explaining the meaning of the law.

Yet, be it permitted to note, such situations could develop and dominate in the church because on the whole canon lawyers were reluctant to be critical of the law;

it causes the contract: this causation must be in the psychological order; a quality cannot cause the contract in any other way than through the person who contracts. The quality becomes the motivating force.

directly and principally intended: directly must mean that it is not intended by any intermediary, as would be the case when a person wants marriage with some absoluteness and at the same time he is glad that the prospective partner enjoys good health; the health would then be a quality indirectly intended. Principally must mean "above all," as when a person wants good health so much in the other that unless it is there, he is not willing to marry her. There is a close affinity between intending a quality directly and principally and conditioning the consent on the existence of that quality. The effect in both cases is the same; if the quality is non existent, there is no marriage; cf. canon 1102 § 2.

But what is the difference between a quality which is the cause of the contract, and a quality which is directly and principally intended? There must be a difference because in the first case the marriage is valid, in the second it is invalid. The legislator did not see the two situations as identical!

In all probability the best explanation is that in the first case when the quality is the cause of the contract, the intention of the person is assumed to center so much on marriage itself that he would be willing to contract even if the quality that moves him were proved non existent. In the second case, his intention is presumed to focus so much on the quality that he would not marry but for that quality.

A precious distinction, no doubt. But, in spite of the seeming similarity of the two situations, the interpreter must follow the

they conceived their task as the expository exegetes of the norms, a kind of canonical fundamentalism. For the sake of the good health of the Christian community, a steady and on going critical examination of its laws is a vital necessity. After all, most of the time in canon law we are dealing with human constructs that, even in the church, are marked by human limitations. They can be improved and perfected only if they are properly evaluated. It follows that an uncritical commentary, composed with the best of intentions, fails to help the church in its progress toward applying the evangelical message "more thoroughly to life" (cf. LG: 12).

ground rule of all interpretations, which is that the law must be presumed to have a reasonable meaning. In this case, too, we must presume that the law presents us with a reasonable distinction, subtle as it may be.

But no matter what the theoretical explanations are, in concrete cases brought before our courts, it will be *very* difficult to determine if a quality merely "caused the contract," or it was "directly and principally intended." The dividing line between the two situations must be drawn in the field of the operations of the human psyche, obscure and complex beyond telling. Moreover, those who intended to marry have not made their decisions according to our fine distinctions. The judges will have to decide if one set of facts (as narrated to them often many years after the event) falls rather into the one than the other category. It is doubtful that the non-technical report of the parties and their witnesses in matters so subtle and delicate can ever provide them with enough evidence to make a well grounded choice instead of a vague conjecture.

It is not prudent to make the validity of marriages to depend on such refined theoretical distinctions that even the experts find them hard to explain.[4]

⸎

What is the effect of fraudulent misrepresentation concerning a quality of the intended spouse?

Canon 1098

**Qui matrimonium init deceptus dolo,
ad obtinendum consensum patrato,**

[4]A puzzling feature of this canon is that so much in the canon law of marriage is based on, or taken from, scholastic philosophy, but if this distinction is explained in the categories of the same system, the difference between a quality that "causes the contract" and the one that is "directly and principally intended" seem to vanish.

According to Aristotle and Aquinas, intelligent and free beings in their moral actions (such as marital consent is) are moved by the end they intend to achieve or obtain. Now, when someone directly and principally intends a quality, that end moves him (*causa finalis*) to want the contract. It follows that if a quality causes the contract, it can only happen because it was directly intended in the first place.

circa aliquam alterius partis qualitatem,
quae suapte natura consortium vitae coniugalis graviter
    perturbare potest,
invalide contrahit.

A person who enters into marriage deceived by fraud,
perpetrated to obtain consent,
concerning a quality of the other party,
which can disturb gravely, by its nature, the *consortium* of
    conjugal life,
contracts invalidly.

To prove the invalidity of a marriage on the basis of this canon, the following facts must be established:
— one of the partners was in error concerning the quality in question,
— the error was due to a misrepresentation,
— the misrepresentation was gravely fraudulent, that is the person who perpetrated it was guilty of premeditated and calculated fraud, *dolus*,
— the intention of the guilty person was to induce the victim into the marriage,
— a potentially disruptive situation was created for the marriage, due to the natural importance of the quality in question.

Fraud must be taken in its strongest sense; it must amount to what is *dolus* in Roman law, a coolly calculated act of deception. It does not matter who its author is, the prospective spouse or a third party.

The purpose of the person perpetrating the fraud must be to induce the prospective partner into marriage; this requirement leads to the need of investigating the intention of the wrongdoer, not always an easy task.

It does not matter now in what way the victim's intention or attention was focused on the quality in question. The nature of the quality is, however, all important. If its presence (a bad quality), or its absence (a good quality) is potentially disruptive of the peace and harmony of the conjugal life, the canon is applicable. There is no need to wait for the disruptive potential to develop; once the threat is "naturally" there, the marriage can be pronounced invalid.

This threat to the *consortium* can be interpreted relative to the partners involved; if it can disrupt the unity of *this* particular marriage, the contract is invalid; it need not be such that it could disturb each and every couple.

This canon clearly tries to protect an innocent person from wilful deception. In doing so it introduces some new concepts which are hard to define; e.g. "quality which by its very nature can disrupt conjugal harmony," or "fraud in view of marriage"; further refinement will have to come through jurisprudence.

The Code singles out one case for the application of this canon: if there has been fraudulent misrepresentation concerning the fertility of the prospective spouse, the marriage may have been invalidly contracted, cf. canon 1084 § 3.

CIC/17 offered no relief or no redress, beyond that of separation, for the victim of a similar fraud. It was concerned with the protection of the institution of marriage to such a degree that it left no room for the protection of an innocent victim of deception. The present Code is more balanced.

～＊～

What is the effect of error
concerning an essential property of marriage?

Canon 1099

Error circa matrimonii unitatem vel indissolubilitatem aut
sacramentalem dignitatem,
dummodo non determinet voluntatem,
non vitiat consensum matrimonialem.

Error concerning the unity of marriage or its indissolubility or
its sacramental dignity,
does not vitiate matrimonial consent,
provided it does not determine the will.

The assumption of this canon is that there are two sharply distinguished species of error: one affects the mind only and does not determine the will; another overflows into the will and determines its choice. This assumption flows from the metaphysical principles the Code uses for the understanding of the structures and operations of the human psyche. Modern empirical psychology, however, has demonstrated not only that the decisions and actions of a human person can be prompted, even determined, by the unconscious self, but also that the knowledge in the conscious self always impacts on our actions, whether we are aware of it or not. Indeed, contemporary empirical research has led to a far better perception of the unity and integrity of the human *psyche* than the metaphysical theories that the Code has embraced.

To apply the principles of this canon wisely it is necessary to take notice of this conflict between the philosophy that inspired it and the findings of empirical sciences that are rather contrary to it. Of course, one can admit in theory that *if* there is knowledge that is so purely cerebral that it does not affect the decisions and action of a person, *then*, that knowledge should be discounted in evaluating a decision. But the question is precisely if such an internal split between knowledge and decision can ever occur in a normal person. The answer of the Code is: yes it can. The answer of depth psychology is: no, it is not likely; if it does, a serious personality disorder may be hiding below the surface.

Notwithstanding the theoretical stance of the Code, judges who are called to handle concrete cases under this canon are entitled to take notice of the findings of empirical psychology as well. This is not going against the law; it is rather reconciling the law with accepted scientific conclusions. If any proof is needed for such an approach, it is found in canon 1095 that displays an extraordinary openness toward modern empirical psychology to the point that one can speak of a veritable "canonization" of it.

The "traditional" philosophical hypotheses should be taken for what they always were: hypothetical positions which can be modified or abandoned if they are contradicted by facts. Aristotle explained many of the physical phenomena by metaphysical principles (e.g. the movements of the stars), but as our knowledge of physics developed we substituted empirically established laws for his theories. As his physics has been corrected, so should be his psychology.

There is another problem in connection with this canon. It implies that a human person can commit himself or herself to a lifelong obligation without knowing about it. Someone believing that marriages can be dissolved can still covenant for an indissoluble union. Again, we have here an understanding of the human psyche that contradicts sharply not only the findings of empirical psychology but even common sense. If an obligation is not known to a person, how could he ever be motivated to observe it?

It is interesting to note that the traditional moral theology always tended to excuse a person from those obligations which were unknown to him at the time of the contract.

The classical argument to support the Code's approach used to be that any person contracting a marriage wants above all "marriage as it is" (e.g. indissoluble), even if he is mistaken about its properties. But again, this assumption is questionable in our culture; the overriding desire to marry is much less prevalent than it was in the feudal society of the Middle Ages when so many of the principles of our laws were formulated. The ordinary assumption should be rather that every person wants marriage as it is known to him: indissoluble or otherwise.

❦

Does the knowledge or the opinion
that the marriage to be celebrated will be invalid
exclude matrimonial consent?

Canon 1100

Scientia aut opinio nullitatis matrimonii
consensum matrimonialem non necessario excludit.

The knowledge or the opinion of the nullity of marriage
does not necessarily exclude matrimonial consent.

A marriage can be invalid for different reasons. If it is known or conjectured null and void for reason of some missing formality, there is internal logic in this canon. It simply states that an external defect cannot cancel out the internal reality of consent. In a convalidation it will be enough to supply the missing formality or simply obtain a dispensation from it.

But if one of the would-be spouses knows that the marriage is null and void for reasons more substantial than a missing formality, the question can be raised as to how far such a person can still undertake a lifelong commitment with any kind of seriousness.

does not necessarily exclude: a rather restrained statement. Each case must be dealt with according to its own merits.

⌒☀⌒

If the consent is an internal and spiritual act,
how can the law ascertain its existence?

Canon 1101 § 1.

Internus animi consensus praesumitur conformis verbis vel signis in celebrando matrimonio adhibitis.

The internal spiritual consent is presumed to correspond to the words or signs used in the celebration of the marriage.

The world of law is the world of external, mainly social, structures and relations. If it wants to bring a judgment over events in the internal world of the spirit, it must gather the necessary evidence from the external world, and then proceed further by way of conjectures that become legal presumptions.

This approach applies to all sacraments: the law can pronounce only on external events, not on the existence of an invisible internal reality.

Matrimonial tribunals operate on the same rule: they cannot pronounce on the existence of a sacrament, only on the amount of the external evidence. When the external signs are such that by any prudent judgment they cannot be consistent with the required internal disposition, the tribunals pronounce that there is evidence for nullity, *constat de nullitate*. They cannot pronounce on the internal reality of the sacrament, known to God alone. There is never any divine guarantee that their judgment is correct, but their prudent decision can give enough assurance to the parties to proceed, with a good conscience, to a new marriage, if they wish to do so.

What is the effect of the wilful exclusion of marriage or
of one of its essential elements or properties?

Canon 1101 § 2.

At si alterutra vel utraque pars
positivo voluntatis actu
excludat matrimonium ipsum vel matrimonii essentiale aliquod
elementum, vel essentialem aliquam proprietatem,
invalide contrahit.

But if one or both of the parties,
with a positive act of the will
exclude marriage itself or an essential element of marriage or an
essential property of it,
they contract invalidly.

a positive act of the will is not opposed to any "negative act of the will" since no such act exists; it simply means an act of the will.

to exclude positively implies an act of rejection; it implies that a person who has become aware of a value decides to reject it.

But what if a person has never become aware of a value, e.g. indissolubility; how could he ever exclude something that is unknown to him? In other terms, the rule of exclusion can apply to those only who are well informed. For the others the Code's answer is the classical answer: anyone intending to marry has the overriding intention to take marriage as it is.

In this context an interesting question can be raised: what if a person steadily and firmly professes a religious creed that *positively* rejects one or more of the essential properties of marriage? Among non-baptized persons it could be unity or indissolubility, among baptized non-Catholics it could be sacramental dignity. There may not be a general answer to this question; each case should be judged on its own merits. But the possibility that an intensely held religious belief can lead (according to our canon law) to a "positive act of the will" must not be excluded.

If a marriage is conditioned on a future event,
can it be valid?

Canon 1102 § 1.

Matrimonium sub condicione de futuro
valide contrahi nequit.

Marriage conditioned on a future event
cannot be validly contracted.

If a condition concerning a future event is attached to the consent, the law gives no effect to the consent; there is no marriage.

If a marriage is conditioned on a past or present event,
can it be valid?

Canon 1102 § 2.

Matrimonium sub condicione de praeterito vel de praesenti
initum
est validum vel non,
prout id quod condicioni subest, exsistit vel non.

Marriage entered into under a condition concerning the past or
the present,
is valid or not,
as the condition is fulfilled or not.

The rule is simple: the validity of the marriage depends on the fulfillment of the condition.

Who can authorize a conditional marriage?

Canon 1102 § 3.

Condicio autem, de qua in § 2,
licite apponi nequit,
nisi cum licentia Ordinarii loci scripto data.

The condition mentioned in § 2, however,
cannot be lawfully [*licitly*] attached,
unless the local ordinary has given his permission in writing.

The permission of the ordinary is not required for the validity of the condition or of the marriage.

Summary of the three canons on conditional consent:
(1) If a condition concerns the future, it can never be lawful; it renders the marriage invalid.
(2) If a condition concerns the past or the present, it can be lawful; the effect of the consent depends on the fulfillment of the condition; if it is fulfilled, the marriage is valid; if not, the marriage is invalid.
(3) For the fully lawful [*licit*] celebration of a conditioned marriage, the written permission of the local ordinary is necessary.

Reflections: A conditioned consent is difficult enough to explain epistemologically, but it is nearly impossible to reconcile it with the nature of the marriage covenant. While it may be perfectly acceptable in a financial transaction, it is not a suitable way for someone to commit himself to another "until death do them part." When the act of consent is conditioned, the covenanting party intends, *with the very same act*, to commit himself *and* to suspend the effect of the commitment. In such an act, the hierarchy of values can be easily perverted by making the validity of the sacrament depend on some flimsy event.

Moreover, it is difficult to conceive of any situation where the conditioning of the consent would be warranted for a serious reason. If the problem is in some lack of information, the marriage should be delayed until it can be obtained.

There is something absolute in the marital promises; to give them conditionally verges on the absurd. A simple and sound way to handle the problem would be to deny any effect to a conditional consent, whether the condition concerns the future, the past or the present.

⤝ ✳ ⤜

What is the effect of force or fear?

Canon 1103

**Invalidum est matrimonium
initum ob vim vel metum gravem ab extrinseco,
etiam haud consulto incussum,
a quo ut quis se liberet, eligere cogatur matrimonium.**

**A marriage is invalid
when entered into under force or grave fear inflicted from the
outside,
even if inadvertently,
from which to be freed, a person must choose marriage.**

force comes from the outside; fear arises inside of a person; both concepts are strongly relative, depending on the capacity of a person to resist force or to handle fear.

from the outside: force is from the outside, fear is not. But the legislator wants to exclude an irrational fear arising without any external provocation; such fear can still amount to undue influence on the consent, but the case would not fall under this canon.

inadvertently, *inconsulte*: the person inflicting the fear did not realize that the words used, the attitudes shown amounted to such forceful "persuasion" that in fact fear was generated in the victim; also, *not in view of marriage*: force and fear were indeed inflicted and the victim suffered from them, although they were not imposed with the intention of compelling the victim to marry, but as a matter of fact he married to escape the situation.

the victim is compelled to choose marriage in order to escape: that is, there was no other exit from the oppressive situation than this particular marriage; if the victim could have done something else to escape the force or to get rid of the fear, e.g. he could have taken up residence elsewhere, this canon is not applicable.

Must the parties be present together at the exchange of the promises?

Canon 1104 § 1.

**Ad matrimonium valide contrahendum
necesse est ut contrahentes sint praesentes una simul
sive per se ipsi, sive per procuratorem.**

**To contract marriage validly,
it is necessary that the contracting parties be present together
either in person or by proxy.**

Classical Roman law had the same requirement for a contract *in verbis*, that is for *stipulatio*; but not for a consensual contract.

Proxy means a duly authorized agent; in Roman law the relationship between the principal and his agent would be that of the *mandans* to the *mandatarius*; the object of the *mandatum* would be to give the promises in the name of the principal. Canon law conceives the appointment of a proxy as a contract of mandate in the classical sense.

How should the consent be expressed?

Canon 1104 § 2.

**Sponsi consensum matrimonialem verbis exprimant;
si vero loqui non possunt, signis aequipollentibus.**

The spouses must express their matrimonial consent by words; or, if they cannot speak, by equivalent signs.

No consensual contract in Roman law had to be made orally, *verbis*, or by equivalent signs, which is another reason why the simple identification of our modern marriage contract with the Roman consensual contract is incorrect. Through the imposition of the compulsory canonical form by the Council of Trent, our marriage contract has become a composite of the *stipulatio* (contractus *stricti iuris*, the validity of the contract depends on the exact observance of the prescribed external formalities) and of the consensual contract (internal consent is essential).

❦

What are the requirements for a proxy to function validly?

Canon 1105 § 1.

Ad matrimonium per procuratorem valide ineundum requiritur:
  1° ut adsit mandatum speciale ad contrahendum cum certa persona;
  2° ut procurator ab ipso mandante designetur, et munere suo per se ipse fungatur.

To enter into a marriage validly through a proxy, it is required
  1° that there be a special mandate to contract with a determined person,
  2° that the proxy be designated by the principal in person, and the proxy fulfill his function in person.

❦

How to compose a valid mandate?

Canon 1105 § 2.

Mandatum, ut valeat,
subscribendum est a mandante et praeterea

a parocho vel Ordinario loci in quo mandatum datur, aut a
   sacerdote ab alterutro delegato,
aut a duobus saltem testibus;
aut confici debet per documentum ad normam iuris civilis
   authenticum.

For the mandate to be valid,
it must be signed by the principal and, in addition,
by the parish priest or the ordinary of the place where the
   mandate is given or by a priest delegated by either,
or at least by two witnesses;
or it must be given by a document recognized as authentic in
   civil law.

What is to be done if the principal cannot write?

Canon 1105 § 3.

Si mandans scribere nequeat,
id in ipso mandato adnotetur
et alius testis addatur qui scripturam ipse quoque subsignet;
secus mandatum irritum est.

If the principal cannot write
it must be noted in the mandate and
another witness must be added who also must sign the
   document;
otherwise the mandate is invalid.

Can the principal revoke the mandate?
Can the mandate lapse?

Canon 1105 § 4.

Si mandans, antequam procurator eius nomine contrahat,
mandatum revocaverit

aut in amentiam inciderit,
invalidum est matrimonium,
licet sive procurator sive altera pars contrahens haec ignoraverit.

If the principal revokes the mandate
or becomes insane
before the proxy contracts in his name
the marriage is invalid,
even if the proxy or the other party to the contract are in
ignorance of the fact.

The consent from the part of the principal must exist at the moment of the exchange of the promises.

Can marriage be contracted through an interpreter?

Canon 1106

Matrimonium per interpretem contrahi potest;
cui tamen parochus ne assistat,
nisi de interpretis fide sibi constet.

Marriage can be contracted through an interpreter;
but the parish priest must not assist
unless he is certain of the interpreter's trustworthiness.

The parish priest has the duty to ascertain the trustworthiness of the interpreter.

Is an invalid marriage compatible with an enduring consent?

Canon 1107

Etsi matrimonium invalide
ratione impedimenti vel defectus formae initum fuerit,
consensus praestitus praesumitur perseverare,
donec de eius revocatione constiterit.

**Even if a marriage has been entered into invalidly
because of an impediment or a defect of form,
the consent given is presumed to persist
until its revocation has been established.**

This canon is a particular application of canon 1101 § 1: the internal disposition of a person is presumed to correspond to the external "words or signs used in the celebration of the marriage." Once such words or signs were given, although invalidly, the person is presumed to continue in the same disposition unless there is evidence to the contrary. Thus, in the case of a missing formality, the marriage can be convalidated by a *sanatio in radice*.

A summary of invalidating causes.

Lack of sufficient use of reason,
grave defect of discretion of judgment concerning matrimonial
   rights and duties,
incapacity to assume the obligations of the marital state, due to
   psychological causes (1095).

Ignorance of the permanent nature of *consortium*,
ignorance of the sexual nature of the human generation (1096).

Error of person,
error in a quality that was intended principally and directly (1097).

Error induced by *dolus* concerning a quality that by its nature can
   be potentially disruptive of the *consortium* (1098).

Error that determines the will
   concerning unity,
      indissolubility, or
      sacramental dignity (1099).

Positively willed exclusion of the marriage, or, of any of its essential elements or properties (1101).

Conditioned consent on a future event (1102).

Force or fear inflicted from the outside leaving no other escape
   than the marriage (1103).

A critical note: law versus life.

For the law to be *ordinatio rationis*, that is "reason bringing order into the life of the community," it must be applicable. No matter how finely a norm is conceived otherwise, if it does not fit the concrete facts of life, it cannot bring order into it.

A significant weakness in the law of consent is in the difficulty of applying some of its fine distinctions to the concrete facts of life, or the other way round, in the difficulty of fitting the external evidence into the subtle categories of the law. Thus, while an abstract distinction can be construed between a quality that "causes the contract" and another that is "directly and principally intended," or between an error that "does not determine the will" and another that "does determine the will," to differentiate the evidential data according to the categories of the law may be nigh impossible.

The categories of the law are so subtle and so remote from the way of thinking of our faithful that when the facts of a case are narrated by them, it is a *tour de force* for an expert to place the facts into the correct category. Often enough, the external signs of the internal state of mind of the person concerned are so ambivalent that the advocate or the judge is compelled to make a guess, which is more of subjective option than an objective decision. But to guess he must because the facts cannot be handled unless they are classified according to the rubrics of the law. This being the case, no matter how refined our procedural norms are, the risk of injustice is there.

There is a discrepancy between law and life.

An explanatory note: the grounds of nullity.

There are many manuals presenting a more or less complete list of the grounds of nullity.[5] The most important ones are: *the lack of sufficient reason and due discretion of judgment, the lack of capacity*

---

[5] *See* the widely used manual by Lawrence G. Wrenn, *Annulments*,4th ed.(Toledo: Canon Law Society of America), 1978.

to carry out the obligations, all of them originating in various personality disorders or at least in some temporary disturbances of the human spirit; *the simulation of consent*, which often covers an intention to exclude the *bona*, the goods of marriage, such as the procreation of children, mutual fidelity and indissolubility; various forms of *error, force and fear*; and others. The question is how far such precise classification of the grounds of nullity is necessary or even desirable.

Since most of these grounds are intimately connected with the doctrine of consent, the question can be best answered by reflecting on the relationship of the law to the act of consent.

Interestingly, the law's approach is mostly negative: it determines the typical cases when consent cannot exist or must not be presumed to exist. It says little positively about what consent is, except that it is an act of the will. It says nothing about the complex internal process through which the act of consent is created.

No wonder; it is not easy for the law to handle consent. The world where it is given or withheld is far away from the world where the laws operate. Consent is born and exists in the internal world of the human spirit; legal norms regulate the external social relations in a visible community. The legislator can do no more than to catch a glimpse of the internal universe of the spirit and then propose some external norms by which the presence or absence of consent can be conjectured. It follows that to handle the issue of consent intelligently and responsibly, some understanding of the two distinct worlds is necessary, that of the human spirit and that of the human society.

Philosophers as well as psychologists have made great strides in presenting us with a unified explanation of the process of knowing and deciding.[6] Consent, of course, is always created by such process, and if the consent is deficient in some way it is always due to some

---

[6]For philosophers *see* (among many others) e.g. Bernard J. F. Lonergan, *Insight* (New York: Longmans, 1958); Michael Polanyi, *Personal Knowledge* (Chicago: University of Chicago, 1962); Joseph de Finance, *L'affrontement de l'autre* (Roma: Universitá Gregoriana,1973). Were our law of marriage as open to modern epistemological insights as it is to the discoveries of empirical psychology, the law would be simpler and closer to life.

For psychologists or psychiatrists: legion is their name! But *see* e.g. the writings of Jung and of those who profess to belong closely or remotely to his school; they present a unified vision of the human psyche and of its operations.

defect in the process of knowing and deciding.

The law, however, can never be more than an imperfect instrument in handling such an internal process; it can never know perfectly all the ways that it can go wrong. For this reason, it will never be able to declare with finality what the grounds of nullity must be. As we keep learning more and more about the operation of the human spirit in gathering information, in understanding the facts, in critically evaluating them, and in coming to a decision, the known grounds of nullity may increase or even decrease.

It follows that the list of the grounds of nullity can never be closed. They are no more than standardized conceptual tools to comprehend how the process of creating consent can go astray.

Since all defects of consent are defects in the process of knowing and deciding, a few pertinent questions concerning that process could probably serve the cause of justice better than so many elaborate categories. Such questions are:

— was the person intending to marry in possession of all the necessary information concerning the nature of the marital life and about the future spouse (cf. the canons on the amount of knowledge required for a valid contract, canons 1096 — 1100)?

— did the person understand the values of marriage (cf. the "sufficient use of reason" and the need for "discretion of judgment" in canon 1095)?

— was the person able and free to come to a moral decision and did he or she have the strength to carry it out (cf. canons 1095 and 1103)?

The consent could then be declared deficient if there is convincing evidence that there was insufficient knowledge, inability to assume responsibility or incapacity to carry out a decision — without any further need to squeeze the great variety of causes into previously determined and fixed categories.

Due to a deep sense of respect for traditional procedures, such an approach may not be acceptable today. Nonetheless, even at present, there is no absolute rule that the judges must limit their inquiries to "canonized" categories only. If the facts postulate a different approach because there is indeed a defect in the process of forming consent but no category for it, the judges should contribute to the development of jurisprudence by creating one. Eventually, a more unified and simpler doctrine may prevail.

CHAPTER FIVE
THE FORM OF CELEBRATION
1108 — 1123

The subject matter of this chapter is the juridical act of marrying; we are now in the field that is the law's own. The purpose of the canons is external, it is to create social structures and regulate social relations. To marry, indeed, is an external and social event; in it the welfare of the individual persons blends with the welfare of the community. Consequently the law takes cognizance of the act of marrying, regulates it, and determines the rights and duties that flow from it. That much is true in any civic community.

With due regard for the differences, the same is true in the church: the church retains jurisdiction over the marriages of Catholics and among many other prescriptions we have the one on the "canonical form."

Historical background.

For the ancient Romans marriage was not a contract but a state of life, consequently their lawyers' attention focused not so much on the initial act of marrying and on the customary formalities that went with it as on the fact that the couple was living together with marital affection, *cum affectu maritali*.

156

From the earliest times, Christians have sought the blessing of God, through the prayers of the church, on their marriages. Appropriate liturgical ceremonies developed rapidly: Tertullian already mentions them (around 200). But the Roman way of thinking was kept alive and Christians too regarded marriage as a state of life and not as a contract. The blessing, given by a bishop or a priest in the form of "imposition of hands" (accompanied by prayer), was an initiation into a new vocation. This ancient tradition is still expressed in the liturgy of the Eastern church through the "crowning" of the couple, a modified version of the imposition of hands.[1]

As from the twelfth century, the West opted for the contractual theory. Consequently, the emphasis shifted to the exchange of promises, to the act through which the union was initiated. If at a later time the validity of the marriage was contested, the fact of living together with marital affection counted for less; the circumstances surrounding the exchange of promises held the clue to the answer.[2]

The model of the marital contract was the Roman consensual contract, which had always a well determined content but required no specific external formality. The marital contract too, which of course had a well defined content, could take place without any formality, privately or publicly.

The private celebrations, however, became the object of strong disapproval; they were repeatedly called unlawful, although never declared invalid by universal legislation until the Council of Trent introduced the "canonical form." The Fathers preoccupied with the spreading of clandestine marriages after prolonged debates imposed a new formality necessary for the validity of the contract. Their decree *Tametsi*, approved in the 24th session of the Council in 1563,

---

[1]*See* L. Godefroy, *Le mariage au temps des Pères*, DTC, 9.2: 2077-2123, for the blessing in particular 2104 — 2105. Tertullian is interesting because he speaks of the couple *asking* the priest for the marriage and the priest *giving* it. In general, not much is known about the ceremonies used in the blessing of the couple.

[2]*See* G. Le Bras, *La doctrine du mariage chez les theologiens et les canonistes depuis l'an mille*, DTC, 9.2: 2123-2317. We do not know any better overall history of the formation of the classical doctrine, nor a better synthesis of it than the ones presented here by the author, 2162-2223. For the issue of clandestine celebrations at the Council of Trent and for a description of the ensuing problems see 2246-2249.

was intended to be clear and straightforward (*see* D-SCH 1813-1816); here is the concluding part of it (D-SCH 1816):

> They who will attempt marriage otherwise
> than in the presence of the parish priest,
> or of another priest by the permission of the parish priest or of the ordinary,
> and of two or three witnesses,
> are made by this holy Synod totally unable to contract,
> and [*this Synod*] declares such contracts to be invalid,
> as they were made invalid by this present decree.[3]

The implementation of this new law, however, was not easy. It had to be promulgated in every parish, and it became effective thirty days later. But in many places, the heralds and the documents of the Council were not welcome. The church was in turmoil, and the parishes who professed themselves "reformed," or the provinces where the secular prince was "reformed," did not allow any publicity concerning the decrees of the Council.

There followed a great variety (more correctly, a great deal of confusion) in the implementation of the law:

— in some parishes it was promulgated before the community became divided, hence the assumption was that Catholics and Protestants were bound by it;

---

[3]Gérard Fransen sees in the introduction of the canonical form a sign of a *nominalisme canonique*, that is a juridical formalism, emerging from and after the Council of Trent and gradually permeating the life of the church and bringing an end to the classical science of canon law that concerned itself with the substance of things. Preoccupation with external formalities and uncritical exegesis of new texts (nothing else was allowed by the order of Pius IV) took the place of the reflective explanation of the ancient sacred canons. Thus the science that through its creativity and originality has contributed so much for the renaissance of the church in the twelfth century has been condemned to sterile and restricted debates about the meaning of the words (no interpretation or commentary or explanation of the decrees of the Council were allowed). This new spirit (or the loss of spirit) became the hallmark of most canonical enterprises after Trent until very recent times. So Fransen. But he is a good historian and his remarks deserve attention, even if he himself calls them *provocant*. The history of our marriage law in the post-Tridentine times certainly displayed a great deal of formalism, nor are we as yet fully free from it.

— in some parishes there was no promulgation, hence no Catholic or Protestant was bound by it.

As if this had not been enough, new complications arose when whole parishes changed their religion, not an exceptional occurrence.

Besides, two principles of interpretation played their own part —and often increased the uncertainties:

(1) the law was personal, hence it continued to bind a person anywhere and everywhere; irrespective of the local law;

(2) they who were not bound by the law communicated their exemption to their intended partners.

The net result was that in the regions affected by the reform movement the decree was virtually defeated by the uncertainties concerning its application.

The first move toward some clarity and uniformity came from Benedict XIV in 1741; he declared that in the Netherlands the decree *Tametsi* was binding only when two Catholics marry each other. Pius X in 1906 extended the same ruling for Germany, in 1909 for Hungary. Then, in 1907 with his decree *Ne temere* he imposed the canonical form on all marriages where one of the parties was Catholic, except in Germany and Hungary.

Finally, CIC/17 put an end to all exceptions and declared all baptized persons to be bound by the canonical form. It granted however an exemption to non Catholic Christians — following a theological opinion, abandoned since, that they were under the jurisdiction of the pope.

Transitions: *From no exceptions to some flexibility.* The old Code displayed a certain intransigence about the observance of the form. Apart from emergency situations (danger of death, no priest availa-

---

It deserves reflection that no other sacrament has two forms, one theological, another canonical. Does the expression "canonical form" cover any reality, or are we simply dealing with an "impediment of clandestinity" disguised under a terminology that does not make good theological sense?

Cf. Gérard Fransen, "L'application des décrets du Concile de Trente. Les débuts d'un nominalisme canonique," *L'anneé canonique*, 27 (1983), 5-16. For a superb documentation of the creativity and originality of canon law in the Middle Ages *see* Harold J. Berman, *Law and Revolution: The Formation of the Western Legal Traditions* (Cambridge, MA: Harvard University Press, 1983).

ble) the form was absolutely binding to the extent that an inadvertent omission of some technical requirement (e.g. about delegation) could invalidate the marriage and deprive the substantially correct intention of the parties from its effect. The form took precedence over the substance.

The new Code is more flexible. Dispensation from the form can be obtained whenever a Catholic marries a non-Catholic person, Christian or not. Delegation has been made easier. In the case of a technical fault the church is more willing to supply what is missing. The substance has come to the fore.

Literary forms: the canons prescribing the requirements for the canonical form are *legal norms in the strictest sense.*

The values that the canonical form intends to protect *are mainly but not exclusively societal values,* such as legal clarity and certainty about marriages; such a protection is for the welfare of individual persons as well.

⤳ ✳ ⤙

What are the requirements for the canonical form?

Canon 1108 § 1.

Ea tantum matrimonia valida sunt,
quae contrahuntur coram loci Ordinario
aut parocho
aut sacerdote vel diacono ab alterutro delegato qui assistant,
necnon coram duobus testibus,
secundum tamen regulas expressas in canonibus qui sequuntur,
et salvis exceptionibus
de quibus in cann. 144, 1112 § 1, 1116 et 1127, §§ 2-3.

Only those marriages are valid,
which are contracted in the presence of the local ordinary, or of
the parish priest,

or of a priest or a deacon delegated by either of them, who must
assist,
and in the presence of two witnesses,
[*and contracted*] according to the rules expressed in the canons
that follow,
save for the exceptions stated in canons 144, 1112 § 1, 1116 and
1127 §§ 2-3.

ordinary, parish priest, delegated priest, deacon, [or lay person, see
can. 1112]; they all are "qualified" witnesses entrusted with a special
task which goes beyond their mere presence: they must "assist" the
parties in the public declaration of their consent; cf. § 2 of this canon
where the technical meaning of "assistance" is defined.

two witnesses: no special appointment is necessary; anyone who is
present, sees, hears and understands what is happening is a witness.

canon 144 authorizes the application of the norms for common
error to celebrations that may have been deficient.

꙳

Who is the "assistant" at a marriage?

Canon 1108 § 2.

**Assistens matrimonio intellegitur tantum
qui praesens exquirit manifestationem contrahentium consensus
eamque nomine Ecclesiae recipit.**

**Only the person who, being present,
requests the manifestation of the consent of the contracting
parties and receives it in the name of the church
is understood to assist at the marriage.**

In other words:

The "assistant" is the person
who is deputed by the church
to request the parties to declare their consent, and,
to receive it in the name of the church.

The terms, **assistant, to assist,** are used in a technical sense throughout the canons on marriage: they refer to the so called "qualified witness" who is the ordinary, the parish priest, or a priest, a deacon or a lay person delegated by either of the two. No other persons present, not even the two required witnesses, should be said to assist, or be called assistants.

requests the manifestation of consent: the assistant must assist actively; he must ask the parties to declare their intentions, that is, to manifest their consent.

receives the consent in the name of the church: this expression does not go well with the contractual theory. If the agreement is strictly between the parties, they should receive the consent from each other. But if to receive the sacrament of marriage is to accept a "consecration" from the church for a new state of life with appropriate rights and duties, the requesting and receiving of the consent "in the name of the church" makes good sense. There is no reason to think, however, that the drafters of the Code would have accepted the theory of "consecration" even if the text can be construed as being favorable to it.[4]

Who are entitled to be "assistants"?

Canon 1109

Loci Ordinarius et parochus,
nisi per sententiam vel per decretum fuerint excommunicati vel
  interdicti vel suspensi ab officio aut tales declarati,
vi officii, intra fines sui territorii,
valide matrimoniis assistunt non tantum subditorum,
sed etiam non subditorum,
dummodo eorum alteruter sit ritus latini.

---

[4]To ask for the consent and to receive it in the name of the church is a puzzling expression. Consent is an internal reality in the human spirit; no one can give it to anybody. The meaning of the expression can be only to ask for the *manifestation* of the consent and to take notice of it when it is done.

> The local ordinary and the parish priest —
> unless they have been excommunicated or interdicted or
> suspended from the exercise of their office
> by a sentence or a decree or they have been declared as such —
> in virtue of their office,
> within the limits of their territory,
> assist validly at the marriages not only of their own subjects,
> but also of those who are not their subjects,
> provided one of the parties is of the Latin rite.

in virtue of their office: their power to assist is an integral part of the ordinary power attached to their office.

within the limits of their territory: valid assistance to marriages is ruled by the territorial principle. The ordinary cannot follow his subjects into another diocese and there assist at their marriage; nor could a parish priest function in another parish.

Canon 1110

> Ordinarius et parochus personalis
> vi officii matrimonio solummodo eorum valide assistunt,
> quorum saltem alteruter subditus sit
> intra fines suae dicionis.

> A personal ordinary and a personal parish priest,
> in virtue of their office [*and*] within the ambit of their
>   jurisdiction,
> assist validly at the marriages of those only
> of whom at least one party is their subject.

This canon is an exception to the principle of territoriality.

This semantic problem should be distinguished from the more substantial one: how does someone receive the sacrament of marriage? Undoubtedly, from the church. But who is acting for the church? In other words, who is the minister of the sacrament? The scholastic doctrine is that each spouse is the minister for the other one. But is another explanation acceptable, such as the priest or the deacon is the minister as the Oriental church assumes? The best answer seems to be in saying that the church has the power to designate the ministers; hence the two conceptions are not opposed, they just manifest the manifold ways the church can handle the administration of a sacrament.

Who has the authority to delegate the faculty to assist?

Canon 1111 § 1.

Loci Ordinarius et parochus,
quamdiu valide officio funguntur,
possunt facultatem intra fines sui territorii matrimoniis assistendi,
etiam generalem,
sacerdotibus et diaconis delegare.

The local ordinary and the parish priest,
as long as they function validly in their office,
can delegate the faculty to assist at marriages,
even generally,
to priests and deacons,
within the boundaries of their own territory.

as long as they function validly in their office: as long as they have not been excommunicated, interdicted, etc.; the same restrictions as in canon 1109.

general delegation is given to a determined person for undetermined marriages. Restrictions can be imposed on it; the grant can be for a certain number of marriages, for a period of time, for a specified place. General delegation granted by the ordinary of the place with no restriction is valid for his territory; one granted by the parish priest is valid for the parish only.

special delegation is given to a determined person for one or several determined marriages.

❧ ✳ ☙

How to give a special delegation?
How to give a general delegation?

Canon 1111 § 2.

Ut valida sit delegatio facultatis assistendi matrimoniis,
determinatis personis expresse dari debet;

si agitur de delegatione speciali, ad determinatum matrimonium
danda est;
si vero agitur de delegatione generali, scripto est concedenda.

For a delegation of the faculty to assist at marriages to be valid
it must be given expressly to determined persons;
if it is a special delegation, it must be given for a determined
marriage;
however, if it is a general delegation it must be given in writing.

determined person: the person must be designated in such a way
that no doubt is possible as to his identity; normally this is done by
naming him, but it could be done in some other way, e.g. designating
him by the office that he holds, such as "the rector of the seminary."

determined marriage: the same rule applies; the designation of the
marriage should leave no room for any doubt; again it could be done
in different ways, such as by naming the couple, or by stating the
place and time of the marriage, etc.

in writing: the meaning of this clause must be construed in function of the introductory statement: "for a delegaton. . .*to be valid*"; it
follows that a written document is required for the validity of a
general delegation (not for the validity of a *special* one).

❧❀❧

Can a lay person be delegated?

Canon 1112 § 1.

Ubi desunt sacerdotes et diaconi,
potest Episcopus dioecesanus,
praevio voto favorabili Episcoporum conferentiae et obtenta
licentia Sanctae Sedis,
delegare laicos, qui matrimoniis assistant.

Wherever there is a lack of priests and deacons,
the diocesan bishop can delegate lay persons to assist at
marriages,

with the previous favorable vote of the episcopal conference
and after having obtained the permission of the Holy See.

The lack of priests and deacons may be relative, e.g. none of those
who are available is able to speak the language of a particular group
of people.

the diocesan bishop can delegate: since there is no restriction in the
law, the bishop can grant either general or special delegation to a lay
person.

lay persons: although in the original Latin the masculine gender is
used, it includes both sexes. To use one gender in reference to both
sexes is a common practice in canon law, cf. e.g. *baptizati, peregrini,
incolae, religiosi*, etc., etc.

favorable vote by the episcopal conference: although this requirement seems canonically analogous to a consultation imposed by the
law (cf. canon 127 § 2), in reality it is not the diocesan bishop who is
consulting the conference but it is the Holy See who does not wish to
grant the permission without the supporting judgment of the
conference.

permission by the Holy See: the bishop's ordinary power does not
include the right to delegate lay persons to assist at marriages; it
follows that the bishop needs the authorization of the Holy See for
the validity of such delegation.

꧁ ❋ ꧂

What qualifications are required in the lay person to be delegated?

Canon 1112 § 2.

**Laicus seligatur idoneus,
ad institutionem nupturientibus tradendam capax
et qui liturgiae matrimoniali rite peragendae aptus sit.**

A qualified lay person should be selected,
competent to give instructions to those to be married,
and able to perform the matrimonial liturgy correctly.

Clearly, the purpose of the law is to facilitate the presence of an "ecclesiastical assistant" at marriages in those regions where there is a scarcity of persons in sacred orders.

ᕙᕗ✳ᕙᕗ

In the case of special delegation,
who is responsible for the investigations?

Canon 1113

Antequam delegatio concedatur specialis,
omnia provideantur,
quae ius statuit ad libertatem status comprobandam.

Before a special delegation is granted,
all [*necessary*] provisions should be made to ensure
that the prescriptions of the law for ascertaining the freedom of
  the parties will be observed.

In other terms, the one who grants the special delegation is responsible for all the necessary investigations. He is not forbidden to hand this duty over to the one who receives the delegation, but if he does so, he must take all the necessary steps to ensure that the prescriptions of the law will be properly observed.

ᕙᕗ✳ᕙᕗ

What are the responsibilities of the "assistant"?

Canon 1114

Assistens matrimonio illicite agit,
nisi ipsi constiterit de libero statu contrahentium ad normam
  iuris atque,

si fieri potest, de licentia parochi,
quoties vi delegationis generalis assistit.

The person who is assisting at the celebration of a marriage acts
unlawfully [*illicitly*] unless
the freedom of the parties to marry in conformity with the law
  has been established to his satisfaction; and
— if he assists in virtue of a general delegation —
he is certain, as far as possible, of the permission of the parish
  priest.

In other words:

> The assistant must satisfy himself
> that the parties are free to marry in conformity with the law.
>
> The person who assists in virtue of a general delegation
> must make sure, as far as possible,
> that he has the permission of the parish priest to assist at that
> particular marriage.

Every person authorized to assist at a marriage is bound to ascertain that the parties are free to marry; this does not mean that he is bound to investigate personally, he may rely on the testimony of the one who *ex officio* conducted the inquiries. A failure to fulfill this duty, however, does not affect either his mandate to assist or the validity of the marriage.

If a person has general delegation, he should not assist at an individual marriage without the permission of the parish priest who is ultimately responsible for ascertaining the freedom of the parties and for providing the necessary "canonical assistance."

What parishes are legally designated for the celebration?
Who has authority to grant an exception?

Canon 1115

Matrimonia celebrentur in paroecia
ubi alterutra pars contrahentium habet domicilium vel quasi-

> domicilium vel menstruam commorationem,
> aut, si de vagis agitur, in paroecia ubi actu commorantur;
> cum licentia proprii Ordinarii aut parochi proprii,
> alibi celebrari possunt.

Marriages should be celebrated in the parish where
either of the contracting parties has domicile or quasi-domicile,
**   or one month's residence; or,**
if they [both] are homeless [vagi],
in the parish where they actually are;
marriages can be celebrated elsewhere
with the permission of the proper ordinary or of the proper
**   parish priest.**

For the celebration of the marriage, the law designates either the parish of the bride or that of the bridegroom; they are free to choose. If they wish to go beyond the boundaries stated in the law, they should request the permission of their own ordinary or parish priest. The couple need not present any special reason, and as a rule the permission should be granted; it is required mainly for pastoral purposes.

━━✳━━

When is it lawful to celebrate a marriage without an "assistant"?

Canon 1116 § 1.

> Si haberi vel adiri nequeat
> sine gravi incommodo
> assistens ad normam iuris competens,
> qui intendunt verum matrimonium inire,
> illud valide ac licite coram solis testibus contrahere possunt:
>   1° in mortis periculo;
>   2° extra mortis periculum,
> dummodo prudenter praevideatur earum rerum condicionem
>   esse per mensem duraturam.

If without grave inconvenience,
the assistant competent according to the norm of the law
cannot be present or cannot be approached,

those who intend to enter into a true marriage
can contract it validly and licitly in the presence of witnesses
only
1° in danger of death;
2° apart from danger of death,
provided it is prudently foreseen that the same conditions will
continue to prevail for a month.

grave inconvenience: a relative concept; there is no way of giving an absolutely and universally valid definition of it; the final decision about it must come from the prudential judgment of those involved in the case. If in doubt, it is legitimate to proceed with the marriage; the celebration will be valid, *ecclesia supplet*.

cannot be present or cannot be approached: this is the translation of *haberi vel adiri nequeat*. The term "cannot" has many meanings; it may refer to a physical impossibility, such as when the roads are not passable, or to a moral inconvenience, such as when there is a danger of losing one's job if it becomes known to the authorities that a priest officiated at the marriage.

danger of death: it is enough that death may occur; there is no need to have certainty that it will follow. When there is a threat, there is no need to wait until the situation becomes critical. If a legitimate "assistant" cannot be secured without grave inconvenience, the law itself grants dispensation from the form.

prudently foreseen: no more is required than an honest judgment whether or not the circumstances are likely to change within a month. If not, again, the law grants dispensation from the requirement of having an "assistant." Once the marriage is celebrated on the basis of such prudent judgment, it is valid, no matter what happens afterwards, e.g. after ten days a priest unexpectedly arrives.

two witnesses are still required for the validity of the contract.[5]

---

[5]The celebration of the marriage without an "assistant" but in the presence of two witnesses is called also the "extraordinary form"; it follows that we have two canonical forms. The extraordinary form is not to be confused with the case where there is no canonical form, as when the couple is dispensed from it. Throughout it all, there is, of course, just one theological form.

Is there a duty to call a priest or a deacon
who has no faculty to assist?

Canon 1116 § 2.

In utroque casu,
si praesto sit alius sacerdos vel diaconus qui adesse possit,
vocari et, una cum testibus, matrimonii celebrationi adesse
   debet,
salva coniugii validitate coram solis testibus.

In either case,
if there is another priest or deacon who can be present,
he must be called and he must be at the celebration together
   with the [*two*] witnesses,
without prejudice to the validity of the marriage in the presence
   of the [*two*] witnesses only.

can be present, must be called: that is without grave
inconvenience.

priest or deacon: he is not called to be present to inquire about the
consent, or to receive it in the name of the church, although if
requested by the parties he may certainly preside over the exchange
of the promises. He also has power to dispense from certain impediments, see canon 1079 § 2. Even if he assists at the marriage, he is not
an "assistant" as defined in canon 1108 § 2.

⌒⋇⌒

Who are bound by the law of the canonical form?

Canon 1117

Statuta superius forma servanda est,
si saltem alterutra pars matrimonium contrahentium in Ecclesia
   catholica baptizata
vel in eandem recepta sit neque actu formali ab ea defecerit,
salvis praescriptis can. 1127, § 2.

The above stated form must be observed
if at least one of the parties contracting marriage was baptized
  in the Catholic church,
or was received into it and has not by a formal act defected
  from it;
the prescriptions of canon 1127 § 2, however, remain in effect.

at least one of the parties: a repetition of the principle enunciated in canon 1059; the church claims jurisdiction over all marriages where at least one of the parties is Catholic.

baptized in the Catholic church: a more adequate translation would be baptized *into* the Catholic church. The intention of the person seeking baptism, or of those who act in the name of that person (e.g. parents requesting baptism for their child) is decisive; the place where the baptism was administered (e.g. a protestant chapel in a hospital), or the religious affiliation of the person who administered the baptism (e.g. a protestant minister) can be irrelevant.

received into the Catholic church: that is formally received, which in ordinary circumstances is a specific liturgical act; it signifies not only the public profession of the Catholic faith, but also the public bond of *communion* with the Catholic church.

defection by a formal act: the "formal act" of defection is not defined by the Code, but no doubt it means an act that could be proved in the external forum. Examples of such an act can be easily given, even if an all-embracing definition of it cannot be easily construed. If a Catholic requests and receives confirmation in a non Catholic community, or asks that his name should be put on their parish register, or publishes a book advocating atheism, there is certainly enough evidence to convince any court that he meant to leave the Catholic church. But if someone for civil purposes states that he left the Catholic church, so as to avoid the paying of church tax collected by the state, his act should be judged with caution; it may not be the rejection of his religious allegiance. See also our comments on canon 1086 § 1.

In the case of a mixed marriage a dispensation from the canonical form can be obtained from the ordinary; see canon 1127 § 2.

In what building should a sacramental celebration take place?

Canon 1118 § 1.

Matrimonium inter catholicos
vel inter partem catholicam et partem non catholicam baptizatam
celebretur in ecclesia paroeciali;
in alia ecclesia aut oratorio celebrari poterit
de licentia Ordinarii loci vel parochi.

A marriage between Catholics,
or between a Catholic and a baptized non-Catholic
should be celebrated in the parish church;
it can be celebrated in another church or oratory
with the permission of the local ordinary or of the parish priest.

Who has the authority to permit the celebration in some other place?

Canon 1118 § 2.

Matrimonium in alio convenienti loco celebrari
Ordinarius loci permittere potest.

The local ordinary may permit the celebration of the marriage
in some other suitable place.

The law favors a sacred place for the celebration of the sacrament of marriage. Ordinarily it should be the parish church, but with the permission of the ordinary of the place or of the parish priest, the couple may choose another church or oratory.

To celebrate the marriage at a not sacred but suitable place, the permission of the ordinary is required.

In what place should a non-sacramental marriage be celebrated?

Canon 1118 § 3.

Matrimonium inter partem catholicam et partem non
  baptizatam
in ecclesia vel in alio convenienti loco celebrari poterit.

A marriage between a Catholic and non-baptized person
may be celebrated in a church or in some other suitable place.

If the marriage is celebrated after a dispensation from the impediment of disparity of cult has been obtained, the law leaves it to the
couple to choose a suitable place for its celebration. They may have it
in a Catholic church, or at any other convenient place. No further
permission is necessary, but no matter where they go, they are still
bound by the canonical form.

꒰ �֍ ꒱

What rites are to be followed in the liturgical celebration?

Canon 1119

Extra casum necessitatis,
in matrimonii celebratione serventur ritus in libris liturgicis,
  ab Ecclesia probatis,
praescripti aut legitimis consuetudinibus recepti.

Apart from a case of necessity,
in the celebration of marriage the rites prescribed in the liturgical
  books approved by the church, or,
[*the rites*] received through legitimate customs must be observed.

case of necessity: e.g. danger of death.

*What is the competence of the episcopal conference
concerning the rite of the celebration?*

Canon 1120

**Episcoporum conferentia exarare potest ritum proprium
matrimonii,
a Sancta Sede recognoscendum,
congruentem locorum et populorum usibus ad spiritum
christianum aptatis,
firma tamen lege
ut assistens matrimonio praesens requirat manifestationem
consensus contrahentium eamque recipiat.**

**The episcopal conference can compose its own suitable rite of
marriage,
to be recognized by the Holy See,
adapting the usages of places and peoples to the spirit of
Christianity,
without prejudice to the law that
the assistant present at the marriage must require the
manifestation of consent and must receive it.**

In the United States the translation of the *Rite of Marriage* published on March 19, 1969, by the Sacred Congregation of Rites, is
used.

Record keeping.

The remaining canons in this chapter are self-explanatory. Their
principal message is clear and simple: the church intends to keep its
records concerning marriages in good order. The canons list those
who are responsible for making the entries in the books, or for
transmitting information to those who are in charge of the books.

Who is responsible for keeping the records?

Canon 1121 § 1.

Celebrato matrimonio,
parochus loci celebrationis vel qui eius vices gerit,
etsi neuter eidem astiterit,
quam primum adnotet in matrimoniorum regestis nomina
   coniugum, assistentis ac testium,
locum et diem celebrationis matrimonii,
iuxta modum ab Episoporum conferentia aut ab Episcopo
   dioecesano praescriptum.

After the celebration of a marriage,
the parish priest of the place of the marriage or his substitute,
even if neither of them assisted at the marriage,
must enter as soon as possible into the register of marriages
   the names of the spouses, of the assistant and of the witnesses,
   the place and the day of the celebration of the marriage,
according to the modalities prescribed by the episcopal
   conference or by the diocesan bishop.

The primary responsibility is with the parish priest.

⌂⟶✳⟵⌂

Who is responsible for providing the information for the recording
of a marriage celebrated without an "assistant"?

Canon 1121 § 2.

Quoties matrimonium ad normam can. 1116 contrahitur,
sacerdos vel diaconus, si celebrationi adfuerit,
secus testes tenentur in solidum cum contrahentibus
parochum aut Ordinarium loci de inito coniugio
quam primum certiorem reddere.

Whenever a marriage is contracted according to the norm of
   canon 1116,
if a priest or deacon was present at the celebration, he is
   bound;

otherwise, the witnesses and the contracting parties are jointly
  bound
to inform, as soon as possible, the parish priest or the local
  ordinary
of the marriage entered into.

jointly bound: the canon uses an expression from Roman law:
they are bound *in solidum*, that is, each of the spouses and witnesses
has the personal duty to provide the information necessary for the
recording of the marriage entered into. None of them is absolved
until one has fulfilled the obligation.

✎ ✳ ✎

*Who are responsible for the registration when the spouses were
dispensed from the canonical form?*

Canon 1121 § 3.

Ad matrimonium quod attinet cum dispensatione a forma
  canonica contractum,
loci Ordinarius, qui dispensationem concessit,
curet ut inscribatur dispensatio et celebratio in libro matrimoniorum tum　　curiae tum paroeciae propriae partis catholicae,
cuius parochus inquisitiones de statu libero peregit;
de celebrato matrimonio eundem Ordinarium et parochum
  quam primum certiorem reddere tenetur coniux catholicus,
indicans etiam locum celebrationis necnon formam publicam
  servatam.

In the case of a marriage contracted with a dispensation from
  the canonical form,
the local ordinary who granted the dispensation should see that
the dispensation and the celebration is entered
into the book of marriages of the curia and of the proper parish
  of the Catholic party
whose parish priest conducted the investigations concerning
  the free state;
the Catholic spouse is bound to inform as soon as possible the
  same ordinary and the parish priest

of the marriage that has been celebrated,
indicating also the place of the celebration
and the public form that was observed.

The primary responsibility is with the ordinary who granted the
dispensation; the Catholic spouse must notify him after the
celebration.

❦

Should a marriage be entered into the baptismal registers?

Canon 1122 § 1.

Matrimonium contractum adnotetur etiam in regestis
  baptizatorum,
in quibus baptismus coniugum inscriptus est.

The marriage contracted should be recorded
also in the baptismal registers
in which the baptisms of the spouses are inscribed.

❦

Who is responsible for providing the information?

Canon 1122 § 2.

Si coniux matrimonium contraxerit non in paroecia in qua
  baptizatus est,
parochus loci celebrationis
notitiam initi coniugii
ad parochum loci collati baptismi quam primum transmittat.

If a spouse contracted marriage elsewhere than in the parish of
  baptism,
the parish priest of the place of the celebration

must send, as soon as possible, a notice of the marriage that has
 been entered into
to the parish priest of the place of baptism.

❦

How ought later events affecting a marriage to be recorded?

Canon 1123

Quoties matrimonium vel convalidatur pro foro externo,
vel nullum declaratur,
vel legitime praeterquam morte solvitur,
parochus loci celebrationis matrimonii certior fieri debet,
ut adnotatio in regestis matrimoniorum et baptizatorum rite fiat.

Whenever a marriage is validated in the external forum,
or is declared null,
or is dissolved lawfully otherwise than by death,
the parish priest of the place of the celebration of the marriage
 must be notified
so that the correct information could be entered into the registers
 of marriages and baptisms.

Such events must be recorded in both the book of baptisms and
the book of marriages.

CHAPTER SIX
MIXED MARRIAGES
1124 — 1129

Mixed marriage is the technical term canon law uses for a marriage between two Christians, one of whom is Roman Catholic and one of whom is not. They share the same baptism but they do not profess the same beliefs. In their personal relationship the tragic state of the Christian churches is displayed: they are united and divided at the same time. Such a complex situation is difficult enough to explain theologically; it is nearly impossible to make satisfactory laws for it.[1]

[1]The theological difficulty is well demonstrated by the expression that became current during the Council: separated brethren, *fratres seiuncti*. It stresses the unity: we are brethren. It states the disunity: we are separated. It shows the tragedy and absurdity of the situation: it is wrong for brethren to be separated. Theology handles the problem by speaking of a partial communio, or of communio by degrees. Now, to conceive clear norms of action for a situation where there is unity *and* there is no unity is nearly impossible. No wonder the legislation of the Catholic church concerning ecumenical matters has been hesitant ever since the Council! Traditionally, it was easy for the law to handle either full membership or radical excommunication; a person was either inside or outside of the community. But just how to make good laws for the complex relationship that we have with our separated brethren? There is a season for learning...!

Transitions: *from inimical opposition to ecumenical cooperation.* The historical origins of our present legislation go back to the bitter confrontations between the Reformers and the Roman Church, although our norms reached their high point in severity and rigidity with CIC/17 only. The starting point of that legislation was the conviction that for a Catholic to marry a non-Catholic Christian was to expose himself to the permanent danger of "perversion," against which he had to be protected. The conscience of the non-Catholic could not be taken into consideration, nor was much attention paid to the "gifts and graces" given to the other community by the Spirit (cf. LG:15). Logically enough, dispensation from the impediment was granted with reluctance and for a "canonically valid" reason only. To obtain it both parties to the marriage had to promise that all the children will be baptized in the Catholic church and educated in the Catholic faith.

The new law on mixed marriages has been inspired by the principles laid down in the Declaration of Vatican Council II on *Religious Freedom*, and, of course, it must be interpreted on the basis of the same ideas:

> On his part, man perceives and acknowledges the imperatives of the divine law through the mediation of conscience. In all his activity a man is bound to follow his conscience faithfully, in order that he may come to God, for whom he was created. It follows that he is not to be forced to act in a manner contrary to his conscience. Nor, on the other hand, is he to be restrained from acting in accordance with his conscience, especially in religious matters (3).

Thus the purpose of the legislator is to uphold old and new values in a delicate balance. Both the Catholic and the non-Catholic must be faithful to their religious conviction and must respect the conscience of the other. As long as the balancing is to be done between the two spouses only, the task may not be all that difficult;but when a child is born, a new person with an undivided mind must be introduced into the divided world of Christians. No one but the parents can have the necessary tact and wisdom to handle that situation; they must take care of the values particular to their family. Rightly, the law leaves much to the discretion of the couple.

The law is concerned with universal values; here are the principal ones:

— the integrity of the movement towards Christian unity; the new Code is significantly more friendly towards mixed marriages than the old one was;

— the integrity of the conscience of both the Catholic and the non-Catholic partner; since this requires a delicate balancing in the concrete order, the legislation is restrained and leaves much to the decision of the spouses;

— the freedom of a person to choose his or her spouse; the issue of the Catholic education of children is not stressed to the point where it could make a marriage impossible;

— the stability of the union; the law assumes that harmony and peace among the spouses can be more important than the specifically Catholic education of the children;

— the baptism and education of the children in the Roman Catholic tradition; the law insists that the Catholic party has a duty to communicate his faith to the children but not without taking into account other values.

All these values can be realized only in a unique and delicate balance with each other, knit together in a kind of hierarchical structure, the more important ones taking precedence over the others without suppressing them. The general demands of the law must be adjusted to the needs and possibilities of a particular couple.[2]

Literary forms: *dogmatic statements, theological opinions, philosophical insights, exhortations, strict legal provisions:* all such forms are represented here and should be taken into account in interpreting the canons.[3]

---

[2]The old law was built on the principle "error has no right," hence Catholic beliefs were upheld irrespective of the conscience of the non-Catholic. The new law is based on the principle "persons have rights," hence the freedom of both persons is upheld. In consequence, they must accept the responsibility of working out a prudent solution for their differences.

[3]Much of what is in CIC/83 on mixed marriages is a consolidation of the post conciliar legislation. The following documents can be considered the principal sources: *Matrimonii sacramentum*, CDF, 18 March 1966, CLD 6:592-597; *Crescens matrimoniorum*, CEO, 22 February 1967, CLD 6:605-606; *Matrimonia mixta*, Paul VI, MP 31 March 1970, CLD 7:711-718.

What is a forbidden mixed marriage?
Is permission obtainable?

Canon 1124

Matrimonium inter duas personas baptizatas,
quarum altera sit in Ecclesia catholica baptizata vel in eandem
    post baptismum recepta, quaeque nec ab ea actu formali
    defecerit,
altera vero Ecclesiae vel communitati ecclesiali plenam
    communionem cum Ecclesia catholica non habenti adscripta,
sine expressa auctoritatis competentis licentia
prohibitum est.

A marriage between two baptized persons,
one of whom was baptized in the Catholic church or was
    received into it after baptism and has not defected from it by
    a formal act,
the other of whom belongs to a church or an ecclesial
    community not having full communion with the Catholic
    church,
without the express permission of the competent authority,
is forbidden.

baptized in the Catholic church: the determining factor is not so
much who administered the baptism and at what place but the intention of the person who asked for it, or the intention of his parents or
sponsors; for more detailed comments see canon 1117.

received into the Catholic church: a formal transition has taken
place from a non-Catholic church or ecclesial community to the
Catholic church so that it can be documented in the external forum;
cf. canon 1117.

has not left by a formal act: there can be many varieties of formal
act, and it would be impossible to list them; for our purposes it is
required and it is sufficient that an external act has taken place that

could prove beyond any reasonable doubt that a person left the Catholic communion, e.g. he asked that his name should be put on the roll of a parish of the Lutheran church. Cf. canon 1117.

belongs to: the original Latin word is *adscriptus*, which is a derivation of the classical word *ascribo*, meaning (among other things) "to enroll or enlist as additional or new members of a body," also "to reckon as belonging, assign, ascribe, include in" (cf. OLD:181). The canon seems to assume that every non-Catholic Christian formally belongs to an organized community, but this is not always the case. In some countries, the USA among them, there are many baptized believers who are not in any sense enrolled among the members of a religious group; the well documented phenomenon of the "unchurched" believer proves it. *Adscriptus* could then be interpreted in a somewhat loose sense, such as "being clearly a non-Catholic Christian without any formal affiliation with a determined community."

In the practical order what matters for the implementation of the law is that (a) the non-Catholic person was baptized; (b) he professes to be a non-Catholic Christian. Beyond that there is no need for any lengthy investigation.

not having full communion: the emphasis here is on the *full* since all baptized persons have at least some partial communion with the Catholic church. Full communion is defined in canon 205:

> Those baptized are on this earth fully in the communion of the Catholic church who are joined with Christ in his visible body, namely by the bonds of profession of faith, sacraments and ecclesiastical government.

is forbidden: this is a simple prohibition. A marriage contracted without permission would be unlawful [*illicit*] but valid. But such marriage could hardly ever happen because if no permission was granted, no priest, deacon, or duly authorized lay person is entitled "to assist" at the marriage; that is, the marriage would be invalid for the lack of the canonical form.

express permission: *express* in this context means that the permission must be given for a determined marriage, without any ambiguity as to what is given. Although the law does not impose any formality, it is prudent to give it in writing.

permission has its own traditional canonical meaning; it comes into play when the legislator is well disposed towards an act but does not want it to be performed until he has the opportunity to check that all the necessary conditions or requirements are in fact fulfilled. Thus, the petition for the permission need not be supported by any special reason. Permission must be distinguished from dispensation, which is a "wound on the law";therefore it should be given for an adequate justifying reason only; the wound on the law should be balanced by some other value to be obtained through the dispensation.

competent authority: it is defined in the next canon.

❦

Who can grant permission for a mixed marriage?
Under what conditions?

Canon 1125

Huiusmodi licentiam concedere potest Ordinarius loci,
si iusta et rationabilis causa habeatur;
eam ne concedat, nisi impletis condicionibus quae sequuntur:
1° pars catholica declaret se paratam esse pericula a fide
  deficiendi removere
atque sinceram promissionem praestet se omnia pro viribus
  facturam esse, ut universa proles in Ecclesia catholica
  baptizetur et educetur;
2° de his promissionibus a parte catholica faciendis altera pars
  tempestive certior fiat,
adeo ut constet ipsam vere consciam esse promissionis et
  obligationis partis catholicae;
3° ambae partes edoceantur de finibus et proprietatibus
  essentialibus matrimonii,
a neutro contrahente excludendis.

The local ordinary can grant such permission
if there is a just and reasonable cause;

he must not grant it unless the following conditions are fulfilled:
1° the Catholic party is to declare that he or she is prepared to
remove dangers of defecting from the faith,
also to give a sincere promise to do all within his or her power
to have all the children baptized and educated in the Catholic
church;
2° the other party is to be informed in good time of the promises
to be made by the Catholic party,
so that it is certain that the other is truly aware of the promise
and obligation of the Catholic party;
3° both parties are to be instructed about the ends and essential
properties of marriage,
which are not to be excluded by either of the parties to the
contract.

the local ordinary: the ordinary of the place to which the Catholic party belongs by reason of his domicile or quasi-domicile, or of the place where the marriage is going to take place provided the Catholic party is there present.

if there is just and reasonable cause: the honest desire of the parties to marry is a just and reasonable cause; no more is required; this interpretation is confirmed by practice.

provided the conditions are fulfilled: they must be fulfilled, that is the Catholic must have given the promises and the non-Catholic must be in possession of the required information before the permission can be granted.

prepared to remove dangers of defecting from the faith: the positive meaning of this clause is that the Catholic is willing to profess and practice his faith in the circumstances of a mixed marriage. The intention of the legislator is to protect the religious freedom of the Catholic party.

to do all within one's power: this is a key expression; *pro viribus* means "as far as one's strength goes" or "as far as one is able to do it." This capacity, however, should not be measured by the internal disposition of the Catholic party only but by the intensity of the religious convictions of both. The law mandates the Catholic to do no more and no less for the Catholic baptism and education of the children than what is feasible and fitting without doing violence to the right hierarchy of values which together make up the fabric of a happy union. The correct judgment can be made, and must be made, by the two spouses together. Therefore, when a Catholic wife is trying to fulfill her promise, she must not bring into peril the peace and harmony of the marriage; she must not violate her husband's freedom of conscience; she must not hamper him in practicing his religion and speaking of it to their children, and vice versa.

To reach a satisfactory solution the spouses and those who are advising them should keep in mind the distinction between the abstract approach of the law and the concrete demands of life. The law assumes that the Catholic is intensely committed to his faith and to his church; in real life it may happen that the non-Catholic is the one who is more dedicated to Christian beliefs and practices. If so, the balance must shift from the ideal which cannot be reached to the concrete good that can be obtained. The Catholic should be humble enough to admit that acting on his religious strength, *vires*, the child would learn less about Christian life than by letting the non-Catholic take care of his education.

the other party is to be informed: it is only fair that the non-Catholic should be informed about the promise and the obligation of the Catholic. Although the law does not say so, it is equally fair that the Catholic should be made aware of the state of the conscience of the non-Catholic, he too may have duties. Through such mutual information the parties should be in position to come to a mutually acceptable solution.

The law requires some kind of evidence that the non-Catholic has come into the possession of the information required and understands it.

in good time: prudential advice to all concerned. The parties should take cognizance of the complex problems they must solve if they want to live together peacefully. If they do not confront those issues before their marriage, the problems are likely to return and haunt them later.

both are to be instructed: the law wants to make sure that both parties know the Catholic doctrine about the sacrament of marriage and that they accept it — a wise rule, but not without some theological difficulty. If the non-Catholic's beliefs concerning marriage are different from ours, e.g. he does not admit that marriage is indissoluble (suppose he is Orthodox and holds to the tradition of his church concerning divorce in case of adultery), are we asking him to change and to conform to our teaching? There is the dilemma: after the Catholic position has been explained, must the non-Catholic be left free to marry according to his convictions, or must he accept ours in order to secure the permission to marry?

The classical, although not very satisfactory answer is that the non-Catholic may be left in his "error." The marriage will be valid, provided he does not exclude one of its essential properties.

not to be excluded: see our comments *re* canon 1099.

❧ ✳ ❧

Who has the authority to determine the modalities of the promises?

Canon 1126

> Episcoporum conferentiae est tum modum statuere,
> quo hae declarationes et promissiones, quae semper requiruntur,
>   faciendae sint,
> tum rationem definire, qua de ipsis et in foro externo constet
> et pars non catholica certior reddatur.

> The episcopal conference must determine
> how these statements and promises, which are always required,
>   are to be made,
> also, it must define how they are to be attested in the external
>   forum,
> and how the non-Catholic is to be informed of them.

The episcopal conference must determine: literally the text says "it belongs to the episcopal conference to determine," that is, the conference has the power and is mandated by the law to determine it. No doubt, in these matters it is healthy to have a uniform procedure within a country or a region. In the United States the NCCB issued particular norms on November 16, 1970; they are still in effect; cf. CLD 7:730-740.[4]

always required: that is, by general legislation. Could the local ordinary dispense from them in a particular case? Yes, since the law requiring the promises and statements is disciplinary (it cannot be constitutive; nor is it procedural in the sense the term is used in Book VII). He must not dispense, however, without a proportionate reason since he is not the legislator. But such cases should be rare because the law is flexible enough to take care of most situations.

attested in the external forum: there are many ways of doing that, e.g. through a signed and sealed document, or through statements made before witnesses, etc. The law of the country may give some direction as to what type of document has probative value.

⌁ ✳ ⌁

In the celebration of a mixed marriage,
what form is required?

Canon 1127 § 1.

Ad formam quod attinet in matrimonio mixto adhibendam, serventur praescripta can. 1108;
si tamen pars catholica matrimonium contrahit cum parte non catholica ritus orientalis,
forma canonica celebrationis servanda est ad liceitatem tantum;
ad validitatem autem requiritur interventus ministri sacri, servatis aliis de iure servandis.

Concerning the form to be used in a mixed marriage
the prescriptions of canon 1108 are to be observed;

---

[4]For regulations issued by various episcopal conferences *see* CLD 7 under canon 1061; the following ones are reproduced or quoted at length: Canada (page 718), India (725), South Africa (727), Ireland (729), USA (730); also, references are given for finding the norms for Australia, Belgium, France, Germany, Holland, Italy and Switzerland (740-741).

but if the Catholic party is contracting marriage with a non Catholic of oriental rite,
the canonical form of the celebration is to be observed for its lawful [*licit*] celebration only;
for validity, however, the active presence of a sacred minister is required;
also, all other prescriptions of the law are to be observed.

In other words:

The parties to a mixed marriage are bound by the law of the canonical form in the same way as two Catholics are: it is required for validity.
There is one exception, however: if the non-Catholic is of oriental rite, the marriage before an oriental sacred minister is valid, although it may be unlawful [*illicit*].

prescriptions of canon 1108: the law of canonical form applies to mixed marriages unless an exception is granted either by law or by the competent authority.

when a Catholic marries a non-Catholic of oriental rite: they are bound to observe the Catholic canonical form, but if they do not the marriage is still valid provided a "sacred minister intervenes," that is a deacon, priest or bishop presides over the liturgical ceremony.

all other prescriptions of the law: a standard sweeping formula, a reminder that all other canons (e.g. about the preparation, impediments, etc.) continue to apply. Each of those prescriptions retains its own specific binding force.

Who can dispense from the canonical form?
Under what conditions?

Canon 1127 § 2.

Si graves difficultates formae canonicae servandae obstent, Ordinario loci partis catholicae ius est ab eadem in singulis casibus dispensandi,

consulto tamen Ordinario loci in quo matrimonium celebratur,
et salva ad validitatem aliqua publica forma celebrationis;
Episcoporum conferentiae est normas statuere,
quibus praedicta dispensatio concordi ratione concedatur.

If grave difficulties exist concerning the observance of the
canonical form,
the local ordinary of the Catholic party has the right to dispense
from it in individual cases,
after having consulted the ordinary of the place where the
marriage is to be celebrated,
and on the condition that, for validity, the celebration is to be in
some public form.
The episcopal conference must enact norms to ensure that the
said dispensation is granted in accordance with commonly
agreed principles.

grave difficulties: the law does not define or specify them; the
parties should be in position to perceive them. The ordinary has the
power to decide if they are serious enough to justify a dispensation.
Examples can be found: objections based on the religious conviction
of the non-Catholic and his family, civic disadvantages that may
follow from a Catholic wedding; and similar ones.

What if no grave difficulties emerge as obstacles but great advantages are likely to follow if the canonical form is not used; e.g.
significant improvement in the mutual relations between two Christian communities in a given locality? There would be a "grave cause"
to justify the dispensation, sufficiently analogous to the grave difficulty required by the law.

The ordinary who has the power to grant the dispensation is the
ordinary of the territory where the Catholic party has domicile or
quasi domicile, or if he does not have any, the ordinary of the place
where he is present. Such an ordinary, to act validly, must consult the
ordinary of the place where the marriage is taking place, although he
is not bound to follow the other's advice (cf. canon 127). Note,
however, that were the consultation omitted, and the dispensation
granted, the marriage would be still valid if the conditions for common error are verified (cf. canon 144).

A **public form** is required for validity: the form must be one that is officially recognized by some religious or civil authority; thus celebration according to the rites of a non-Catholic religious community, or according to the law of the land certainly satisfies the requirements of canon law.

Moreover, the Pontifical Commission for the Interpretation of the Decrees of the Second Vatican Council decided that

> the diocesan bishop, when he grants a dispensation from canonical form in a mixed marriage in accord with the *motu proprio, Matrimonia mixta,* can place limits to the scope of this concession by attaching clauses affecting validity. *See* CLD 9:659).

Episcopal conferences have the right to coordinate policies and procedures in this matter; the very fact that they are authorized to do so implies that a fair amount of discretion is left to them to adapt the universal law to the particular needs of their country or region.

⟋⟍ ✳ ⟋⟍

Are two religious ceremonies permitted?
Are two inquiries about the consent admitted?

Canon 1127 § 3.

Vetatur, ne ante vel post canonicam celebrationem ad normam
   § 1,
alia habeatur eiusdem matrimonii celebratio religiosa
ad matrimonialem consensum praestandum vel renovandum;
item ne fiat celebratio religiosa,
in qua assistens catholicus et minister non catholicus insimul,
suum quisque ritum peragens,
partium consensum exquirant.

It is forbidden to have, either before or after the canonical
   celebration prescribed in § 1,
another religious celebration of the same marriage
in order to give or to renew the matrimonial consent;
further, no religious celebration is to take place
where the Catholic assistant and the non Catholic minister
[*functioning*] together, each in accordance with his own rite,
inquires about the consent of the parties.

no two religious celebrations should take place in order to give or
to renew the consent: the purpose of the law is to avoid confusion;
once the sacrament is completed, there should be no repetition of the
sacramental sign. There is no objection in the law, however, to
another religious celebration which does not include the giving or
renewing of the consent, elaborate as it may be. Such celebrations
may be even advisable from an ecumenical point of view.

There is no objection either to a merely secular ceremony that
includes the usual exchange of promises, before or after the religious
ceremony, if it is so prescribed by civil law.

no two ministers should jointly request and accept the consent:
this clause reflects the same preoccupation with the clarity of the
sacramental sign as the above one. Either the Catholic form should
be observed, and no other one used; or a dispensation from the
canonical form should be obtained and a public form used; no other
option is made available. But two ministers may be present at the
wedding, they may offer prayers together, offer their blessing jointly,
etc., provided the rule about the consent is respected.

ᑯᑭ✳ᑫᑐ

What should be the principal aims of pastoral care?

Canon 1128

Locorum Ordinarii aliique animarum pastores curent,
ne coniugi catholico et filiis e matrimonio mixto natis
auxilium spirituale desit ad eorum obligationes adimplendas
atque coniuges adiuvent ad vitae coniugalis et familiaris
    fovendam unitatem.

Local ordinaries and others entrusted with pastoral care
should see to it that the Catholic spouse and the children born
    of a mixed marriage
are not deprived of spiritual help to fulfill their obligations,
also they should assist the spouses to foster the unity of their
    conjugal and family life.

The sense of the canon is: since those living in mixed marriages are
bound to experience special difficulties due to the tension arising

from their different beliefs, they should be given special care. Indeed the church should watch such families with particular interest and concern because while they experience the tragedy of division, they can be also pioneers on the road to unity.

⌒⌒ ✳ ⌒⌒

Are the norms given for mixed marriages
applicable to marriages with disparity of cult?

Canon 1129

Praescripta cann. 1127 et 1128
applicanda sunt quoque matrimoniis,
quibus obstat impedimentum disparitatis cultus,
de quo in can. 1086, § 1.

The prescriptions of canons 1127 and 1128
are applicable also to those marriages
which are impeded by the impediment of disparity of cult,
mentioned in canon 1086 § 1.

The broad norms given for mixed marriages are applicable also when a Catholic marries a non-Christian. There is an internal logic in extending the scope of the norms: the problems are similar. The faith of the Catholic ought to be protected and the conscience of a non-Christian must be respected.

Summary

The law recognizes that marriages between Catholics and non-Catholic Christians are of ordinary occurrence. The canons uphold the rights and duties of the Catholic party, but they leave no doubt that their exercise must be balanced with the analogous rights and duties of the non-Catholic person. This balancing requires well thought out prudential judgments, which being concerned with con-crete actions, can be made only by those who are in possession of all the factual information. They are the spouses, and the spouses only.

The permission of the ordinary is required. Its grant is conditioned on the promise of the Catholic to fulfill his obligations. But such a promise does not cancel out the duty of the Catholic to respect the conscience of the other and to uphold the stability and the harmony of marriage. The task of loving and helping each other obtains a priority over the issue of the confessional education of the children.

The non-Catholic is required to state that he is aware of the rights and duties of the Catholic. Implied in the law is that he too should respect the conscience of the other and make an effort to reach balanced solutions in religious matters, keeping in mind the right hierarchy of values.

The parties are bound to observe the Catholic canonical form, but a dispensation can be obtained when there are grave difficulties. A public form, however, remains necessary.

No matter what form the spouses follow, their consent should be manifested only once, binding them forever. Beyond this restriction they are free to have an "ecumenical celebration."

Reflections

The issue of mixed marriages is part of the broader scene of the movement of Christian churches towards unity. The practical legal provisions reflect the prudential judgments of the Catholic church at a specific moment of history, in this case at the time of the promulgation of the new Code.

These official judgments are cautiously ecumenical. The concern of the post-Reformation period that someone may lose the faith through a mixed marriage is still there: the Catholic must watch out and avoid what may imperil his faith. There is none of the quiet assurance of St. Paul, who saw in the marriage of a Christian to an unbeliever a source of sanctification for all, children included. He did not try to impede such marriages; he only provided a radical remedy if the unbeliever did not want to leave the believer in peace because of his conversion (cf. 1 Cor 7).

The law supports the rights and duties of the Catholic party on the basis of general principles but it leaves enough room for adjustments according to the unique qualities and circumstances of the couple. As long as the Catholic is a truly committed Christian all is good and well, but if he is weak in his faith, the assumptions of the law may not be applicable — a good illustration of the old adage: no matter how wise general laws are, they can lead to unwanted consequences in particular situations. Fortunately, our laws are not so rigid that they would hamper an equitable approach in an individual case.

It may be asked if a need exists at all for a specific "prohibition" when the honest intention to marry is enough to obtain the necessary permission. Besides, the spouses are allowed to use their own discretion concerning religious education of the children. To involve the ordinary in each case seems an unnecessary administrative complication. Mixed marriages could be handled on the parish level, exactly as marriages among Catholics are. A step toward such development of the universal law can be taken by the ordinaries: they can delegate the power to grant permission to priests working in the parishes.

Ideally, the pastoral care of families of mixed religion should be taken on jointly by the churches to which they belong; they should do it in mutual respect and understanding.

"Domestic church"

In the case of a mixed marriage, the religious composition of the family reflects the state of the Christian church: there is unity, there are divisions. It is good to recall, however, that unity antecedes all divisions. Those who are baptized in Christ are one in his Spirit, even if they are divided in matters of belief. This unity is the solid foundation for a "domestic church"; the couple needs only to have the "eyes of faith" to perceive it before their minds dwell on the problems that spring from the divisions. If they are able to do that, they can become an "ecumenical family," an inspiration to all Christians of whatever denomination.

CHAPTER SEVEN
THE CELEBRATION OF
MARRIAGE IN SECRECY
1130 — 1133

At times the public knowledge that a marriage has been celebrated may cause serious inconvenience, even harm, to the couple. An obvious example would be the case when civil law imposes an impediment which cannot have any validity in canon law, such as the outlawing of "interracial" marriages and making them into a criminal offense. To protect the couple, the church not only allows the canonical marriage to be celebrated in secrecy, but provides safeguards for keeping it secret. In such a case, **the value the law intends to protect** is the *right of the faithful to marry.*

Transitions: there is *virtually no change* from the old Code to the new Code.

The canons are disciplinary norms. They are mostly self-explanatory.

Who has the authority to permit a secret celebration?

Canon 1130

Ex gravi et urgenti causa loci Ordinarius permittere potest, ut matrimonium secreto celebretur.

The local ordinary may permit, for a grave and urgent cause, that a marriage be celebrated in secret.

grave and urgent cause: it would be idle to try to compose a list of such causes. They can be of the greatest variety, originating in personal circumstances or in public situations. The law wisely leaves the concrete determination of a justifying cause to the local ordinary.

celebrated in secret: it means that *in fact* no publicity about the marriage is required or allowed. The exchange of promises, however, remains a public juridical act; the "assistant" must request and accept the consent in the presence of two witnesses. Also, the performance of the ceremony must be properly documented.

What does the permission imply?

Canon 1131

Permissio matrimonium secreto celebrandi secumfert:
1° ut secreto fiant investigationes quae ante matrimonium peragendae sunt;
2° ut secretum de matrimonio celebrato servetur ab Ordinario loci, assistente, testibus, coniugibus.

Permission to celebrate a marriage in secret implies:
1° that the investigations to be done before the marriage are carried out in secret;
2° that the secret about the marriage that has been celebrated is

observed by the local ordinary, the assistant, the witnesses and the spouses.

the permission implies: the permission dispenses the couple from the customary publicity before the marriage and protects them from unwarranted publicity afterwards; for this purpose it imposes the duty of observing the secret on all who are officially involved in the celebration of the marriage.

❧ ❊ ❧

Are there circumstances
in which the duty of observing the secret ceases?

<h2 align="center">Canon 1132</h2>

Obligatio secretum servandi, de qua in can. 1131, n. 2, ex parte
    Ordinarii loci cessat
si grave scandalum aut gravis erga matrimonii sanctitatem
    iniuria ex secreti observantia immineat,
idque notum fiat partibus ante matrimonii celebrationem.

The obligation of observing the secret, mentioned in canon 1131,
    n. 2, ceases to bind the local ordinary
if from the observance of the secret a threat of grave scandal or of
    grave harm to the sanctity of marriage arises;
this [*rule*] must be made known to the parties before the
    celebration of the marriage.

There are times when the common good must take precedence over the particular good of individual persons. The judge is the local ordinary but fairness demands that he should consult with the couple before he reveals what has happened. The spouses will have to carry the burden of the publicity.

How to record a secret marriage?

Canon 1133

Matrimonium secreto celebratum in peculiari tantummodo regesto,
servando in secreto curiae archivo, adnotetur.

A marriage celebrated in secret is to be recorded in a special register only,
which is to be kept in the secret archives of the curia.

For the rules concerning the establishment and the administration of the secret archives see canons 489 and 490. The documents must be kept under lock and key all the time and the bishop alone is to have the key.

CHAPTER EIGHT
THE EFFECTS OF MARRIAGE
1134 — 1140

The effects of marriage described in this chapter are the *bond* that arises from the valid exchange of promises and the *equal rights and duties* that flow from the spouses' new status, especially concerning the education of children. The canons provide also some guidelines for determining the legitimacy of the children at the time of their birth or for conferring it later if they were born illegitimate.

Transitions: there is *no substantial change* from the old Code to the new Code but there is more emphasis on the specific character of a Christian marriage and the equality of the spouses.

Literary forms: the canon on the nature of the bond (1134) is ambivalent: when applied to natural marriages, it represents a statement of social and moral *philosophy,* when referred to sacramental unions the same words acquire a *theological meaning*; similarly, the canons on the rights and duties of the spouses (1135, 1136) can be interpreted in a philosophical or theological context; the remaining canons about legitimacy are *legal texts* in the full sense.

The values the canons proclaim are *the permanency and the exclusivity of the bond, the rightful autonomy of each of the spouses and the education of the children.* The issue of canonical legitimacy is of much lesser significance today than it was once when the transmission of wordly goods and honors depended on it. The continued use of the term "illegitimate" could be questioned since it still marks unfavorably an innocent person. In the Christian perception a child, even when born out of wedlock, is a gift from God; his creative act is not "illegitimate."

⌬ ✳ ⌬

What is the bond of marriage?
What is the difference in a Christian marriage?

Canon 1134

Ex valido matrimonio enascitur inter coniuges vinculum
natura sua perpetuum et exclusivum;
in matrimonio praeterea christiano
coniuges ad sui status officia et dignitatem
peculiari sacramento roborantur et veluti consecrantur.

From a valid marriage arises a bond between the spouses,
perpetual and exclusive by its nature;
moreover, in a Christian marriage the spouses are strengthened
and, as it were, consecrated by a special sacrament
for the offices and dignity of their state.

marriage here means the act of the initial commitment, the exchange of promises, the very act of creating a lifelong right-and-duty situation, natural or sacramental. In classical canon law this act was described as "marriage coming into existence," *matrimonium in fieri,* distinct from "marriage in existence," *matrimonium in esse.* The distinction should not be pushed too far; the moment of birth cannot be separated from the life that follows it. The canon does not distinguish between natural and sacramental marriages although they represent different values: while a natural marriage perfects the humanity of the spouses, a sacramental marriage is part of the redemptive act of Christ.[1] *See* also our comments on canon 1055. As there is a difference between these two types of marriages, there is also a difference in the "effects" they produce, cf. canon 1056 that states that unity and indissolubility have a "particular firmness" in a Christian union.

The expression a **bond arises** cannot mean that some kind of new physical entity or new substance is created, either in the material or in the spiritual order.[2] It can mean only that in each partner a set of new obligations arises. The spouses, by committing themselves mutually to each other, give a new orientation to their own life. They choose the values that marriage represents and they make their decisions and direct their actions accordingly. This is very much of a real change in a person, but it happens internally, in the world of the human spirit. Nothing is added to the persons involved from the outside; their transformation is from the inside. When this new orientation is sealed by God's grace, it belongs to the saving events of the Kingdom.

To speak about the bond as a separate entity can be confusing and misleading if not properly interpreted. A clearer and simpler way of conveying the same meaning would be to say that the spouses are bound to each other. Their obligation is real enough. Also, one understands easily that such obligation when sealed by the grace of

[1] When classical scholastic theologians spoke of the sacrament of marriage as a "remedy of concupiscence," *remedium concupiscentiae*, they meant much more than "a legitimate outlet for sexuality" as the expression has often been interpreted. They meant that this sacrament conferred grace, as all sacraments did, and therefore it strengthened a person against all evil desires and inclinations that could lead someone to revolt against God. For them, *grace* was the principal remedy of concupiscence. *See* e.g. *Summa Theologiae*, Suppl. q. 42, art. 3.

[2] *Bond* is often spoken of as if it had an autonomous existence in itself as physical substances have. In reality it is the creation of the law, human or divine, as the case may be; cf. the famous definition of Justinian *obligatio est vinculum iuris* (Inst. 3:13), "obligation is a legal bond." The nature of the bond, *vinculum*, is determined by the law (human or divine, secular or sacred) that creates it.

the sacrament has indeed a "particular firmness" as canon 1056 states.[3]

by its very nature perpetual: it is perpetual because it is total within the context of human relationships. A commitment for a term of years, or conditioned in its permanence on some future event, cannot be a total commitment. Virtually all Christian churches recognize that much when they impart their blessing on those marriages only where the parties intend to stay together "until death do them part." Even such an overriding commitment, however, must take its place within the overall hierarchy of values. The church recognizes that there are cases when it can or must cede its place to a higher value, such as when a situation warrants the grant of a privilege of the faith or a dispensation from a sacramental commitment that has not reached consummation.

exclusive: one person cannot be bound to several persons, either simultaneously (polygamy or polyandry) or successively (a new mar-

---

[3]At this point scholastic philosophy can help us to clarify further the nature of the bond. It is not any kind of substance, or *esse in se*; it is an accident that belongs to a substance; the substance in question being that of a human person. The bond is the specific marital relationship of a man to a woman and vice versa, an *esse ad*; that is, a general orientation in the world of their intentionality; an orientation that permeates and dominates their judgments and decisions. Quite appropriately it could be called "conversion" (turning to in a radical sense) to another person. In the case of a sacramental marriage God himself grants a special grace-filled dimension to this bond.

We use this scholastic terminology to convey a point: no new physical or spiritual substance is created either in a natural or a sacramental marriage. If it were so, it should follow that whenever the church dispenses from a natural or a sacramental marriage, this physical substance is "annihilated" — a patently absurd proposition.

In the case of a dispensation nothing more or less happens than the person dispensed is allowed or authorized to terminate his or her orientation to the former spouse, and be free to assume a new one.

Marriage is not one of those sacraments that have for their effect what traditionally has been described as "character," an indelible sign on the soul; baptism is the obvious example. Precisely, because such sacraments bring about a permanent transformation in the person, they cannot be repeated. Although some theologians tried to apply the same doctrine to marriage, (e.g. Hugh of St. Victor, +1141) their opinion never gained acceptance (*see* DTC 9.2:2144-2147).

riage is contracted while the bond of the previous one is still in existence). A total commitment for life can be only to one person; apart from any other reason, our human nature is too limited to carry more than one relationship with the intensity that true marriage demands.

The Christian tradition concerning the exclusivity of the bond has been firm and uniform throughout: it always excluded the simultaneous marriage of one person to several others.

Christian marriage: up to this point the canon did not distinguish between the two types of marriage; now it focuses on the Christian marriage. In it all the elements of a natural commitment remain good and valid, but they are lifted up and integrated into a higher spiritual order; in the sacrament the secular and temporal meet the sacred and eternal.

Thomas Doyle in COM-USA uses the following expressions to describe the nature of the bond: an "ontological reality" (766), "an integral and not partial reality," "a separate reality" (808). A way of testing the meaning and correctness of these expressions is to try to locate the bond within the categories of being as they are referred to in nearly every work of Aquinas. Can the bond be a substance? Certainly not, it has no autonomous existence. So it must be an accident. Among the accidents, a rapid survey of the categories shows that the only one that can accommodate it is relation, *esse ad.*

Now a relation can most certainly be an ontological reality, as long as it remains attached to a substance. No relation can, however, have a separate existence from the substance, not even in the Trinity — if we may go that far.

It follows that the bond is a relationship. Because it is not a relationship based on a "character," it can be only a relationship of obligation. But, due to the sacrament, such a relationship is sealed by God's grace and his commitment to the spouses. Therefore, it should not be described in terms of a merely natural obligation; it is a grace-filled obligation in the Kingdom.

When the church terminates such a grace-filled obligation through dispensing from the bond of a sacramental non-consummated marriage, it simply frees the person *in the name of God*, on the strength of a power of divine origin, from a *vinculum*, "chain," that is binding him or her.

Although we used the categories of scholastic philosophy and theology to explain the nature of the bond with some clarity and precision, the essential validity of our explanation does not depend on that system. It could be expressed in other ways.

Be that as it may, in this matter one should aim for the greatest precision obtainable — for the sake of those who eventually will have to carry in real life the burden of our theoretical conclusions.

the spouses are strengthened: this strength ultimately comes from God, who through the sacrament becomes a partner to the covenant. In a grace filled world marriage too is redeemed and has a sanctifying role to play.

consecrated: the law uses this term in an analogous sense: *veluti, as it were*, but from a theological point of view, the sacrament of marriage is indeed a "consecration" for a new state of life.

❧ ✳ ☙

Is there an equality between the spouses?

Canon 1135

Utrique coniugi aequum officium et ius est ad ea quae pertinent ad consortium vitae coniugalis.

Both spouses have equal office and right to whatever belongs to the *consortium* of conjugal life.

The equality of rights and duties is defended. Conjugal life should not be conceived on the pattern of an "authority and obedience" relationship.

❧ ✳ ☙

What are the parental rights and duties?

Canon 1136

Parentes officium gravissimum
et ius primarium habent prolis educationem
tum physicam, socialem et culturalem,
   tum moralem et religiosam
   pro viribus curandi.

The parents have a very grave office
and the primary right to do all in their power
for the physical, social and cultural,
also, for the moral and religious education of their children.

This canon simply states a duty that existed long before humanity turned to drafting legal norms, a duty so far reaching and all embracing that no man-made law can ever fully state it.

A practical application of this parental office is mentioned in canon 914: when the appropriate time comes for it, the parents should see that their child is introduced into the participation in the eucharist.

※

How is the legitimacy of a child determined?

The following three canons are basically procedural norms, setting presumptions to decide issues of legitimacy and fatherhood. They are self-explanatory. Accordingly, our comments will be restrained.

Canon 1137

Legitimi sunt filii concepti aut nati ex matrimonio valido vel putativo.

Children conceived in, or born from, a valid or putative marriage are legitimate.

To invoke any other presumption would be absurd; not to invoke this presumption would be an outrage.

When an ecclesiastical court decides that a marriage has been null and void from the beginning, the children born from that marriage do not become illegitimate; they are children of a putative marriage. They remain legitimate in the fullest sense of the term.

Canon 1138 § 1.

Pater is est, quem iustae nuptiae demonstrant, nisi evidentibus argumentis contrarium probetur.

The father is the one who is designated by a lawful marriage unless the contrary is proved by evident arguments.

See our first comment after the preceding canon.

Canon 1138 § 2.

Legitimi praesumuntur filii,
qui nati sunt saltem post dies 180 a die celebrati matrimonii,
vel infra dies 300 a die dissolutae vitae coniugalis.

Children who were born not less than 180 days after the day of
the celebration of the marriage,
or within 300 days from the day of the dissolution of the
conjugal life,
are presumed to be legitimate.

A reasonable definition of the limits of the legal presumption for establishing the legitimacy of the child.

Canon 1139

Filii illegitimi legitimantur per subsequens matrimonium
parentum sive validum sive putativum,
vel per rescriptum Sanctae Sedis.

Illegitimate children are legitimated by the subsequent valid or
putative marriage of their parents,
or by a rescript of the Holy See.

Historically, in many countries where there was a close relationship between church and state, canonical legitimacy or the lack of it had momentous consequences in civil law. In modern times, wherever the doctrine of separation of church and state has been accepted, the effects are confined to the internal life of the church.

Even in canon law, the distinction has lost its importance; no special restriction or inability is mentioned in the new Code. For this, and for an even deeper reason, it would be no loss to abandon the term "illegitimate" altogether. The deeper reason is that in a community of "saints" (one of St. Paul's favorite expressions), no one should be marked for life as "illegitimate."

Canon 1140

**Filii legitimati, ad effectus canonicos quod attinet,
in omnibus aequiparantur legitimis,
nisi aliud expresse iure cautum fuerit.**

**Legitimated children, concerning the canonical effects,
are regarded equal in everything to those who were born
   legitimate,
unless the law expressly provides otherwise.**

as regards the canonical effects: the status of a legitimated child in canon law is exactly the same as that of a child born legitimate; they have the same standing and capacity in the law.

The universal law has no provision to the contrary.

CHAPTER NINE
THE SEPARATION OF
THE SPOUSES
1141 — 1155

A paraphrase title of this chapter could be: "The place of the marital obligations within the hierarchy of other religious obligations." Or "The place of the values of marriage in the context of other religious values."

The legislator recognizes that

(1) the essential properties of marriage do not have the same firmness in natural and sacramental marriages (cf. canon 1056), and,

(2) the values represented by a given marriage in some cases may be abandoned for the sake of other values.

Consequently,

— in some well defined circumstances natural marriages can be dissolved, provided it is for the benefit of the faith, and,

— in some cases sacramental non-consummated marriages can be dissolved for the benefit of even one of the spouses, and,

— at times prudence postulates that the marital rights and duties of the spouses, even in a sacramental consummated marriage, should be permanently suspended and the spouses should remain separated, if necessary, for life.

The values protected are manifold: a peaceful environment for the believer, a new marriage grounded in Christian faith, a new state of life in a religious institute, or simply an opportunity to lead a life free of deception, turmoil or harassment.

Transitions: in their form the canons in the new Code represent a *consolidation of several earlier documents*, in their content they do not differ substantially from the rules and norms found in the old Code.

Literary forms: there are some doctrinal statements in the canons but most of them are concerned with *right-and-duty situations*.

A summary of the main issues in this chapter can serve as an introduction into its complex doctrine:

first, the legislator situates the value of a sacramental and consummated marriage bond: it is so supreme that it can never be dissolved, cf. canon 1141;

then, he determines the value of a sacramental but non-consummated marriage bond: it can be dissolved for some greater good; cf. canon 1142;

further, he determines the value of a non-sacramental bond: it can be dissolved in different ways for the sake of the faith, cf. canons 1143-1150:

finally, he provides norms for the practical suspension of the marital rights and duties in the case of a justified separation, cf. canons 1151-1155.

Article One: THE DISSOLUTION OF THE BOND

꩜✻꩜

Can a ratified and consummated marriage be dissolved?

Canon 1141

> **Matrimonium ratum et consummatum**
> **nulla humana potestate nullaque causa,**
> **praeterquam morte, dissolvi potest.**

**A ratified and consummated marriage
cannot be dissolved by any human power
nor by any cause other than death.**

The canon is a doctrinal and legal statement about the nature of a Christian marriage. Because it is doctrinal, its theological meaning ought to be determined from theological sources. Because it is legal, it lays down a norm of law: no human power is competent to dissolve a sacramental consummated marriage.

Obviously, there is more than "human power" in the church: the eucharist is celebrated, sins are forgiven, the sacramental bonds of non-consummated marriages are dissolved, all in virtue of a power of divine origin. The canon does not touch, still less does it resolve, the issue whether or not the church could dissolve a sacramental consummated marriage in virtue of the same power — not of human origin.

ratified: is the translation of *ratum*; it means that the sacramental sign has been correctly enacted, the marital promises have been exchanged, a Christian marriage has come into existence.

consummated: sexual intercourse has taken place *modo humano*, that is the spouses have given themselves knowingly and freely to each other.

to dissolve: here means more than separation; it means the termination of the bond, that is the cancellation of the obligation of fidelity for the life of the spouses.

by any human power: this clause means what it says: no power of human origin is enough to cancel the obligation; it does not pronounce in any way on what a power of divine origin can do.

cause: an event that would either dissolve the marriage, or would give the right to dissolution, as e.g. adultery does in the Orthodox tradition.

It follows that in the case of a ratified and consummated marriage,

(1) the spouses cannot withdraw their consent and opt for dissolution; the marriage cannot be dissolved from the inside; it has "intrinsic indissolubility";

(2) no secular authority of any type (state, tribe, etc.) can break the bond; it cannot be dissolved by such an authority from the outside; it has "extrinsic indissolubility";

(3) in our present state of knowledge, it cannot be stated as an article of faith that the church does not have the power to dissolve such a bond.

In the restricted legal context, as distinct from the theological, the canon certainly implies that the Latin church is not willing to dissolve sacramental consummated marriages, even if it had the power to do so. That much is enough to explain indissolubility in canon law; theology has the task to investigate further. The issue is really a problem about the extent of the sacred power given to the church.

༄ ✳ ༄

Who can dissolve a non-consummated marriage?
In what circumstances?

Canon 1142

Matrimonium non consummatum inter baptizatos
vel inter partem baptizatam et partem non-baptizatam
a Romano Pontifice dissolvi potest iusta de causa,
utraque parte rogante
vel alterutra, etsi altera pars sit invita.

A non-consummated marriage between baptized persons,
or between a baptized party and a non-baptized party,
can be dissolved by the Roman Pontiff for a just cause,
at the request of both parties,
or of one of them even if the other is unwilling.

non-consummated marriage here refers to marriages between two baptized persons (sacramental), and to marriages between a baptized and a non-baptized person (non-sacramental), whether they have taken place in the Catholic church or any other church or ecclesial communion, provided they are recognized as valid by the Catholic church.[1]

can be dissolved, that is, the obligation, sacred or secular, can be terminated, provided the marriage has not been consummated.

Note that in the case of a ratified but not consummated marriage the sacrament is fully there before any consummation. So is the duty of lifelong fidelity; there is indissolubility in the sense of moral obligation. But the marriage still can be dissolved, and the sacramental obligation is terminated.

Therefore, we must be careful in speaking of the indissolubility of the *sacrament* of matrimony. The sacrament certainly generates the obligation but not to the point that it could not be terminated. Consummation confirms the obligation to the point that it cannot be terminated. Consummation is not part of the sacramental sign. The sacrament itself can be, and is often dissolved by the church.

by the Roman Pontiff: the reservation of these cases to the Roman Pontiff cannot be more than an administrative measure; there is no evidence that it is a doctrinal necessity; there are firm proofs to the contrary. The very same power has been given by Gregory XIII in his Constitution *Populis* in 1585 "to ordinaries and parish priests, and presbyters of the Society of Jesus," working in foreign missions. The present Code is even more generous; it grants the same dispensation by law to all those who are forcibly separated from their spouses; for precise details *see* canon 1149. By the principle of subsidiarity, the diocesan bishops should be competent to handle such cases.

for a just cause: this requirement reflects the law's assumption that the Roman Pontiff in dispensing from the bond does so in virtue of his "vicarious" power, he is dispensing from God's law not his own,

---

[1]The earliest evidence of papal dispensations from non consummated marriages comes from the pontificate of Alexander III (1159-1181), *see* Erich Sauerwein, *Der Ursprung des Rechtsinstitutes der Päpstlichen Dispens von der nicht vollzogenen Ehe* (Roma: Università Gregoriana, 1980). The book contains also a fair amount of documented information concerning the development and final acceptance of the "consent theory."

therefore he is not entitled to act without a justifying cause.

Here are some justifying causes used in the past: intention to receive sacred orders, to enter the religious state, to contract a new marriage.

a request is necessary: not even the Roman Pontiff has the right to interfere with the bond if none of the parties asks for it.

at the request of both or of one only: in other terms the termination of the bond can be imposed on a reluctant party.

❧❁❧

What marriage can be dissolved by the Pauline privilege?
How does it operate?

Canon 1143 § 1.

Matrimonium initum a duobus non baptizatis
solvitur ex privilegio paulino
in favorem fidei partis quae baptismum recepit,
ipso facto quo novum matrimonium ab eadem parte contrahitur,
dummodo pars non baptizata discedat.

A marriage entered into by two non-baptized persons
is dissolved in virtue of the Pauline privilege
in favor of the faith of the party who has received baptism
by the fact that a new marriage is contracted by the same party,
provided the non baptized party departs.

a marriage entered by two non-baptized persons: this is an absolute *sine qua non* condition for the applicability of the Pauline privilege; it cannot be invoked if at the time of the marriage one of the spouses was already baptized.

Pauline privilege: a specific form, with its own exclusive rules, of the privilege of the faith; it is so named after Paul's ruling in his first epistle to the Corinthians:

> To the rest I say, not the Lord, that if any brother has a wife who is an unbeliever, and she consents to live with him, he should not

divorce her. . . .But if the unbelieving partner desires to separate, let it be so; in such a case the brother or sister is not bound. For God has called us to peace. (7:12, 15)

The evidence that the church has interpreted this passage as authorizing the dissolution of the bond goes back no further than the fourth century.[2] The correct interpretation of the text remains uncertain; Paul speaks of "separation," which need not include necessarily the freedom to marry again.[3] Thus, the possibility that the practice arose not from an apostolic concession but from a custom introduced later by the church cannot be excluded.

the marriage is dissolved by the Pauline privilege, that is, this privilege can enter into operation and dissolve the bond whenever the required conditions are there and the baptized party wishes to benefit from them; it is granted by the law; there is no need for a dispensation from any authority. The dissolution itself cannot be anything else than the termination of all moral and legal obligations originating in the marriage that is now dissolved.

in favor of the faith: the expression admits a fairly broad interpretation, *see* also our comments on § 2 of this canon.[4]

[2]Cf. Richard Kugelman, "The First Letter to the Corinthians" in *The Jerome Biblical Commentary* (Englewood Cliffs, NJ: Prentice Hall, 1968), 51:40.

[3]The literal translation of the original Greek text is: "But if the unbelieving separates himself, let him be separated. . ." The Greek equivalent used in this passage for the verb "to separate" does not include in any way the freedom to marry again; it does not exclude it either (cf. *xōrizō* in GEL, 898). It follows that there is no indication in the text whether or not Paul contemplated the possibility of a second marriage. Thus the "Pauline privilege" may have been introduced by the church. If so, we have an important piece of historical evidence to help us to assess the power of the church over the marriages of Christians. One has to remember in this context that all the enlargements on the Pauline privilege have indeed been introduced by the church.

[4]The expression "privilege of the faith" is used in different ways in canon law; the context should be the guide for its precise significance in a given text. At times it is all embracing: it includes the Pauline privilege and all other privileges of the faith; at times it excludes Pauline privilege and is used only for the other types of privileges. Sometimes one encounters the expression "Petrine privilege"; it always refers to

by the very fact that the same party contracts a new marriage: the dissolution takes place at the moment of the new contract. This clearly cannot be a Pauline doctrine since it supposes the contractual theory, a relative late comer in the field of canon law. The preoccupation itself to determine the precise moment when the obligations contracted by the first marriage cease displays an analytical mentality alien to the ways of thinking of the early church. The determination of the moment of dissolution must have been of ecclesiastical origin.[5]

provided is the translation of the classical *dummodo* which indicates that the validity of the act is at stake.

the non-baptized party departs from the other: the operation of the Pauline privilege is conditioned on the fact that the unbeliever "departs" from the believer. The Latin *discedere* indicates "departing," "moving out," "going away," but the law is not so strict. It does not require that the unbeliever should physically abandon the conjugal home, nor does it prohibit the application of the privilege if the believer is the one who walks out of a difficult situation.

What does it mean "to depart"?

Canon 1143 § 2.

Discedere censetur pars non baptizata,
si nolit cum parte baptizata cohabitare
vel cohabitare pacifice sine contumelia Creatoris,

privileges which are not of the Pauline type. It is a recently coined terminology, it places side by side the power of Paul with that of Peter (that is, the pope). Since Peter himself did not introduce it, for the sake of historical accuracy, the expression is best left to oblivion.

[5]The same authority that determined that the first marriage is dissolved at the moment of the second marriage could probably fix any other moment for the dissolution, e.g. when the local ordinary determines that the conditions for the application of the privilege are there. That much seems theologically certain.

nisi haec post baptismum receptum
iustam illi dederit discedendi causam.

The non-baptized party is considered to depart
if he or she is unwilling to live with the baptized party, or
to live [*with the same*] peacefully without offense to the Creator,
unless after the reception of baptism,
the baptized party has given the other just cause to depart.

considered to depart: "to depart" has been given a technical meaning; a person is considered as "departing" or "departed" even if he or she has not moved away physically but refuses to live in peace with the other one, or, behaves in a way that is offensive for a Christian.

unless is the translation of *nisi* which ordinarily introduces a condition for validity. In this case the text states that the privilege is canceled out if the believer has given a just cause for the unbeliever to depart. It should be recalled though that even if the application of the Pauline privilege is excluded, the use of the privilege of the faith in a broader sense can be still invoked.

⚜

What is the "rule of interpellation"?

Canon 1144 § 1.

Ut pars baptizata novum matrimonium valide contrahat,
pars non baptizata semper interpellari debet an:
1° velit et ipsa baptismum recipere;
2° saltem velit cum parte baptizata pacifice cohabitare, sine
contumelia Creatoris.

For the baptized party [*to be free*] to contract a new marriage
validly,
the non-baptized party must be always interpellated whether he
or she
1° wants to receive baptism;
2° or, at the least, is willing to live peacefully with the baptized
party, without offense to the Creator.

to interpellate, interpellations are technical legal terms used in connection with the Pauline privilege only. They are the first step in a quasi-judicial inquiry to ascertain whether or not the non-baptized party is indeed "departing" in the sense explained in the preceding canon. Such inquiry is an absolute requirement, a *conditio sine qua non*, for the canonical validity of a new marriage.

Clearly, in our ecumenical times the questions must be handled with tact and understanding; not even a semblance of an interference with the conscience of the other should be given.

⊂⊃ ✳ ⊂⊃

When is the interpellation to be made?
Can the ordinary dispense from it?

Canon 1144 § 2.

Haec interpellatio post baptismum fieri debet;
at loci Ordinarius, gravi de causa,
permittere potest ut interpellatio ante baptismum fiat,
immo et ab interpellatione dispensare,
sive ante sive post baptismum,
dummodo constet modo procedendi saltem summario et
   extraiudiciali
eam fieri non posse aut fore inutilem.

This interpellation must be made after baptism;
but the local ordinary, for a grave reason,
can permit that the interpellation be made before baptism,
he may even dispense from the interpellation,
either before or after baptism,
provided it has been established,
at least through a summary and extra judicial process,
that it cannot be done or that it would be useless.

This canon pays respect to the special status of a catechumen; although not baptized, he or she already belongs to the community, hence can receive some of the benefits ordinarily reserved to those who are baptized.

The catechumen can initiate the proceedings for the application of the Pauline privilege, provided the evidence for the "departure" of the partner is there.

By whose authority should the interpellation be made?

Canon 1145 § 1.

Interpellatio fiat regulariter de auctoritate loci Ordinarii partis conversae;
a quo Ordinario concedendae sunt alteri coniugi,
si quidem eas petierit, induciae ad respondendum,
eodem tamen monito ut,
si induciae inutiliter praeterlabantur,
eius silentium pro responsione negativa habeatur.

As a rule, the interpellation must be made by the authority of
the local ordinary of the converted party;
the same ordinary must allow a period of time for reply to the
other spouse if he or she asked for it,
with the warning, however, to the same
that if the period elapses with no reply
silence will be taken for a negative response.

The ordinary acts in a quasi-judicial capacity.

Can a privately made interpellation be valid?

Canon 1145 § 2.

Interpellatio etiam privatim facta ab ipsa parte conversa valet, immo est licita, si forma superius praescripta servari nequeat.

An interpellation made privately by the converted party is valid, it is even lawful [*licit*] if the procedure prescribed above cannot be observed.

An important distinction: the interpellation is required for validity but to make it through the ordinary is not required for validity.

Question: what if the interpellation appears useless but the ordinary cannot be reached (e.g. for reason of distance or political disturbances) to obtain a dispensation? Is the believer still bound to take this useless step privately? The answer is: no, he is not bound. The Code does not consider this case but canon 19 on the *lacuna legis* can be invoked.

⟡

Must the interpellation be documented?

Canon 1145 § 3.

In utroque casu de interpellatione facta deque eiusdem exitu in foro externo legitime constare debet.

In either case the fact of the interpellation and its outcome must be documented in the external forum.

Precisely because the interpellation is for validity, there should be legal evidence that it has taken place. Otherwise doubts about the marriage may arise.

⟡

When is the baptized party free to marry again?

Canon 1146

Pars baptizata ius habet novas nuptias contrahendi cum parte catholica:
1° si altera pars negative interpellationi responderit,
aut si interpellatio legitime omissa fuerit;
2° si pars non baptizata, sive iam interpellata sive non,
prius perseverans in pacifica cohabitatione sine contumelia Creatoris,
postea sine iusta causa discesserit,
firmis praescriptis cann. 1144 et 1145.

The baptized party has the right to contract a new marriage with
a Catholic party:
1° if the other party responded negatively to the interpellation,
or,
if the interpellation was legitimately omitted;
2° if the non-baptized party, already interpellated or not,
at first continued to live with the other without offense to the
Creator
[*but*] later departed without just cause;
the prescriptions of canons 1144 and 1145, however, remain in
effect.

The right to contract a new marriage is granted by the law, not by
an office holder. Thus, the local ordinary may take steps to ascertain
before the second marriage that all the conditions for the application
of the privilege are there, but otherwise he must not interfere with the
case.

with a Catholic party: a clear restriction; but see the following
canon.
There is a slight inconsistency in the legal system: the baptized
person has a right to contract a new marriage when the earlier one is
still good and valid![6]

⚫➤❋⬅⚫

Is the baptized party free to marry a non-Catholic?

Canon 1147

Ordinarius loci tamen, gravi de causa, concedere potest
ut pars baptizata, utens privilegio paulino,
contrahat matrimonium cum parte non catholica
sive baptizata sive non baptizata,
servatis etiam praescriptis canonum de matrimoniis mixtis.

---

[6]There is a classical description for such occurrences: *inelegans lex*, the law lacks
elegance.

> The local ordinary, however, can permit for a grave cause,
> that the baptized party using the Pauline privilege
> contract a marriage with a non-Catholic party,
> whether baptized or non-baptized,
> [*provided*] the prescriptions of the canons on mixed marriages
> are also observed.

This canon makes clear that to enjoy the benefit of the "privilege of the faith" (in a broad sense, including the Pauline privilege) it is not necessary that the new marriage should be between two Catholics or even two Christians; it could be a marriage between a Catholic and a non-Christian, provided the necessary dispensations are obtained.

How does the privilege of the faith operate when a husband with several wives, or, a wife with several husbands receives baptism?

There are three basic rules to follow in such situations:
(1) the baptized person is free to choose a new spouse among the several partners: *see* canon 1148 § 1;
(2) for this union all ordinary formalities must be observed (as for a new marriage): *see* § 2;
(3) the obligations of justice and equity toward the earlier partners and the offsprings remain binding, *see* § 3.

We are now in the field of the so called "privilege of the faith" cases. They are analogous to the case handled by Paul but they embrace a much greater variety of situations. While the Pauline privilege is applicable only in rather restricted circumstances as described above, the privilege of the faith can be invoked (in diverse ways) in all non-sacramental marriages provided it is requested for the sake of the faith of a Catholic.

Canon 1148 § 1.

Non baptizatus, qui plures uxores non baptizatas simul habeat, recepto in Ecclesia catholica baptismo,

si durum ei sit cum earum prima permanere,
unam ex illis, ceteris dimissis, retinere potest.
Idem valet de muliere non baptizata,
quae plures maritos non baptizatos simul habeat.

When a non-baptized man, who has simultaneously several non-baptized wives,
has received baptism in the Catholic church,
[*and when*] it is hard for him to remain with the first of the wives,
he can retain one of them while dismissing the others.
The same [*norm*] applies to a non-baptized woman
who has simultaneously several non-baptized husbands.

This canon is a summary and adapted version of some rules, contained in two papal documents, enacted in the sixteenth century for "missionary" countries, governing the transition of a polygamous man, converted to the faith, to a monogamous marriage.

Paul III in his Constitution *Altitudo*, in 1537, ruled that those who remembered who their first wife was had to keep her; those who could not remember it were free to take any of the several. The ruling caused wide spread problems, as the missionaries reported, because some converts simply stated that they could not remember which of the several wives had been the first one, and no one knew if they were honest or not in describing the state of their memory. Yet, the validity of the marriage depended on their sincerity. Mainly to avoid such problems of conscience, another document followed.

Pius V in his Constitution *Romani Pontificis*, in 1571, ruled that a polygamous convert, when baptized, may keep as his wife any one of the several, provided that she, too, received the sacrament of baptism.

The theological and canonical assumption of both Constitutions was that a valid natural bond existed between the man and his first wife, therefore he needed a dispensation from that bond in order to marry another woman. Interestingly enough, the dispensation was granted by law, applicable without any formality, without any need for recourse either to the pope or to the ordinary. It was understood that such a ruling represented a legitimate extension of the traditional Pauline privilege.

Our modern canon applies in the cases of simultaneous polygamy and polyandry. It does not apply when a person has several wives or husbands through successive marriages and divorces.

If the conditions described in the canon are verified, there is no need for any dispensation. The ordinary or the parish priest should simply check the facts and ascertain that the person or persons involved are entitled to the privilege, hence free to marry.

Canon 1148 § 2.

In casibus de quibus in § 1,
matrimonium, recepto baptismo, forma legitima contrahendum
    est,
servatis etiam, si opus sit, praescriptis de matrimoniis mixtis
et aliis de iure servandis.

In the cases described in § 1,
after the reception of the baptism the marriage must be
    contracted in legitimate form,
observing also, if necessary, the prescriptions on mixed marriages,
and other requirements of the law.

This paragraph prescribes no more than what is the norm anyway. The marriage with the chosen partner must be contracted in the canonical form and, if any dispensation or permission is needed, it must be obtained in the usual way.

Canon 1148 § 3.

Ordinarius loci, prae oculis habita condicione morali, sociali,
    oeconomica locorum et personarum,
curet ut primae uxoris ceterarumque dimissarum necessitatibus
    satis provisum sit,
iuxta normas iustitiae, christianae caritatis et naturalis aequitatis.

The local ordinary, taking into account the moral, social, and
    economical conditions of the places and persons,
must ensure that there are adequate provisions to take care of
    the needs of the first wife and of the other ones dismissed with
    her,
according to the norms of Christian charity and natural equity.

This paragraph is an exhortation, which does not mean that it is any less binding than the legal rules. In the practical order, however, no one is so well placed as the local ordinary to determine what should be done.

How does the privilege of the faith operate when the spouses are forcibly separated from each other?

Canon 1149

**Non baptizatus qui, recepto in Ecclesia catholica baptismo,
cum coniuge non baptizato ratione captivitatis vel persecutionis
cohabitationem restaurare nequeat,
aliud matrimonium contrahere potest,
etiamsi altera pars baptismum interea receperit,
firmo praescripto can. 1141.**

**A non-baptized person who has received baptism in the Catholic church
and for reason of captivity or persecution,
cannot live together with the non-baptized spouse,
can contract another marriage,
even if meanwhile the other party, too, has received baptism;
canon 1141, however, remains in effect.**

This canon, too, is a summary and modified version of a sixteenth century papal enactment that provided for those situations where the non-baptized spouses were forcibly separated, then one of them or both received baptism but the couple remained unable to resume their conjugal life.

Gregory XIII in his Constitution *Populis*, in 1585, ruled that the spouse so separated is free to marry again after the baptism, irrespective of the first marriage (whether it was polygamous or not) and that he can remain in the new marriage contracted after the baptism, even if the first spouse, too, has received baptism, provided that in no time after their baptism have they consummated their first marriage.

This Constitution was different from the others. The grant of the privilege was not by the operation of the law whenever the circumstances were verified. A dispensation had to be requested; the ordinaries, the parish priests, and the priests of the Society of Jesus were empowered to grant it.

This canon, however, follows the approach of canons 1143 and 1148; the grant of the privilege is by law; it operates whenever the required conditions are present. It even goes beyond those two canons since it includes, if needed, a dispensation by law from a sacramental non-consummated marriage.

The warning about the continuing validity of canon 1141 is a reaffirmation of the principle that no dispensation is ever granted from the bond of a sacramental marriage that has been consummated.

❧ ✳ ❧

How to proceed
when the applicability of the privilege of faith is doubtful?

Canon 1150

In re dubia privilegium fidei gaudet favore iuris.

In a doubtful matter the privilege of the faith enjoys the favor of the law.

The meaning of this canon can be correctly understood and explained only in balance with canon 1060 that states that "Marriage enjoys the favor of the law." We are dealing with two procedural norms; each has been conceived to resolve a doubt with the help of a presumption. They ought to work together.

Canon 1060 refers to all marriages, sacramental or not sacramental. Its meaning is simple: whenever a doubt arises about the validity of a marriage, the church stands for its validity, until proved otherwise. Invalidity must be established beyond reasonable doubt.

Canon 1150 operates within this context but for non-sacramental marriages only. It does not destroy the first presumption, they still must be presumed to be valid. But if both or one of the spouses wishes for the dissolution of their non-sacramental marriage through the privilege of the faith, he or she is entitled to the grant even if reasonable doubt remains about its applicability to this case. The privilege of the faith enjoys the favor of the law. In other words, whenever it is possible that the privilege is applicable, the law favors its granting. Therefore —

(1) whenever a reasonable doubt emerges about the validity of a natural marriage, the application of the privilege of faith takes precedence over invoking the favor of law for that marriage; this rule has had some importance historically but today it has little significance since the privilege of the faith is granted whether or not there is any doubt about the validity of the marriage;

(2) whenever there is any reasonable doubt whether or not the conditions for the privilege are present (e.g. doubt concerning the process of interpellation, about the intention of the non-Christian to depart, about the Christian having given a cause for the other's departure, etc.), the decision should be in favor of the privilege.

Note, however, that if there is doubt whether or not the marriage is sacramental or non-sacramental (e.g. because the baptism of one or of both is doubtful), canon 1150 cannot be invoked since the favor of the law for a doubtfully sacramental marriage is absolute; the application of the privilege of the faith is excluded. The reasoning behind this strict rule is that by granting the privilege of the faith in the case of a doubtfully sacramental marriage, the church could in fact attempt to dissolve a sacramental marriage. Cf. *Decree, HO*, 10 June 1937, CLD 2:343.

Canon 1150 should not be construed as introducing a presumption against the validity of all non-sacramental marriages. There is no supporting evidence in our canonical tradition for such an interpretation; besides, to hold such view would be an insult to non-Christians who most certainly have the ordinary human capacity to marry. No religious authority is entitled to say that their marriages should be presumed invalid until the contrary is proved.

Addendum to the Code

∽ ✱ ∾

What are the conditions for the grant of the privilege of the faith by the Holy See?

Instruction *Ut notum est,* CDF, 6 December 1973.

In all previous cases the grant of the privilege was by law; the role of any authority was restricted to ascertaining that the conditions for the privilege were there; its application was in substance "automatic."

There are, however, many cases of non-sacramental marriages which do not fall into any of the categories above. Then the only way of obtaining the dissolution of the marriage through the operation of the privilege of the faith is by requesting its grant from the pope. The Code does not mention this well approved practice, but an instruction from the Congregation for the Doctrine of Faith describes the conditions for the grant of the privilege; *see* CLD 8:1177-1184. The norms given in the Instruction remain valid law even after the promulgation of the new Code, consequently they have the same binding force as the canons. For this reason, we quote them:

> ...His Holiness, Pope Paul VI, has deigned to approve these new norms in which are declared the conditions for a grant of dissolution of marriage in favor of the faith, whether the petitioner is baptized or is a convert or is not.
>
> I. In order that a dissolution may be validly granted, *three* conditions are *absolutely (sine quibus non)* required:
>
> *a)* lack of baptism of one of the two spouses during the whole time of their married life;
>
> *b)* nonuse of the marriage after the baptism perchance received by the party who was not baptized;
>
> *c)* that the person who is not baptized or baptized outside the Catholic Church yields freedom and ability to the Catholic party to profess his own religion and to baptize and educate the children as Catholics: this condition must be safeguarded in the form of a promise (*cautio*).
>
> II. It is further required:
>
> § 1. that there is no possibility of restoring married life because of persistent radical and irremediable discord.
>
> §2. that from the grant of favor no danger of public scandal or serious wonderment be had.
>
> §3. that the petitioner is not the culpable cause of the wreckage of the valid, non-sacramental marriage and the Catholic party with whom the new marriage is to be contracted or convalidated, did not provoke separation of the spouses by reason of fault on his own part.

§4. that the other party of the previous marriage be interpellated if possible, and does not offer reasonable opposition.

§5. that the party seeking the dissolution take care that children who may have been born of the previous marriage be brought up in a religious manner.

§6. that equitable provisions be made according to the laws of justice for the abandoned spouse and for the children who may have been generated.

§7. that the Catholic party with whom a new marriage is to be entered live in accord with his baptismal promises and take care of the new family.

§8. that when there is question of a catechumen with whom marriage is to be contracted, moral certitude be had regarding the baptism to be received shortly, if the baptism itself cannot be waited for (which is to be encouraged).

III. Dissolution is more readily granted if on some other ground there is serious doubt about the validity of the marriage itself.

IV. A marriage between a Catholic party and a party not baptized entered into with a dispensation from disparity of cult can also be dissolved provided that the conditions set down in nn. II and III are verified and provided that the Catholic party, because of the particular circumstances of the region, especially because of the very small number of Catholics in the region, cannot avoid marriage and cannot live a life consonant with the Catholic religion in the said marriage. Moreover, this S. Congregation must be instructed about the publicity of the marriage celebrated.

V. Dissolution of a valid, non-sacramental marriage entered into with a dispensation from the impediment of disparity of cult is not granted to a Catholic party who petitions to enter a new marriage with a non-baptized person who is not a convert.

VI. Dissolution of a valid, non-sacramental marriage is not granted if it was contracted or convalidated after a dissolution had been obtained from a previous valid non-sacramental marriage.

In order that these conditions may be duly met, "*new procedural norms*" have been drawn up. All future processes must be instructed according to them. These norms are appended to the present instruction.

These new norms completely abrogate the previous norms which were passed for the instruction of these processes.

Some comments on the Instruction:

(1) Currently the privilege is granted by the pope in person only;

the task of the CDF is to instruct the case and submit it to the pope. There appears to be no dogmatic necessity for such an elaborate and cumbersome procedure, which, even with the best of intentions, is likely to produce delays. The apostolic constitutions quoted above have been vald for centuries; implicitly they testify that the privilege of faith can be granted in many other ways than by the pope in person. If the local bishop is the Vicar of Christ in his diocese, it is certainly fitting that he should be able to grant the privilege of the faith to his own people.[7]

(2) When the second marriage is with a Catholic Christian (mixed marriage), or with a non baptized person (impediment of disparity of cult), the strict rules of CIC/17 are applied for the *cautiones*, not the norms given in CIC/83, *see* above I.c) in the Instruction. The text clearly says that the non-Catholic must yield freedom and ability to the Catholic party to baptize and educate the children as Catholics. In other terms, the norms conceived on the basis of the Decree on Ecumenism and the Declaration of Religious Freedom and incorporated into the New Code, in this case do not apply. It is difficult to see the reason for such severity; in fact, it could be argued on good grounds that the Instruction on this particular point has been superceded by the Code.[8]

(3) The Instruction contains also procedural norms concerning the preparation of a case on the local level; they are not quoted here since our primary interest is in the more substantive rules.

Summary: Patterns in the Application of the Privileges

Pattern One: *Pauline privilege*, 1143 — 1147.

There is a marriage between two non-baptized persons,
one of them is baptized,
the other one "departs" out of an animosity towards the faith.

---

[7]"Bishops govern the particular churches entrusted to them as the vicars and ambassadors of Christ." (LG 27).

[8]The practice of the Holy See is to ask for full compliance with the norms of the Instruction concerning the *cautiones*.

To be free to marry again,
the believer must "interpellate" the unbeliever,
or must obtain a dispensation from the duty to interpellate.
If the response is negative,
the believer has the right to marry again.
The new marriage dissolves the old one.

The process is carried out on the strength of the law,
not on the authority of the ordinary except for the
interpellation.
The ordinary is entitled to ascertain the facts
and to grant any necessary dispensation for a second marriage,
should it be needed.

Pattern Two: *Privilege of the faith, polygamy or polyandry,* 1148.

A non-baptized man has several non-baptized wives.
He is baptized.
If he does not want to keep the woman who is his first wife,
he is entitled to choose any one among the others,
but the marriage between the two must take place in the canonical
form.

The same rule applies if a non-baptized woman has several
husbands and wishes to receive baptism.

The law dispenses from the natural bond,
all other necessary permissions and dispensations should be
requested and granted according to the relevant canons.

Pattern Three: *Privilege of the faith, separated spouses,* 1149.

(1)
There is a marriage between two non-baptized persons,
they become separated.
One is converted and baptized in the Catholic church,
the other is not.

They cannot restore their conjugal life
because of some adverse circumstances.
The baptized person, and consequently the other one,
become free to marry again.

They can do so on the authority of the law,
no dispensation is necessary,
only the circumstances must be verified by the authorties.

(2)
There is a marriage between two non-baptized persons;
they become separated.
One is converted and baptized in the Catholic church,
also, the other one is baptized,
not necessarily in the Catholic church.
They cannot restore their conjugal life
because of some adverse circumstances.
The Catholic person, and consequently the other,
become free to marry again.

They can do so on the authority of the law;
no dispensation is necessary,
only the circumstances must be verified by the authorities.

In the first case the law frees the spouses from a natural bond; in
the second case the law frees them from a sacramental non-
consummated bond.

Pattern Four: *Privilege of faith by particular grant, cf. Ut notum est.*

There is a marriage between two non-baptized persons, or,
between a baptized and non-baptized person.
One or both of them requests the grant of the privilege of the faith
from the Holy See.

The privilege is granted or denied at the discretion of the Holy
See.

***

Article Two: SEPARATION WITH THE BOND REMAIN-
ING.

⌒※⌒

Can the spouses be excused from the duty of common life?

Canon 1151

Coniuges habent officium et ius
servandi convictum coniugalem,
nisi legitima causa eos excuset.

**The spouses have the office [*duty*] and the right
to preserve common conjugal life,
unless a legitimate cause excuses them.**

The canonical determination of these rights and duties is rooted entirely in morality, natural and Christian. Although theoretically this canon gives the right to an action for the resumption of conjugal life, in practice litigation before a court may not be the best way of restoring *consortium.*

The canon lays down the principle that the spouses can be legitimately excused from the obligations of conjugal life. For this a proportionately grave cause is required.

⌒※⌒

*In the case of adultery by one,
what are the rights and duties of the other?*

Canon 1152 § 1.

Licet enixe commendetur ut coniux,
caritate christiana motus et boni familiae sollicitus,
veniam non abnuat comparti adulterae
atque vitam coniugalem non disrumpat,
si tamen eiusdem culpam expresse aut tacite non condonaverit,

ius ipsi est solvendi coniugalem convictum,
nisi in adulterium consenserit aut eidem causam dederit
aut ipse quoque adulterium commiserit.

Although it is strongly recommended that a spouse
moved by Christian charity and solicitous for the welfare of the
family
should not deny pardon to the partner guilty of adultery and
should not disrupt the conjugal life,
nonetheless, if that spouse has not expressly or tacitly pardoned
the other's fault,
he or she has the right to terminate the common conjugal life
unless he or she consented to the adultery or gave cause for it,
or
also committed adultery.

The simple meaning of the canon is that if one of the spouses is guilty of adultery, the other has a strict right to terminate the conjugal life. It follows that the guilty one has the duty to consent to such a termination.

This statement about the legal right of the innocent party is presented in a moral context; before invoking the right, he or she should consider the welfare of the whole family, and if charity so dictates, should forgive the trespass.

There is clearly a conflict of values. The right to separation is presented as an absolute right, not subject to any serious moral restraint. The duty of forgiving is described as an act of generosity, never quite binding. In reality, the values to be preserved by staying together can be so high, and the risk of losing them through separation so great, that the innocent party may be morally bound to forgive, especially if otherwise the marriage proved to be successful.

From the point of view of Christian charity it may be morally wrong to claim the right to separation for one act of infidelity when such a move could do irreparable harm to the family, especially to the children. In such case, the demands of charity can overrule a concession granted by the law.[9]

---

[9]In the hierarchy of virtues justice is the minimum of charity; hence there are cases when law must cede to charity. All authorities in the church are bound to respect this hierarchy and if necessary give official sanction to it.

What are the signs of tacit pardon?

Canon 1152 § 2.

Tacita condonatio habetur si coniux innocens,
postquam de adulterio certior factus est,
sponte cum altero coniuge maritali affectu conversatus fuerit;
praesumitur vero, si per sex menses coniugalem convictum
servaverit,
neque recursum apud auctoritatem ecclesiasticam vel civilem
fecerit.

There is tacit pardon if the innocent spouse,
after having learned about the adultery,
has spontaneously engaged in marital relationship with the other
spouse;
it is presumed, however, if [*the innocent spouse*] persevered for
six months in common conjugal life, and
has not had recourse to ecclesiastical or civil authority.

☙ ✻ ❧

Who is competent to authorize the termination of common life?

Canon 1152 § 3.

Si coniux innocens sponte convictum coniugalem solverit,
intra sex menses causam separationis deferat ad competentem
auctoritatem ecclesiasticam,
quae, omnibus inspectis adiunctis,
perpendat si coniux innocens adduci possit ad culpam
condonandam
et ad separationem in perpetuum non protrahendam.

If the innocent spouse spontaneously terminated common
conjugal life,
he or she must bring within six months a case for separation
before the competent ecclesiastical authority;
this authority, after having examined all the circumstances,
should consider whether the innocent spouse could be adduced

to pardon the fault
and not to perpetuate the separation.

the competent ecclesiastical authority and the procedure that it has to follow are described in Book Seven of the Code under the Title "Cases of Separation of Spouses," canons 1692-1696.

As a matter of fact, cases of separation are rarely brought before ecclesiastical authorities. Many couples sue for a civil divorce only.

If one spouse becomes a source of danger, or makes common life hard to bear, what are the rights of the other?

Canon 1153 § 1.

Si alteruter coniugum grave seu animi seu corporis periculum alteri aut proli facessat,
vel aliter vitam communem nimis duram reddat,
alteri legitimam praebet causam discedendi,
decreto Ordinarii loci
et, si periculum sit in mora, etiam propria auctoritate.

If one spouse is causing a grave danger of soul or of body
to the other or to the children, or
in some other way makes the common life too hard to bear,
that spouse gives a legitimate cause to the other to depart,
either by a decree of the local ordinary, or,
if there is danger in delay, even on his or her own authority.

Cruelty would be a typical example; in the practical order the grounds would be as numerous as the types of human misbehavior can be.

If the cause of separation ceases,
what are the duties of the spouses?

Canon 1153 § 2.

In omnibus casibus, causa separationis cessante,
coniugalis convictus restaurandus est,
nisi ab auctoritate ecclesiastica aliter statuatur.

In all cases when the cause of the separation ceases,
the common conjugal life must be restored,
unless otherwise decided by ecclesiastical authority.

The canon implies that an ecclesiastical authority may overrule the decision of the parties not to continue conjugal life. One wonders if it is wise for any authority to impose on them the duty to live together. Besides, how could such decision be enforced?

The law as it stands is anachronistic. The response of the authorities to such difficult situations should be through pastoral care. An attempt to invoke legal rights or duties is likely to exacerbate the situation and makes the reconciliation more difficult.

☙❊❧

How should the children be cared for?

Canon 1154

Instituta separatione coniugum,
opportune semper cavendum est
debitae filiorum sustentationi et educationi.

After the separation of the spouses has taken place,
as it is opportune, provisions must always be made
for the support and education of the children.

As a rule, provisions for the children are made by the secular court where the couple obtained the decree of divorce.

In case of reconciliation,
what happens to the right to separation?

Canon 1155

Coniux innocens laudabiliter alterum coniugem ad vitam
coniugalem rursus admittere potest,
quo in casu iuri separationis renuntiat.

The innocent spouse can laudably readmit the other spouse to
conjugal life,
in which case he or she renounces the right to separation.

The law states the minimum: the innocent spouse has no legal duty to seek the reassumption of conjugal life. Christian morality at times can ask for more, and its demands can be binding in conscience. Law often does no more than to express the minimal demands of charity. There are cases when the law must cede to charity; there are no cases when charity must cede to the law.

CHAPTER TEN
THE VALIDATION OF MARRIAGE
1156 — 1165

The purpose of the canons in this chapter is to provide a legal mechanism for transforming an existing union, created and sustained with marital affection but having no juridical status, into a canonically valid marriage.

Therefore, the starting point in every kind of validation is the fact that there is an existing union, but due to some irregularity, it cannot be recognized as a valid marriage. Through the juridical act of validation, the defect is healed.[1]

[1]There *is* a problem with translating the Latin technical terms into English. *Convalidatio* can be rendered as "convalidation," an archaic word but much used among canonists. *Sanatio in radice* can be literally translated as "sanation in root," an unusual and obscure expression; or "radical sanation," used in TRL-USA, but giving a special meaning to the term "radical." We let ourselves be inspired by the terminology used in TRL-GBI where *convalidatio* is rendered by "validation" and *sanatio in radice* by "retroactive validation"; hoping that one day these expressions will become standard among English speaking canonists. They are fairly simple, clear and contemporary.

As every canonist knows the Latin *sanatio in radice* is a misleading expression. Someone who is not an expert easily assumes that the marriage is made valid right in its "root," that is from the beginning of the invalid union with marital affection. This is, of course, not the case; the *sanatio* is from *now*, the legal fiction alone goes back to the "root."

In the case of a **simple validation**, after the defect has been identified, the parties themselves can play the principal role in the healing action, even if, depending on the nature of the initial irregularity, the intervention of a competent authority is required as well.

In the case of a **retroactive validation** the impediments are dispensed and the requirement of the canonical form is waived by the competent ecclesiastical authority so that the marriage can be healed on the strength of the consent of the couple. In addition, as a rule, the effects of a valid marriage are retroactively attributed to the invalid union.

Historical antecedents: references to the renewal of consent for the validation of a union can be found from the thirteenth century onward. Originally, this renewal meant probably the external manifestation of consent on the model of the Roman consensual contracts, not the highly polished philosophical concept of "eliciting a new act of the will." The purpose of such a renewal must have been to avoid uncertainty about the validity of a marriage in an age when there was no compulsory canonical form.

The first evidence for a *sanatio in radice* comes from the reign of Innocent III (1198-1216). His primary purpose was to confer legitimacy on children born illegitimate, for this purpose he "validated," *sanavit*, the marriage of the parents. When after the Council of Trent the lack of canonical form became a frequent source of invalidity, the use of this grant increased greatly. (*See* DDC 4:549; LTK 6:516)

Transitions in the law of simple validation: according to the old Code the renewal of consent was required when it became certain that the marriage was invalid; according to the new Code the party who *knows or conjectures* the marriage to be invalid may proceed to the renewal; this makes the process more expeditious in doubtful cases; **transitions in the law of retroactive validation:** the power of the local ordinary has been greatly extended.

Literary forms: while there is a strong theological background to the canons, they regulate right-and-duty situations.

The canons are upholding and protecting the values *present in a union created and sustained with marital affection* but having no canonical validity. They provide a relatively easy and speedy mechanism for these unions to obtain the status of a legitimate or sacramental marriage.

Article One: SIMPLE VALIDATION.

This article is organized around three causes that can make a marriage invalid:
— a diriment impediment,
— lack of consent,
— lack of form.

(1) Invalidity caused by an impediment

꒰ᐩ꙳ᐩ꒱

What are the requirements for simple validation?

Canon 1156 § 1.

**Ad convalidandum matrimonium irritum
ob impedimentum dirimens,
requiritur ut cesset impedimentum vel ab eodem dispensetur,
et consensum renovet
saltem pars impedimenti conscia.**

**To validate a marriage that is invalid
because of a diriment impediment,
it is required that the impediment either cease or be dispensed,
and
that, at least, the party who is aware of the impediment
renew the consent.**

validation, to validate are the translations of *convalidatio, convalidare*; they belong to the technical vocabulary of canon law used in circumstances when there is no valid marriage but there is a union with marital affection, a "semblance" or "image" of marriage, *species* *vel figura matrimonii.* Validation is the name of the juridical act through which the situation is rectified and the invalid union becomes a valid marriage.

invalid because of a diriment impediment: CIC/17 distinguished between prohibitive and diriment impediments; in CIC/83 all impediments are diriment.

The party who is **aware of the impediment** is not bound to inform the other about the invalidity; that is, the one who knows has the lawful freedom to leave, but the other may be kept ignorant of the truth. There is an element of unfairness in this rule; if the spouses have equal rights and duties in matters concerning their marriage (cf. canon 1135), surely, they should be equally informed in a matter as vital as the validity of their marriage.

❦

By what law is the renewal of consent required?
What is the effect of its omission?

Canon 1156 § 2.

**Haec renovatio iure ecclesiastico requiritur
ad validitatem convalidationis,
etiamsi initio utraque pars consensum praestiterit
nec postea revocaverit.**

**This renewal [*of consent*] is required by ecclesiastical law
for the validity of the validation,
even if in the beginning both parties had given consent and
neither had revoked it.**

by ecclesiastical law: a provision by the church, not required by any kind of natural justice. Does it bind the non Catholic party? It does not seem so since non-Catholics are not bound by ecclesiastical laws, cf. canon 11:

> Merely ecclesiastical laws bind those who have been baptized in the Catholic church or received into it . . .

yet, canon 1059 says:

> The marriage of Catholics. even if one party is Catholic, is governed not only by divine law but also by canon law. . .

The question is then if the law requiring this new act of consent regulates the behavior of an individual person, in which case it does not bind the non-Catholic, or, regulates the marriage, in which case it binds them both.

Our position is that since this law is part and parcel of the whole fabric of the canon law of marriage, regulating the requirements for the covenant, it binds both sides, the Catholic and the non-Catholic. The opposite opinion, if it wants to be thorough and logical, should conclude also that an impediment that is on the side of the non-Catholic only, sush as age, is no impediment at all. Further, the non-Catholic would not be bound by several other norms concerning validation.[2]

for validity: an absolute requirement; without it the act of validation has no effect.

❦

What is the renewal of consent?

Canon 1157

Renovatio consensus debet esse novus voluntatis actus in matrimonium,

---

[2]The opposite opinion is held by Thomas Doyle, *see* COM-USA, 824. As far as we were able to ascertain, the question is not raised in other commentaries on the new Code published to date. Under the old Code the issue was raised in connection with the validation of marriages where one party was not baptized: was the "unbeliever" bound to elicit this "new act of the will"? Cappello at one place affirms this obligation *speculative loquendo*, at another place denies it. *See* CAPPELLO, 781 and 783. Pietro Gasparri is straightforward:

> *One is baptized, the other is not:* both are bound, one is bound directly and the other indirectly because of the one-ness of the contract, as e.g. in the impediment of disparity of cult the law of the church binds the baptized, and indirectly and

quod pars renovans scit aut opinatur
ab initio nullum fuisse.

The renewal of consent must be a new act of the will
ratifying the marriage
that the party renewing [*the consent*] knows or
thinks was null from the beginning.

new act of the will: the expression has become a standard one in the canonical literature, virtually never questioned, still less critically examined. Yet a "new act of the will" is difficult to define, even more difficult to ascertain legally since it is not subject to any direct verification; it can be conjectured only through external signs. Besides, how can there be a "new" act of consent when the spouses "converse with marital affection" day and night? In what precisely should the "newness" consist? How can anyone prove this "newness"? Perhaps the law should have said simply "the party must give new external evidence of the existing consent." Then the law would have remained within its domain, which is the world of external and social relations.[3]

By the ordinary rules of interpretation, the requirement of a "new act of the will" should not be extended beyond those unions which are invalid for a past or present impediment. It is mentioned only in the first group of canons which deal with invalidity due to an impediment; hence, it should stay there.

To transfer it to unions which are invalid for defect of consent does not make any sense because the problem is that there was no consent in the first place; something that did not exist cannot be renewed.

---

per accidens the non-baptized party.
See GASPARRI, 255. It would be difficult to fault Gasparri's logic.

[3]The proper domain of the law is the so called external forum; the field of external social relations. They can be seen, witnessed, ascertained at a court. To legislate about a "new act of the will" is to create often insoluble difficulties for all involved. An act of the will is a purely spiritual act, it happens in the depth of the human spirit, its existence can be conjectured only through external signs that must be interpreted. When the external signs are recounted years after the event (as it happens in many marriage cases), it is difficult to achieve sound objective knowledge.

If the law judges that in the case of a validation it is prudent to ask for some new external evidence of the internal consent, it should say so.

To transfer it to unions which were invalid for defect of form does not make much sense partly because canon 1160 does not ask for it, and partly because it would warrant an extraordinary inquiry. The person charged to inquire about the consent and to receive it in the name of the church (cf. canon 1108 § 2) should question the spouses twice, first if they consented, second if they consented with "a new act of the will." That much seems to follow from the analysis of the texts.[4]

Law is, however, more than a logical construct on the basis of the texts. By judicial custom a "new act of the will" may have become a requirement for simple validation when the cause of invalidity was lack of form, *defectus formae*, which refers to both the total absence of the canonical form and the absence of an absolutely required element in the form.

knows or thinks: it is not necessary to have a firm knowledge of the invalidity; validation can take place also if both or one of the spouses are of the opinion that the marriage *may be* invalid. Technically, canon 1060 should take care of such doubtful situations (marriage enjoys the favor of the law); but understandably, some couples would prefer to clear up all doubts through the process of validation. The new Code lets them do it, if they so wish.

---

[4]The jurisprudence of the Rota appears to take the opposite view. A statement in *Dubuquen., coram* Rogers, 21 January 1969 (SRR 61 [1969]: 64) could hardly be more explicit:

[*The Law, in iure*]. . .Although marital consent once given is presumed to endure until there is evidence of its revocation (can. 1093), the positive disposition of the law requires the renewal of consent for the simple validation of a marriage contracted by a baptized person invalidly either because of a diriment impediment, or because of lack of consent or, finally, because of lack of form,. . .*ob impedimentum dirimens, vel ob defectum consensus, vel denique ob defectum formae.*

The above decision relies on *Beryten, Maronitarum, coram* Wynan, 1 June 1940 (SRR 32 [1940]: 431-432):

[*The Law, in iure*:]. . .the renewal of consent. . .is always required for the simple validation of a marriage invalid because of lack of form [*defectus formae*] (can. 1137), it follows therefore by the nature of things that they who are contracting anew should be aware that the previous marriage was null and that they should elicit a new consent.

In spite of such statements, the puzzling question still remains if more is required in the case of a simple validation with the canonical form than in the case of an

How to renew the consent when the impediment is public?

Canon 1158 § 1.

**Si impedimentum sit publicum,
consensus ab utraque parte renovandus est forma canonica,
salvo praescripto can. 1127, § 2.**

**If the impediment is public
the consent must be renewed by both parties in the canonical
form,
the prescription of canon 1127 § 2, however, remains in effect.**

Whenever the invalidity of the marriage can be proved in the external forum, the validation must take place in the external forum, too. There is a balance between the defect and the remedy.

The present canon does not cancel out canon 1127 § 2 which authorizes the ordinary to grant a dispensation from the canonical form in the case of a mixed marriage. In practice, however, the opportunity to marry without the canonical form but in a public

ordinary marriage. Is it conceivable that in some cases there could be an authentic consent habitually and firmly in place, but because no new internal act of the will is elicited *at the moment of the wedding*, the validation remains without effect??? Or should we simply say that the very manifestation of consent in the ordinary form is sufficient evidence of the required new consent?

Major commentators on the first Code seem to take for granted that to contract in valid canonical form is equivalent to the renewal of consent. Cappello is typical of them:

> For the validation of a marriage in this case [*invalid because of lack of form, defectus formae*], previous knowledge of the invalidity on the part of the spouses-to-be is not required. The renewal can be explicit and implicit, or equivalent, provided the condition about the required and received consent, according to the norm of can. 1095, § 1, n. 3° is verified. (*See* CAPPELLO, 787)

As it is, there is no ultimate clarity. In the practical order the issue may come up in a petition for nullity; e.g. one of the parties may claim that although he had habitual consent when he agreed to the validation in the canonical form, he did not elicit a new act of the will at the time of the ceremony.

Once again, such difficulties could be easily cleared up if the law demanded no more than a new external sign of consent.

form, as canon 1127 § 2 prescribes, may be nonexistent if the couple is already married according to the civil law.

෴

How to renew the consent when the impediment is occult?

Canon 1158 § 2.

Si impedimentum probari nequeat,
satis est ut consensus renovetur privatim et secreto,
et quidem a parte impedimenti conscia,
dummodo altera in consensu praestito perseveret,
aut ab utraque parte, si impedimentum sit utrique parti notum.

If the impediment cannot be proved,
it is enough that the consent be renewed privately and secretly,
by the party who is aware of the impediment,
provided the other one perseveres in the consent already given;
or,
by both parties, if the impediment is known to both parties.

Whenever the invalidity of the marriage cannot be proved in the external forum, there is no need for validation in the same forum. The private and secret renewal of the consent can take any form; and, of course, no witnesses are necessary.

(2) Invalidity caused by defect of consent

෴

How to validate a marriage if there was no consent?

Canon 1159 § 1.

Matrimonium irritum ob defectum consensus convalidatur,
si pars quae non consenserat, iam consentiat,
dummodo consensus ab altera parte praestitus perseveret.

**A marriage invalid for defect of consent is validated
if the party who failed to consent now consents,
provided the consent already given by the other party perseveres.**

An obvious principle: if there was no consent, it must be given. The marriage comes into being when the consent of the one joins the consent of the other.

Canon 1159 § 2.

**Si defectus consensus probari nequeat,
satis est ut pars, quae non consenserat,
privatim et secreto consensum praestet.**

**If the defect of consent cannot be proved,
it is enough that the party who did not consent
gives his consent privately and secretly.**

Whenever the lack of consent cannot be proved before a court, to remedy the situation there is no need for a judicially ascertainable process.

Canon 1159 § 3.

**Si defectus consensus probari potest,
necesse est ut consensus forma canonica praestetur.**

**If the defect of consent can be proved,
it is necessary that the consent be given in the canonical form.**

Whenever the invalidity of the marriage can be proved, the validation must be in proper legal form.

(3) Invalidity caused by defect of form.

How to validate a marriage invalid for defect of form?

Canon 1160

**Matrimonium nullum ob defectum formae,
ut validum fiat,
contrahi denuo debet forma canonica,
salvo praescripto can. 1127, § 2.**

**For a marriage that is null because of defect of form
to become valid
it must be contracted again in the canonical form,
the prescription of canon 1127 § 2, however, remains in effect.**

Whenever the form was either absent or substantially deficient, there was no canonically valid marriage. The obvious remedy is to contract the marriage in due legal form. See also our comments under canon 1157 *re* the renewal of consent.

Summary: Patterns in simple validation

There are three causes of invalidity:
(1) an impediment not dispensed: 1156, 1157, 1158;
(2) defect of consent: 1159;
(3) defect of form: 1160.
The process can be put into motion whenever there is a firm knowledge or a probable opinion of invalidity.
A simple principle governs the procedure of validation: *the forum of the defect (public or occult) determines the forum of the validation.*
Whenever the invalidity could be proved before a court, the validation must take place in a public (legally ascertainable) form. Whenever the invalidity cannot be proved before a court, the validation can take place in an occult form.

Pattern One: *The marriage is invalid because of an impediment:*

The impediment must cease either naturally or by dispensation and the consent must be renewed, according to the following rules:

If the impediment was *public*, either by its very nature or because proofs of it are available,
> both parties must be informed of it,
> both must renew their consent publicly in the canonical form.

If the impediment was *occult* and is known to both:
> both must renew their consent;
> they may renew it privately and secretly.

If the impediment was *occult* and is known to one spouse only:
> the spouse so informed has no duty to notify the other,
> but he or she must renew the consent,
> may renew it privately and secretly.

Pattern Two: *The marriage is invalid for defect of consent:*

The general rule is that the consent of the one must join the consent of the other; they need not be given simultaneously but at some point they must exist simultaneously.

If neither of the spouses consented:
> both must consent.

If one did not consent:
> he or she must consent.

If the defect of consent was public:
> the canonical form must be used for validation.

If the defect was occult:
> the consent may be given privately and secretly.

Note that the issue of "a new act of the will" cannot come up under this heading since there was no correct act of the will in the first place.

Pattern Three: *The marriage was invalid for defect of form.*

Since there was no valid canonical form, there was no marriage in canon law. The rule for validation is that the marriage should be contracted in due canonical form.

Article Two: RETROACTIVE VALIDATION.

The juridical act of retroactive validation has two facets:
one: it removes impediments and dispenses from formalities, so that the union can become a valid marriage here and now; in this facet there is no retroactivity at all;
two: it creates a legal fiction; it attributes the ordinary effects of a valid marriage to the invalid union right from its beginning; in this facet there is retroactivity.
Although this type of validation is called *sanatio in radice*, the "healing of the marriage in its root," strictly speaking no retroactive healing takes place because the fact of past invalidity cannot be changed ever, not even by God. The healing regards the future; the past receives a new standing in law.

◦━☀━◦

What is retroactive validation?

Canon 1161 § 1.

**Matrimonii irriti sanatio in radice est eiusdem,
sine renovatione consensus, convalidatio,
a competenti auctoritate concessa,
secumferens dispensationem ab impedimento, si adsit,
atque a forma canonica, si servata non fuerit,
necnon retrotractionem effectuum canonicorum ad praeteritum.**

**Retroactive validation of an invalid marriage is its validation
without the renewal of consent,
granted by a competent authority,
including [*the necessary*] dispensation from an impediment if**

there is one, and
from the canonical form if it was not observed,
also the retroaction of the canonical effects on the past.

retroactive validation is the translation of the classical canonical expression *sanatio in radice*, "healing in the root."

The operational structure of this institution is complex and unique:

— in the first place there must be a union with marital affection, that is a "semblance" or "image" of marriage, *species vel figura matrimonii*, but no canonically valid marriage,

— then the competent authority must be satisfied that both parties want the marriage, that is, the consent of each is alive,

— if there is an impediment, it is removed by a dispensation (included in the grant),

— the requirement of the canonical form is waived (by the grant);

— thus, the parties become free to marry, and, not being bound to marry in canonical form, their consent produces the covenant without any formality; they become married then and there, at the moment of the grant; —

— further, the authority granting the validation not being able to change the past fact of an invalid marriage does what it can to extend his favor to the past: by the use of a legal fiction, he regards the past union as if it had been valid right from the moment of its inception.

— in particular, he regards all the children born from the validated union as if they had been born from a valid marriage, therefore legitimate.

Canon 1161 § 2.

Convalidatio fit a momento concessionis gratiae;
retrotractio vero intellegitur facta ad momentum celebrationis matrimonii,
nisi aliud expresse caveatur.

The validation is from the moment of the concession of the grace,

the retroaction, however, is understood to reach back to the moment
when the marriage was celebrated,
unless it is provided expressly otherwise.

validation: note again that the marriage is not the effect of the grant, the consent of the parties brings it into existence; the grant merely removes all the obstacles.

grace: the word is used to underline that no one has a strict right to the grant of retroactive validation; it is given *ex gratia*, that is at the discretion of the competent authority.

the retroaction of the canonical effects takes place in the world of the law; a world where presumptions and fictions play their own part in the service of justice, equity and Christian mercy.
Some exceptions are stated in the following canons.

❦

What are the requirements for retroactive validation?

Canon 1161 § 3.

Sanatio in radice ne concedatur,
nisi probabile sit
partes in vita coniugali perseverare velle.

**No retroactive validation must be granted unless
it is probable that
the parties want to persevere in their conjugal life.**

The competent authority should be cautiously prudent in granting a *sanatio in radice*. Intemperate zeal in "regularizing marriages" may lead to an increase of petitions for nullity.

Canon 1162 § 1.

**Si in utraque vel alterutra parte deficiat consensus,
matrimonium nequit sanari in radice,**

sive consensus ab initio defuerit,
sive ab initio praestitus, postea fuerit revocatus.

If in one or both of the parties the consent is lacking,
the marriage cannot be validated retroactively,
whether the consent was absent from the beginning, or,
was given in the beginning but revoked afterwards.

A union with marital affection is an absolute condition for a retroactive validation. In the absence of consent, no such union can exist.

Canon 1162 § 2.

Quod si consensus ab initio quidem defuerat,
sed postea praestitus est,
sanatio concedi potest
a momento praestiti consensus.

If the consent was absent in the beginning
but it was given afterwards,
retroactive validation can be granted
from the moment the consent was given.

Explanation by way of an example: a civil marriage cannot be validated retroactively as from the date of its celebration if at that time the consent of one of the parties was defective. But it can be validated from the moment when the defect was corrected, that is when the same party consented "with marital affection" to the union.

Note that the language of this paragraph is somewhat ambivalent; its meaning is that *the retroactive attribution of the canonical effects* reaches back to the moment when the consent was given.

Canon 1163 § 1.

Matrimonium irritum ob impedimentum
vel ob defectum legitimae formae

sanari potest,
dummodo consensus utriusque partis perseveret.

**A marriage invalid because of an impediment or
because of the lack of legitimate form,
can be validated retroactively,
provided the consent of both parties perseveres.**

provided translates *dummodo* which is used in canon law to introduce a clause with requirements for validity.

Canon 1163 § 2.

**Matrimonium irritum ob impedimentum iuris naturalis
aut divini positivi
sanari potest solummodo postquam impedimentum cessavit.**

**A marriage invalid because of an impediment of natural law or
of divine positive law,
can be validated retroactively only after the impediment has
ceased to exist.**

The legal fiction must not be extended to a time when no marriage
could have existed because of a prohibition of the natural or divine
law.[5]

---

[5]There is a reported decree of the Holy Office, issued in 1953, granting a *sanatio in
radice* when total impotence has occurred subsequent to an attempted marriage. The
fact of the total impotence (antecedent to the *sanatio* and perpetual) is not in dispute;
if anything it is emphasized in the document. The decree is certainly at variance with
the traditional understanding of the *sanatio in radice*. As far as one can see, the HO
assumed that the sacrament could come into existence in spite of an impediment
believed to be of natural law and present at the time of the *sanatio*. The text of the
decree, as it is reported, insinuates strongly that it was issued by the special mandate
of the pope, Pius XII.
Different interpretations are possible; none of them absolutely certain.
*One: the decree presents a new understanding of a natural union with marital
affection, even if it is canonically invalid.* In this interpretation the decree regarded
the canonically invalid union as possessing the internal structure of a real marriage,
which structure continued to endure even after the supervening impotence. The

Canon 1164

**Sanatio valide concedi potest
etiam alterutra vel utraque parte inscia;
ne autem concedatur nisi ob gravem causam.**

**Retroactive validation can be granted validly
even if one or both of the parties are unaware of it;
but it should not be granted without a grave cause.**

sanatio simply removed an external impediment, and thus, on the strength of their original consent the parties obtained the sacrament. Explanations published in the periodical literature suggest that such reasoning may have inspired the decision. If so, through these decrees the church accorded an unusual degree of recognition to a canonically invalid marriage. If this explanation is correct, the consequences for the recognition of merely civil marriages, contracted by persons who are bound to the canonical form, are far reaching.

Two: the decree is a small step toward a new understanding of the purposes of marriage. At times the church may feel its way toward a new development through hesitating and even seemingly conflicting practices. For some decades now, the official documents of the Holy See displayed an increasing broadness in interpreting the impediment of impotency; this decree could therefore be explained as a small step in a larger process. In practice, it comes close to sanctioning a marriage for companionship only when there is no natural capacity for sexual relations. *If* the decree was inspired by such thoughts (we have no evidence for it), the consequences should be far reaching once again.

But the story does not end here. It has been reported also that another decree of the same HO in 1963 denied *sanatio* in a virtually identical case.

Both decrees have been private replies, never published officially, hence the interpreter cannot work on the original texts. Yet, their existence can hardly be doubted.

Finally, it shold be kept in mind that the decree mentioned in the first place, even if it had been issued by the special mandate of the pope, remains a somewhat singular and isolated event. It would be incorrect to attribute a major doctrinal significance to it. The real issue behind the request of the couple was a simple and touching one: they have repented and wished to receive the sacraments again. Pius XII granted their wish.

A theologian from our sister church in the East would probably explain the grant as an act of "economy," *oikonomia*; the healing power of Christ, through the ministry of the bishop of Rome, brought to those in need. He would see no reason to inquire any further.

For appropriate references concerning the decrees and commentaries *see* CLD 5:549-551 and 6:665.

the parties are unaware of it: this is a concession to be used with the greatest caution. After all, when such validation is granted without the couple being informed about it, the "competent authority" decides for them whether or not they should be validly married. Of course, it may happen that they have unmistakably manifested their intention to marry but their desire was frustrated by a technical mishap. To validate the marriage in such circumstances is no more than to respect and to give due effect to the original decision of the couple.

⌒⁕⌒

Who are the competent authorities?

There are two competent authorities to grant retroactive validations: the Holy See and the diocesan bishop.

Canon 1165 § 1.

Sanatio in radice concedi potest ab Apostolica Sede.

Retroactive validation can be granted by the Apostolic See.

The radical authority to grant retroactive validations is vested in the Apostolic See. Naturally, this canon should not be taken as a dogmatic statement; it means that in the present order of discipline such authority is reserved to the Holy See, in practice to the Congregation of the Sacraments.

Canon 1165 § 2.

**Concedi potest ab Episcopo dioecesano in singulis casibus,
etiam si plures nullitatis rationes in eodem matrimonio
  concurrant,
impletis condicionibus, de quibus in can. 1125,
pro sanatione matrimonii mixti;
concedi autem ab eodem nequit,
si adsit impedimentum
cuius dispensatio Sedi Apostolicae reservatur**

ad normam can. 1078, § 2,
aut agatur de impedimento iuris naturalis aut divini positivi
quod iam cessavit.

It can be granted by the diocesan bishop in individual cases,
even if the same marriage is null for several reasons,
provided that for the validation of a mixed marriage
the conditions stated in canon 1125 are implemented;
it cannot be granted, however, by the same [bishop]
if there is an impediment
from which the dispensation is reserved to the Apostolic See
according to the norm of canon 1078 § 2, or,
if there was an impediment of natural or divine positive law,
[notwithstanding] that it has already ceased.

The power of the diocesan bishop to grant retroactive validation
for a marriage is described and circumscribed in the following ways:

— he can grant it to a determined couple only; he could not grant
it for instance "to all couples in the diocese who neglected to observe
the canonical form";

— he cannot grant it if there is an impediment from which the
Holy See only can dispense, cf. canon 1178 § 2;

— he cannot grant it if there was an impediment of natural or
divine law even if the impediment ceased to exist.

The provisions for mixed marriages or for marriages with disparity of cult (cf. canons 1125 and 1086) remain in effect.

PROBLEM AREAS AND
DISPUTED QUESTIONS

Why this chapter? Because the law of marriage, like any other part of canon law is subject to the law of history, it must change as our understanding of the mystery develops. It must change also in response to legitimate needs that emerge in succeeding ages and at different places. It cannot be any other way since the church is a living body, and the sign of life is movement.

Indeed, ever since the Apostles began to legislate at the Council of Jerusalem for the young communities, the production of new structures and norms of action has continued, by assemblies of bishops, by the rulings of the popes, or by customs quietly arising and received in the communities.

So the system of the canonical norms that we have today comes to us from the distant past and moves into the future. On the surface, the rules may look fixed and rigid; in reality they are part of an evolving reality. As the church progresses in the articulation of the evangelical message, as it works to bring this message to all nations with a new freshness, the church keeps adjusting old structures to new needs; it keeps creating new norms of actions in response to the demands of an evolving community.[1]

---

[1]Canon law as a whole reflects the nature of the church which is a human community endowed with divine gifts. Because it is a human community, it is subject to the limitations of our nature and in its members it is marked by sin.

Such developments in the legal system can originate also in new theological insights. Indeed, most of the changes that have taken place recently in the law of marriage are the practical consequences of the new insights into the Christian mysteries by the Fathers of Vatican Council II.

It follows that there is nothing unusual in the fact that in spite of a fairly extensive revision of the Code, problem areas in the field of canon law still abound. The law of marriage is not an exception. The purpose of this chapter is precisely to list these problem areas and to report on the on-going discussions, and to do so in a more ordered and systematic way than it was possible in our comments on the canons.

Problems, however, are best articulated in questions. Good questions can provoke healthy arguments; also, they can expose the weaknesses of flawed reasonings. Therefore, no question should ever be feared, still less suppressed; if it is not a good one, it will defeat itself sooner or later; if it is well put, it will dispel errors and misconceptions. This was certainly the mind of many medieval teachers and writers, Aquinas being the most prominent among them. They persisted in raising questions, even when, as yet, the answers evaded them. Progress in knowledge can emerge out of such vigorous dialectics only.

In this spirit, the chapter on *Problem Areas and Disputed Questions* is presented.

Because it is a community endowed with divine gifts, through faith it can see beyond the limits of merely human knowledge; through hope and charity it can transcend the dictates of ordinary human prudence.

The clue to the understanding of canon law is in the realization that in this body of norms the complex nature of the church is manifest. Some rules have their origin in divine revelation (e.g. concerning the sacraments), some others in human deliberations (e.g. the technicalities of procedures), many have it in both in varying proportions. Once this realization is there, it is easy to see that there is an on-going need to adjust the laws as the church progresses in the understanding of divine mysteries, or, as humanity progresses in wisdom, in organization and government.

Such flexibility, however, must be balanced with the demands of stability — not an easy task. A legal system is functioning well when it can respond to legitimate requests for change and, at the same time, it can inspire confidence through its permanency.

Question 1: What is the right balance between protecting the institution and respecting the person?

Why the question? Because in the course of history, there have been changes and the problem is still with us.

There have been changes. In the first millennium, the pastoral care of the church in connection with marriage centered mainly on individual persons; on their needs, duties, and above all, on their salvation. With the arrival of the scholastic age, however, the emphasis shifted: the protection of the institution of marriage became the object of overriding concern. This was just one facet of a new orientation that put greater emphasis on institutions; it was a change in direction in both thinking and practical enactments, due mainly to the influence of Roman law and Aristotelian philosophy.

Ever since, the institution of marriage enjoyed the favor of the law, at times, over and against the welfare of the individual. Provided the well defined institutional ends could be fulfilled, the intention of persons counted for little. A complex and far reaching system of impediments developed; rigorous external formalities were imposed. Further, a complex system of courts and precedures was introduced, and it was taken for granted that the individual had no other right or duty than to wait for a decision, no matter how long it took for the judges to reach it. Immense delays were justified by the idea of "protecting the institution."

It is interesting to note that although the right of a person to marry without the prescribed formalities has been recognized for a long time (e.g. when no ecclesiastical assistant is available for a month), the right of an individual to free himself from an invalid bond when no ecclesiastical justice is available for many years has never been recognized; nor are emergency provisions in the law (e.g. discretionary power to decide, granted to the bishop) for those regions or circumstances where the courts cannot function because of great distances, government interference, language difficulties or other similar reasons.

The problem is still with us. Vatican Council II brought an immense change, even upheaval, by stating and acknowledging the importance of the individual person over so many institutions. Respect should be given to the honest conscientious convictions of a person even if they do not promote, or may even be contrary to, the welfare of a respectable institution. Hence, the principle of religious freedom. Hence, the insistence on fundamental rights, inside and outside of the church.

The result of this new stance is a sometimes subtle, sometimes open conflict between the inspiration that comes to us from the Council and the classical structures that we have inherited from the past.

In the new canons on marriage the conflict and the resulting tension between the two trends, institutional and personalistic, is noticeable. There has been a shift toward giving greater importance to the rights of the individual persons, but many structures and rules conceived for the protection of the institution remain in effect.

Maybe, the correct balance between the protection of the institution and the respect for persons is an ideal toward which we can and must strive but which we cannot reach; that is, there is no universally valid formula to determine the right measure on each side. Yet, excesses in either direction are not difficult to diagnose in practice. From the twelfth century, and even more from the sixteenth, the emphasis has been all too heavily on the side of the institution. Presently the trend is toward increased respect for the rights of individual persons; this trend needs to be strengthened both in legislation and in handling marriage cases. After all, institutions exist for the sake of persons, and God came to save individual persons.[2]

---

[2]God indeed judges human persons according to the criterion whether or not they followed the honest light of their conscience, see St. Paul in Rom 2:12-17:

All who have sinned without the law will also perish without the law, and all who have sinned under the law will be judged by the law. For it is not the hearers of the law who are righteous before God, but the doers of the law who will be justified. When Gentiles who have not the law do by nature what the law requires, they are a law to themselves, even though they do not have the law. They show that what the law requires is written on their hearts, while their conscience also bears witness and their conflicting thoughts accuse or perhaps excuse them on that day when, according to my gospel, God judges the secrets of men by Christ Jesus.

In the ultimate analysis, this text proclaims that God judges human persons according to their honest conscience. There is the strongest argument for the primacy of persons over institutions.

Question 2: Does *consortium* have one precise meaning applicable everywhere?

Why the question? Because marriage is a human reality before it can be a saving mystery, and this human reality can be perceived in different ways.

Reflections. There is no doubt that the understanding of marital *consortium* has always been conditioned by the culture of an age and by the customs of a people. The expectations of a couple in the farming communities of Europe in the Middle Ages were certainly vastly different from the expectations of university students in the same continent today. History apart, divergences exist in our own times, the demands of companionship vary significantly from one continent to another, from one country to another, even from one social group to another. Yet, in each case, the human reality, although perceived, understood and lived in different ways, must become part of the one saving mystery. It follows that our canonical definition of *consortium* should be broad enough to accomodate its multiple variations and strict enough to preserve a common substance. No one, to our knowledge, has produced such a perfect definition.

The wisdom of the ancient Roman *jurisprudentes* may come to our help. They were reluctant to define foundational concepts because once their meaning was fixed they would have lost their flexibility. So the lawyers, prudent as they were, left ample room for life to shape the law.

For the future, it seems that this problem can be solved better by judicial decisions on the concrete level where life meets the law than by abstract definitions which may be too narrow to include all the variations that life can produce. The tribunals should be entitled, within reasonable limits, to take into account the particular expectations rooted in the culture of the parties. In other terms, they can, even must, take judicial notice of the difference in the understanding of the human reality of marriage.[3]

[3]There is a contrast between the two joined ends of marriage: the propagation of life is accomplished through the act of generation,which can be defined in law with satisfactory precision; the *consortium* is accomplished by multiple acts on every level, physical, emotional,intellectual, and spiritual, over the life-long association of the parties, which process does not lend itself to any "clear and distinct" definition.

Question 3: How can consummation be the cause of absolute indissolubility?

Why the question? Because consummation is not part of the sacrament (in the classical sense, of the rite that signifies and confers grace); yet, it is consummation that renders marriage definitely indissoluble. In other terms, there appears to be a causal relationship between the physical consummation of a sacramental marriage and the special firmness of its essential property, indissolubility.

Our question is about this apparent cause-and-effect relationship between consummation and indissolubility. Before any answer, however, two theological principles must be recalled:

(1) the sacrament is fully given and received when the promises are exchanged;

(2) as long as the marriage is not consummated it can be dissolved by the church.

The speculative difficulty clearly lies in the fact that an act, which is not part of the sacramental sign, confers the quality of indissolubility "with special firmness" on the bond created by the sign.

A theological explanation can be found in the *Summa Theologiae* of Aquinas:

> ...matrimony before its consummation [*ante carnalem copulam*] signifies the union that Christ has to the soul through grace, which can be dissolved by a contrary spiritual disposition. that is, by sin. But through its consummation [*per carnalem copulam*], matrimony signifies his union with the church, the assumption of human nature into the unity of the person, which is absolutely indivisible. (Suppl. q. 61, a. 2, ad 1)

Although Vatican Council II has abandoned the hierarchical conception of the ends of marriage, the propagation of life and the act of generation continues to get more attention in canon law than the *consortium*, e.g. in the matter of consummation, also, in explicating the symbolism of marriage (the "one flesh" is the symbol of Christ's union to the church). This is due partly to an intention to preserve traditional structures, but it is due also to the fact that canon law has still to come to grips with the reality of *consortium* as one of the principal ends and draw the legal consequences. It has taken many centuries to work out the traditional structures; it will take a long time to let the law assimilate fully the insights of Vatican Council II.

This explanation that Aquinas himself inherited from earlier ages gained wide acceptance; it has become a standard statement in textbooks of theology or canon law. Yet, while it clarifies the symbolism in the act of consummation, it does not explain the causality: how can the act of consummation confer a "a new firmness" on the bond? Even more difficult is to see how the act of consummation can have an impact on the dispensing power of the church by taking it away. The effect transcends the cause.[4]

A historical factor in the development of this doctrine may have been the influence of Roman law which in certain types of contracts (especially the so called innominate contracts) allowed the parties to rescind the agreement as long as there was no delivery or compliance. In fact, there is a reference to this idea in the same article of the *Summa Theologiae* (ad 2).

The very fact that the discussion continues shows that on this speculative issue, as yet, no consensus has been reached among theologians and canonists. Such lack of a theoretical solution need not disturb the traditional practice which is well established. The law can be ahead of the theory. But faith seeks understanding; the search for a satisfactory explanation must continue.

Question 4: Is there a spiritual consummation of marriage?

Background to the question: The institution of marriage has two joined ends: mutual help and procreation of children. Our long standing tradition and the present practice of the church tells us that the sacrament does not become *absolutely* indissoluble unless the marriage is physically consummated. But no "consummation" of

---

[4]After Vatican Council II another question can be raised: if the propagation of human life and *consortium* are joint ends, why should the act of generation alone be the symbol of the union of Christ with his church? Should not the mutual love and help given to each other by the spouses have a substantial sign value?

This question could be reinforced from the findings of modern empirical psychology (not to be discarded easily): sexuality is just one (and not necessarily the principal one) expression of the union of the minds and hearts that should exist between the spouses. Are we not captives of an antiquated biology and psychology by insisting that the sign value of marriage is in the sexual act?

Obviously, such questions are raised to initiate research; not to anticipate answers. More on this issue in the next two questions.

the spiritual relationship of the spouses is required as a condition for indissolubility; hence, there seems to be a lack of balance. Should we say that for the sacrament of marriage to be absolutely indissoluble, the spouses should consummate it in both the physical and the spiritual order?

Jean Bernhard argues *in favor of introducing the new concept* of "existential consummation and in faith," and proposes that as long as the marriage is merely "established" *(instaure)* and not consecrated *(consacré)* the "pastoral authority of the church" could dissolve it. He builds his hypothesis on the new understanding that Vatican Council II reached about marriage, and also on the less legal and more pastoral character that our norms must assume in the future.[5]

Against such a concept it can be argued that unless the ways and means of spiritual consummation can be determined with some precision, no law, no matter how pastoral it is, can handle it. It could lead to a new invasion by the law of the internal world of human persons, with many distinctions and few certainties. Bernhard would probably reply that the whole process should take place outside the field of the law; it should be part of the pastoral care of the church.

On balance, the internal logic of reaching out for some kind of parallelism between the realization of the purposes of marriage cannot be denied. Yet, in the practical order, no one has succeeded in determining the legal criteria for spiritual consummation; nor is it likely that the legislator would be willing to transfer such cases from the field of the law to that of pastoral care: the new Code has reaffirmed the legal approach.[6]

---

[5] See Jean Bernhard, "Indissolubilité du mariage et droit canonique," in Pierre L'Huillier & Others, *Divorce et indissolubilité du mariage*, (Paris: Cerf, 1971).

[6] Here we are touching a fundamental issue in the life of the church: what issues are best handled by legislation; what issues are best left to pastoral care? After the Council of Trent a trend developed to bring more and more issues under the law; more trust was placed in the efficacy of legal precepts than in the effectiveness of pastoral action. Vatican Council II, a strongly pastoral council, reversed this trend, but the adjustment of structures and norms to this reversal is bound to be a long and painful process.

This process, however, can be helped and even speeded up if all those who have to implement or interpret the law are faithful to the spirit of the Council and use the

Canon 1095, 3°, however, may not be so far from the recognition that the lack of some kind of spiritual consummation may invalidate a marriage. It provides that if a person does not have the capacity to carry out the essential obligations of marriage, the union should be declared invalid. Such obligations certainly include mutual help. The incapacity to give this help is likely to be revealed after the wedding only — how could it be known beforehand with any certainty? This means that when one of the parties is not able to fulfill the obligations of *consortium*, there is a strong argument against the validity of the marriage. Surely, the canon does not say that "if there is no spiritual consummation, the bond can be dissolved," but it does say that if there is no capacity to fulfill the obligations of *consortium* the marriage was null and void from the beginning.

No doubt, we are witnessing a new direction in the development of our marriage laws.

Question 5: Can the contract be separated from the sacrament?

Why the question? Because, as a matter of fact, there are many baptized persons who do not believe in Christ. So the question is, can they have the human reality of marriage without participating in the saving mystery?[7]

---

pastoral character of canon law as a hermeneutical principle in their dealing with the law.

One should recall also that in our perception and reception of the laws we must think and act as if we were between two poles: explaining the present law and pointing toward the future law — whenever so warranted. In this way only can we make our contribution toward the progress of a living community, rooted in a sacred past and moving into a rich future.

[7]The problem of the professed unbelievers must be distinguished from the problem of how to handle those who are weak in their faith. Our question refers to the first issue. The second issue raises another question: what can we do for those who need to be strengthened in their faith?

Different answers can be given:

(1) **If the contract cannot be separated from the sacrament,** it follows that

(a) no baptized person can marry without receiving the sacrament,

(b) no marriage can be recognized by the church as valid unless it is a sacrament.

This position, however, leads to absurd consequences:

(a) those who are baptized but have no faith, cannot marry at all; not naturally because the contract is inseparable from the sacrament; not sacramentally because they have no faith;

(b) the church would be forcing a sacrament of Christ on persons who do not believe in Christ.

(2) **If the contract can be separated from the sacrament,** those who are baptized but have no faith, can contract marriage as can all those who are not Christians; they have the human reality but they do not participate in the sacramental mystery.

This position seems the only tenable one:

(a) an adult person cannot be Christian in the full and integral sense of the term unless he is baptized and believes in the mysteries of Christ; never in our tradition was the name "Christian" given to persons who did not believe in Christ; still less were they given the sacraments;

(b)— baptized unbelievers have the natural right to marry like anybody else; moreover, they have the right to marry as they can, that is, in any naturally valid form, without the sacrament.

If this last position is accepted, it follows that the church needs to find some way of recognizing the natural marriages of baptized unbelievers. The possibility of such recognition would also open the way for a dignified refusal of the sacrament when a baptized person clearly professes unbelief.[8]

As a matter of fact, the church may be edging toward such recognition: it admits the possibility of the existence of an authentic matrimonial consent between baptized persons who live in a canonically invalid marriage. It even validates such marriages through a *sanatio* which can be given without the knowledge of the parties. Clearly, when the church grants the validation, it recognizes a

---

[8]That is, the clue to the solution of this issue is in the Declaration on Religious Freedom, *Dignitatis humanae,* by Vatican Council II.

pre-existing union, which currently has no name in canon law but which is very close to being a natural marriage.

If eventually the grace of God leads a couple of baptized unbelievers to the profession of Christian faith, they could indeed receive the sacrament not as validating what was invalid but perfecting by the gift of grace what was already good according to our human nature.[9]

Question 6: What is the nature of the bond?

Why the question? Because the term "bond" is a central concept in the theology and law of marriage. It is referred to constantly, yet hardly ever defined or described with precision.

---

[9]We should also advert to the fact that this disputed question can be and should be nuanced in many ways.

It can be raised on the level of *morality*:

*Is it permissible for a baptized believer to intend the contract only, not the sacrament? The answer is *no, it is not permissible* because his faith binds him to receive the divine gift offered.

*Is it ethical for a baptized unbeliever to ask for the sacrament? The answer is, *no, it is unethical* because the sacrament belongs to a religious community that he rejects.

On the *"ontological"* level, too, there are nuances:

*Does a baptism take away the natural capacity to marry? The official position of the church is that baptism does not take such capacity away because when a baptized person marries a non-baptized one, there is marriage but no sacrament.

* Can the same pattern operate when a baptized believer marries a baptized unbeliever who for his lack of faith cannot receive the sacrament? Logically the answer should be, *yes, it can and it does.*

* Is it conceivable that two baptized believers could exclude the sacrament and yet achieve a "natural marriage"? The issue here is in the efficacy of their intentionality. Theoretically, it can be argued that they can do so; morally, they would be going against their own convictions and commitments.

* Is it conceivable that two baptized believers intending to get the fullness of God's gifts in nature and in grace would ever get less than the sacrament? It is not conceivable that they would ever get less than the sacrament. In such circumstances contract cannot be separated from the sacrament — ever.

Whenever this question is discussed without adverting to these many nuances, the conclusions may be flawed.

Some answers cannot be sustained philosophically or theologically.

There is certainly a difference in the very nature of the bond if the marriage is in the order of human realities or is one of the saving mysteries.

But in neither case can one claim that a new physical reality, independent from the persons, would be created. Not in the order of nature; one could not even conceive what such a physical reality could be. Not in the order of grace; there is not a shred of evidence for it. At most, one could conceive of the possibility of a "sacramental character," but the best of our theologians always rejected such an idea when it was proposed — in very isolated instances, too.

Since in ordinary parlance the term "bond" is often used as if it signified an autonomous physical entity, this negative clarification is necessary.

In the order of beings, only one positive answer can be sustained: the term "bond" signifies a relationship. Now, a relationship does not exist in itself; it is the quality of a person, an orientation toward another. To that extent, it is of course, real. So the next question is: what kind of relationship is the bond?

In the human reality of marriage the relationship consists in the orientation of one person to another. The general foundation for this relationship is the difference between the two sexes: "male and female he created them" (Gen 1:27). The particular aspect of this relationship is in the fact one man and one woman entered into a matrimonial covenant; they are together with marital affection, *cum affectu maritali*, as the Romans liked to say it.

Because this relationship is entered freely and for a purpose that transcends the good of one single individual, each of the partners has a duty to sustain and nourish the relationship; a bond of mutual respect and love exists between them.

So, when we speak of the human reality of the bond, we are speaking of two persons whose life has taken a new orientation, which affects their whole personality, their thoughts, their desires, their decisions. It is a real relationship between two human persons.

In the saving mystery of marriage nothing is lost of the human reality we have just described. But there are significant changes that lift everything into a higher order; the human reality is permeated by

God's mysterious grace and he himself enters into a new relationship with the couple.

The two Christians are part of a new creation, clothed with eternal life. Their promises take place within the Kingdom that is now at hand. Through the sacrament God himself covenants with them and promises to sustain them in their weakness.

The bond is still relationship, but because of the grace that supports it. There is also a specific relationship of the couple to their saving God. All very real for the believer.

Once we understand the marriage bond is a person-to-person relationship, that is, a permanent orientation of the whole internal world of a person to another, we can understand and explain rationally what happens when the "bond" is terminated. In the case of a natural marriage (e.g. through a grant of the privilege of the faith), the spouses become free to give a new orientation to their personal life; hence a new bond can come into existence. In the case of a sacramental non-consummated marriage (e.g. when a dispensation is granted) the obligations are "loosened" by the power of the keys, which is not a human power, and the spouses become free to give a new orientation to their life. In either event, there is no need to assume some "physical" annihilation of a bond. The old saying still holds: beings should not be multiplied without necessity: *entia non sunt multiplicanda sine necessitate*.

Once we know the nature of the bond, we are in much better position to discuss the issue of indissolubility.[10]

---

[10]For those who are familiar with Aristotelian Thomistic categories and terminology, the following may be helpful:

There is simply no way of conceiving of the bond as "substance," *esse per se*; it can be only "accident," *esse in alio*; and within that category it cannot be anything else than "relationship," *esse ad*. Now the foundation for a relationship can be physical: a son is physically related to his father, and vice versa. The foundation for a relationship can be also "moral"; it can be in the orientation that a person gives to his life. Such orientation, however, does not create a substance, physical or spiritual, somehow superimposed on the person.

Question 7: How is marriage the sign of the union of Christ with his church?

Every sacrament is a sign: it signifies a specific gift of grace and it is instrumental in the grant of that grace. Marriage alone, however, has been held traditionally to possess an additional sign value: it signifies the union of Christ with his church.

The scriptural origin of this doctrine.

The origin of this special understanding of the symbolism of marriage is in the Epistle to the Ephesians:

> Husbands, love your wives, as Christ loved the church and gave himself up for her, that he might sanctify her having cleansed her by the washing of water with the word. (5:25-26)

This passage has an exhortative character: the love of Christ for his church should be the model for conjugal love. No love can ever be greater than that. It clearly includes the moral obligation of life-long fidelity, modeled on the self-giving of Christ. Another sentence, however, goes beyond a mere exhortation:

> For this reason a man shall leave his father and mother and be joined to his wife, and the two shall become one. This is a great mystery, and I take it to mean Christ and the church. (*Literally:* this mystery is great, I say as to Christ and as to the church). (31-32)

The best explanation seems to be that the writer of the epistle is referring to the mystery of the first couple: in their union the mystery of Christ and his church was already prefigured, a statement pregnant with dogmatic meaning.[11]

Later tradition not only found in these passages a proof of the indissolubility of marriage, but also construed over it a theory (mainly through the works of medieval canon lawyers) that linked the symbolic character of marriage to its consummation. It became

---

[11]For a fuller explanation *see Jerome Biblical Commentary,* 56:29-41; also Heinrich Schlier, *Der Brief an die Epheser,* 7th ed. (Dusseldorf: Patmos, 1971), pp. 250-283.

a sign of the mystery of Christ and the church through the sexual union of the spouses. The logic of development went this way: Marriage becomes a sign of the union of Christ with his church when it is consummated. Once it is a sign, it takes on the nature of the signified. The signified union cannot be dissolved. Therefore, after its consummation, no marriage can be dissolved either.[12]

This teaching, common to this day, certainly goes beyond the meaning of the doctrine of the epistle. Hence the question: how much of this development is an authentic unfolding of the Pauline doctrine, therefore an integral part of our Catholic faith, and how much of it is of human construction, therefore potentially subject to revision?

Contemporary discussions.

Assuming that marriage is a sign, questions can be raised about the nature of the sign itself. Is it linked to the institution of marriage, or is it linked to the lived reality of the union of the spouses?

* In the first case, marriage is always a sign, no matter how it is lived, or not lived at all — as happens after total separation. Such a position is not without difficulties because every sign exists to convey a message. When a marriage has broken down and the spouses are separated, it is hard to see how and to whom it can convey a message about the mystery of Christ and his church. There is no marital union, and there is no propagation of life; there are only memories of past events. How can a union that has been emptied of all content speak of the vital union of Christ to his church? Can a sign be nominal and still be a sign?[13]

Further, in this theory the sign value of marriage is connected nearly exclusively with the physical consummation of it. Consider-

---

[12]There is no one who had done more to unravel the development of this tradition than Jean Gaudemet. (*See* in Bibliography: Gaudemet)

[13]Horvath raises the question as to what happens when in the concrete order the sign ceases to exist. Can one say that the sacrament of matrimony comes to an end, no less than the presence of Christ comes to an end in the eucharist when the consecrated species are destroyed? His answer is in the affirmative. He speaks of marriage as the fallible symbol of God's infallible love. *See* Tibor Horvath, "Marriage" in *The Sacraments*, ed. by Francis A. Eigo (Villanova, PA: Villanova University, 1979), pp. 143-181.

ing the doctrine of Vatican Council II, it would seem that the sign should be rooted in both, consortium and sexual union.

* In the second case, the sign arises from the lived reality of a Christian marriage. Whenever there is love in the household, according to the ideal described in the letter to the Ephesians, the marriage speaks to the whole world of the living reality of the union of Christ with his church. This theory not only seems to be in harmony with the exhortatory part of the Epistle to the Ephesians but also it explains the role of sign in a wholesome way. There is nothing nominal about it; it speaks of a living bond in faith, hope and love.

Question 8: What is the power of the church over sacramental consummated marriages?

It is not in dispute that

(1) the church can dissolve a marriage between two unbaptized persons for the "benefit of the faith";

(2) the church can dissolve a marriage between a baptized and an unbaptized person through a grant of the "privilege of the faith";

(3) the church can dissolve a sacramental non-consummated marriage;

(4) the church can allow separation in the case of a sacramental consummated marriage; that is, the church can dispense from the actual implementation of all offices that follow from the two ends, consortium and the procreation of children.[14]

---

[14]The use of ambivalent expressions can obscure the proclamation of our beliefs; e.g. if we preach that "all marriages are indissoluble" without qualifying this statement, whenever a privilege of the faith or a dispensation from a sacramental non-consummated marriage is granted, we expose ourselves to the accusation of hypocrisy. We should rather proclaim that "in all marriages there is a life-long obligation of fidelity, with no exception," but we should add that in this imperfect world the church is willing to dispense, for a grave reason, from this obligation —provided the marriage is not a sacramental consummated marriage. Such words would describe our belief and our practice as they are.

The question raised here concerns the power of the church over the bond that remains even after a legitimate separation of the spouses has taken place.

Our query could be put in this way, too: when we say that a sacramental and consummated marriage is indissoluble, do we mean that the church has simply no power to grant dispensation from the bond, *or*, that the church has such power but in the course of history came to the prudential judgment that in order to obey the evangelical mandate and to support the stability of marriages, it would not grant dispensation in the case of sacramental and consummated marriages?[15]

Both positions are within the parameters of Catholic faith. The first one (no power) seems to be held by the majority of theologians and canonists, the second one (firm prudential judgment) seems to be a minority opinion. We say "it seems" because few scholars examine all the meanings of indissolubility and even fewer do a careful analysis of the self-understanding of the church concerning these matters.

There is no doubt that the law of indissolubility has been proclaimed by the Lord as part of the new laws of the Kingdom. This law imposes an obligation on the church as a whole and on every Christian to respect and support the stability of marriages. In the case of married persons, the obligation is to be faithful to each other until "death do them part." Obedient to this mandate, the church never blesses a marriage if the parties intend to exclude indissolubility.

---

[15]There is often a difficulty in interpreting ancient texts or even modern documents. If they say "the church cannot dissolve a sacramental consummated marriage" the "cannot" may signify

(a) the church is not given such power; or,

(b) the church, in obedience to the evangelical mandate to support life-long unions, has formed the judgment that it would be imprudent to grant such dispensations. In the first case the church "cannot" do it because it has no authority to do it; in the second case the church "cannot" do it because it cannot go against its own moral judgment.

The correct method in interpreting a text, ancient or modern, is to ask whether or not the author raised and answered the question of the meaning of "cannot"; if he did not, he left the issue open. Caution is especially advisable in interpreting patristic texts.

But this divinely imposed moral obligation is different from the question of the power of the church over the bond.

If the hypothesis of the church not having the radical power to dissolve the bond is accepted, it is easy to explain a steady and uniform practice in more recent times (the second millennium) but it becomes hard to explain a number of other facts, such as:

— the church can dispense from a sacramental marriage; why and how does consummation take away the church's power;

— there were concessions given to innocent persons, especially in the first millennium;

— the Eastern church developed a different understanding and practice, yet, overall the church of Rome exercised much prudence and great restraint in judging them; while in other matters the Latins were inclined to attack the "Greeks," in this matter by and large they were more cautious, even when they kept urging their own point of view;

— the Council of Trent acknowledged that there were different opinions among the ancient Fathers, and among contemporary Catholic doctors; so the Council exercised extreme care to avoid condemning them, and also to avoid condemning the "Greeks."

If the hypothesis of the church having the radical power to dissolve the bond is accepted, all these facts are easily explained. Through a historical process, the church has formed the prudential judgment that for the sake of the common good, no dispensation from the bond of a sacramental and consummated marriage must be given. To this day, the church stands by this judgment.

In this hypothesis, the church appears as indeed the intelligent and free agent of Christ, solicitous to uphold in the best way the stability of marriages. If ever in history prudence would dictate a different judgment, the light and strength of the Spirit will be there again to guide the church.

Question 9: Can a marriage heal itself?

Why the question? Because it happens that the mutual commitment of the parties is quite imperfect in the beginning — even to the point that the marriage could be judged invalid — but later on, as time goes by, they find each other in love and become united with marital affection in the fullest sense of the term.

Now, it is not unusual in our imperfect world that an enterprise should begin in an imperfect way but eventually it should mature into something that is thoroughly good. Presumably marriage should not be an exception. After a shaky start, through sufferings and reflections, the spouses may come to a perfection of married life. Since such things do happen, the question arises, if in this process of purification the marriage can heal itself, so that the sacrament that was not there in the beginning is there at the end.

The answer is that our canonical system does not have effective provisions for the recognition of such a natural process; a marriage cannot heal itself. If it can be proved that it was invalid at the moment of the exchange of promises, no matter what happens later, invalid it must remain until it is formally validated.[16]

This greatly simplifies the work of the tribunals, should a crisis develop later. They can ignore years of true marital affection and dedication; they can disregard the testimony of children concerning the union of their parents; by law they must judge the marriage according to the disposition of the parties on their wedding day, more precisely, at the moment of the exchange of their promises.

This approach is a deficiency in our laws, mainly because it goes so much against the ordinary course of nature and because it perpetuates a defect instead of letting it be healed.

The approach of the ancient Romans to marriage was different; if it could be shown that the parties lived together with obvious marital affection, there was marriage. The church did not question this understanding and practice for many centuries, just quietly accepted it. An existing union with publicly displayed marital affection generated the presumption of a valid marriage.[17]

The introduction of the compulsory canonical form has changed all that. The marriage contract, because it was a contract in the eyes of the canonists, became also a verbal contract, *stipulatio,* notwithstanding the fact that the authors kept repeating that it was a consensual contract. They were right — partially. Some elements of

---

[16]The parties can heal the marriage themselves when valid consent was not given by one or both provided that this deficiency cannot be proved in the external forum.

[17]There is the origin of the so-called "common law marriage," which was canon law marriage in the first place. That is, after the Reformation in England, on this particular point, canon law became the law of the land.

the consensual contract remained, but the validity of the transaction from then on had to be judged according to the state of things at the moment when the ritual words were pronounced.

We can hardly do anything more here than to record the unsatisfactory character of the law that does not allow a marriage to heal itself from the inside. Even if God is ready to give his healing grace and bring the couple to the maturity of the sacrament, we must stand by the initial invalidity.

To remedy the situation would be relatively easy: if a defective consent in the beginning was followed by obvious public display of marital affection, the marriage should be considered healed and canonically valid.[18]

Question 10: How is the law of consent likely to develop in the future?

Why the question? Because the law of consent kept developing ever since the Middle Ages, and as recently as with the publication of the new Code underwent an extensive revision. There is no reason to think that this process has come to an end. Quite the contrary: our current problems indicate the need for further progress.

As it is, the canons on consent display a somewhat uneasy compromise between upholding traditional scholastic categories and opening the door to modern psychology; also, between highly abstract philosophical distinctions and the concrete demands of life.

(1) The law does not present a unified understanding of what "defect of consent" means; it works with the fragmentary approach of "grounds of nullity" which is akin to the ancient "forms of action." While this approach has the advantage of offering well defined practical categories to the courts, it also hampers the devel-

---

[18]It could be objected that if we admitted that a marriage could heal itself, a great deal of legal uncertainty would result. On the one hand, there would be evidence of its initial invalidity, on the other hand, no obvious evidence of its healing.

The answer is that the question would come up only in the case of a nullity suit. Then, the courts would have to raise one additional question: have the spouses lived together with marital affection? If so, the presumption is that the marriage was healed.

There is a value in legal clarity and certainty; there is an even greater value in granting healing to those who need it even if it can confuse our books.

opment of jurisprudence since it refuses to move any further in the process of legal abstraction.[19] Canon 1095, however, has gone a long way to change the situation; the grounds it presents are so broad that several particularized ones are likely to be absorbed under its general headings.

(2) Thus the tribunals will play a more important role in the future in determining the requirement for true consent. This may well be good for particular regions since the local expectations concerning married life can be taken into account, but inevitably it will obscure the general expectations of the law. For the careful observer it is already clear that in some regions the tribunals tend to set very high standards for a legally effective consent (with the result that a larger number of marriages are found null and void); in other regions they seem to be satisfied with rather minimal requirements (with the result that only a few marriages are declared invalid). Such development is not necessarily wrong; after all the human reality of marriage may vary, but in one way or another it is a source of problems. For instance, just what standards should the Roman Rota use?

(3) The crux of the consent issue is in the intentionality required for the reception of the sacraments in general, and of the sacrament of marriage in particular. Rigorous comparative studies would be needed, e.g. what is the difference between the intention required for ordination and the one required for marriage? Both sacraments, each in its own way, consecrates a person for a state of life and brings with it heavy responsibilities.

As an answer to our main question this much can be said: the law of consent, being a fusion of old and new, exhibits built-in tensions. Such tensions are likely to lead to new developments, first, through

---

[19]The movement away from the "forms of action" toward judging cases on the basis of general principles is a fairly common phenomenon in legal history. Progress consists in abstracting common guidelines from the multiplicity of the individual forms. As this happens the law becomes less rigid and able to handle new problems. The Romans virtually completed this unifying process in the law of delicts as they moved away from the ancient categories of their civil law and subsumed nearly all wrong doing under the heading of *being at fault, culpa*. A similar process has taken place in common law through the abolition of the forms of action, even if in practice they continue to influence the law.

A similar movement concerning the "grounds of nullity" can be observed in canon law but we are still far from its completion.

jurisprudence, then by statutory legislation. Both judicial prece-
dents and the new Code show the trend: away from the abstract
theories and subtle distinctions inherited from the Middle Ages and
toward the best insights of modern cognitional theories and psychological discoveries. The forces of life are shaping the law.[20]

Question 11: Should the law continue to impose the canonical form for validity?

The introduction of the canonical form by the Council of Trent was
a disciplinary measure and a most unusual one: on marriage alone,
among all the sacraments, a "canonical form" as distinct from, and
additional to, its "theological form" was imposed. After some four
hundred years, it is legitimate to raise the question whether or not
the church should stay with the discipline of Trent (a good deal of
which has been abrogated by Vatican Council II) or should continue with it in this particular matter.

The gist of the question is whether the public ceremony should be
a matter for pastoral care, as it was until the sixteenth century, or
should be a matter for strict legislation as it has become after the
Council of Trent.

Perhaps the fairest way of presenting the problem is to set forth
both sides of the issue, listing the advantages and disadvantages that
would flow from a return to the pre-Tridentine law.

It seems that many *advantages* would flow from the abolition of
the compulsory canonical form:

(1) the validity of the matrimonial covenant would cease to
depend on a technical formality;

(2) canon law would uphold the obligations born from a true
although informal covenant;

---

[20]It took several centuries for the law of consent to develop in the Middle Ages.
In our age, new elements that originated in fresh insights are trying to find their way
into an old but cohesive and logical system. It is understandable that there is a fair
amount of resistance in the system itself, and that the process of assimilation is
slow. In ancient Rome, it took a long time for the equitable system of law,
introduced by the *praetor peregrinus*, to penetrate into the traditional civil law and
to replace its formalities with the new law's humanity.

The simple point that we are trying to make through these examples is that legal
development has always been a slow process.

(3) the validity of a marriage would not depend strictly on the momentary disposition of the parties at the time of the exchange of the promises;

(4) the validity of a marriage would be judged much more on the basis of true facts; that is, whether or not the couple have come together and are living together with marital affection;

(5) those who have not married in the church would not feel themselves to be cut off from the church; nor would the community regard them as such;

(6) the same rule would apply to Catholic and non-Catholic Christians; that is, to all potentially sacramental marriages.

The abolition of the canonical form, however, would not be without *disadvantages:*

(1) if the couple did not wish an ecclesiastical ceremony, the church would have less opportunity for pastoral contact before the marriage and no possibility to investigate if the conditions for a Christian marriage are there;

(2) the church would have no official records of all the Catholic marriages; only of those which were celebrated before ecclesiastically designated witnesses;

(3) there would be widely spread uncertainty about the validity of the marriages of those Catholics who have not opted for a religious ceremony in the Catholic Church.

On the basis of these arguments, it is difficult to say which solution should prevail. The trend seems to be to retain the form but with some modifications. In the new Code, the severity of the Tridentine law has been tempered; it is possible now to obtain a dispensation from the canonical form in the case of a mixed marriage; and if the mixed marriage is between a Catholic of Latin rite and a non-Catholic of Eastern rite the promises exchanged before a sacred minister of the Eastern rite, are recognized as valid.

A further prudent step may well be in finding a canonical way of recognizing the marriages of baptized unbelievers (as we formally accept the marriages of unbaptized persons) as valid unions, without trying to compel them to go through the canonical form.

We have to recognize, too, that the main (virtually exclusive) motive of the Council of Trent in introducing the canonical form for validity was to put an end to clandestine marriages, which problem does not exist, certainly not to the same extent, today since there is everywhere compulsory civil registration of marriages. If tne canonical form is retained, it must be for other reasons.

A prudent answer to our disputed question could be formulated in this way: there are strong arguments for further relaxations of the law of the canonical form. Whether or not such a process of relaxation should lead to the law's eventual abolition, could well remain a disputed question; not all the evidence is in as yet.[21]

Question 12: Is the tribunal system satisfactory?

The tribunals are fulfilling an important balancing role in the legal life of the church. Their task is to uphold the demands of the common good and at the same time protect the rights of individual persons. Also, in the cases that come before them, they must reconcile the abstract and impersonal norms of the law with the concrete and personal situation of those involved. No mean task.

Understandably, there has been a great deal of discussion among canon lawyers on the issue of tribunals. To situate the problem, however, we must keep in mind that our ordinary diocesan courts have become marriage tribunals pure and simple. In theory they are general courts of justice; in practice, apart from rare exceptions, they are highly specialized institutions to handle marriage cases.

---

[21]One of the principles governing the drafting of the new Code was: "Pastoral care should be the hallmark of the Code" (cf. COM-USA, p. 6).

Could some future revisors of the law go even further and say: "Whatever can be reasonably provided by pastoral care, should not be the object of canonical legislation" — adding perhaps "We want this in fidelity to Paul who warned us against the danger of laws bringing sin into the life of the community."?

There is no doubt that in the course of Christian history many practices that originated in a generous spirit and for a long time were objects of pastoral care, have been transferred into the field of law and then their non-observance or even different observance bacame an occasion for new sins; the law indeed did create sins; the laws of fasting and abstinence were typical examples.

There is no good theological, or for that matter, canonical, reason why such practices should not be returned to where they belong: the generous offerings of the Christian people — supported by pastoral care but not made by law into an issue of sin and damnation. The question is: should the ecclesiastical ceremony be a matter of Christian practice supported by pastoral care — without inflicting the sanction of invalidity, sin and the threat ef eternal damnation on those who do not obey, or should it be a matter for legislation?

Most of them may never see another one. Our disputed question is not about the administration of justice in general but about the "marriage tribunals" in particular.

Typical arguments against the present system:

(1) Historically, their procedure was conceived for circumstances different from ours. The procedure for judging the validity of marriages was created in times when in many countries no civil divorce was possible and ecclesiastical annulment was the only way of terminating a marriage and opening the way for another one. Naturally, the church had to protect itself against deceptions, pressures and other abuses. Thus, it created a procedural system that was strict and strong enough to protect the dignity of marriages and of the tribunals as well.

The circumstances, however, changed radically. In most countries a civil divorce is easily available and those who approach the church do so "for conscience's sake": they want peace with God. It follows that the response of the church to their request should be at least as much pastoral as it is judicial. They should be granted the presumption of good faith and their case should be handled through a relatively simple procedure that not only judges a case but has also the capacity to heal the persons.

(2) Experience shows that no matter how uniform the laws may be the operation of the tribunals remains uneven. In one place immense delays may occur and the cases are judged with extreme severity. In another place there is speed and declarations of nullity are granted with some generosity. In other terms, the way our tribunals operate raises serious questions about equal justice for all the faithful.

(3) For a tribunal to function efficiently, there must be well trained judges, a supporting staff and a sufficient outlay in money, which may mean that a great deal of energy must be siphoned away from other works in the diocese. This can lead to a lack of balance in pastoral care: too many are working for the welfare of a few. Or, if the tribunal is not well provided for, cases are accepted reluctantly, judgments are given with long delays, and individuals suffer.

Arguments for the present system:

(1) The procedure has for its purpose the protection of the institution of marriage; its primary end is the common good and not the private good of an individual. The parties to the case are interested parties; for the sake of truth a tightly woven procedural system remains necessary; otherwise there is no way of preserving objectivity and legal stability.

(2) Tribunals are important instruments in developing the law; as a matter of fact their jurisprudence pioneered many advances that have been incorporated into the new Code, for instance in the matter of matrimonial consent. They ought to continue this work.

(3) Pastoral help should certainly be given to the parties, and the tribunals should listen to them with understanding and compassion. But the requirements for forming an objective and detached judgment about the marriage are different from the approaches that dedicated pastoral care demands.

Some clarifications are necessary before any evaluation:

(1) In evaluating the role and function of the tribunals we are not dealing with an issue of belief but with a matter for prudential judgment. Hence, free debate is legitimate.

(2) Precisely because the issue is a prudential one, it cannot be decided on the basis of abstract principles; concrete historical circumstances and experiental facts must be taken into consideration. The question cannot be what is the best in all circumstances but what is most helpful at this point of history, taking into account the actually available resources of the church.

(3) No human tribunal can pronounce infallibly about the existence of the sacrament of matrimony; that is known to God alone. All that a tribunal can do is to formulate a fallible human judgment on the strength and extent of the evidence: whether or not it can support a declaration of nullity, *constat de nullitate*. In other words, no tribunal can judge the validity of a marriage; it can pronounce only on the nature of the available evidence.

(4) The judgment of the court is valid and binding in the external forum only. If the parties know that the true state of facts is

different, they must follow their own conscience.[22] In most cases, however, the parties can rely safely on the judgment of the court in forming their own conscience. Thus, besides protecting the institution of marriage, the tribunals help the persons involved to form their own consciences.

(5) In the practical order the import of the judgment of the tribunal is in permitting a second marriage with full participation in the eucharist.

(6) Finally, the issue whether or not the church has the radical power to dissolve consummated sacramental marriages has nothing to do with the disputed question of the tribunal system: even if the church has such power it can still decide for prudence's sake that no dispensation from the bond will be given, but no invalid agreement will be enforced either.

After these clarifications, let us return to our disputed question: is the tribunal system satisfactory?

(1) It does contain unsatisfactory elements. If favors heavily, even in its revised form in the new Code, the institution over the individual. It has carefully built in devices to protect the marriage that may be valid; it has no parallel provisions for protecting the individual person who may have the right to marry. Thus, if the tribunal is efficient, all may go well, but if not, the right of the person to obtain justice *within reasonable time* is jeopardized, which in the practical

---

[22]In traditional moral theology these cases are known as *casus perplexus*, not improperly rendered by "insoluble cases"; e.g. when a person knows that his marriage was valid although the court judged it invalid, he can marry according to the law but this will not help him before God. Vice versa: if a person knows that her marriage was invalid but the court refuses to grant a declaration of nullity for lack of sufficient proofs, she is free to marry before God but not according to the law. Such cases, which do occur, prove that no legal system can provide for all honest needs of the community; law by its nature is limited. Justice, however, postulates that there should be ways and means to help those persons who find themselves in such perplexing situations. Aristotle's remedy was in the application of *epieikeia*, the Romans invoked *equitas*, and the Eastern church to this day recurs to *oikonomia*. (For the explanation of these institutions *see* COM-USA, pp. 42-44.) In the Latin church such cases are handled in the internal forum.

order may well mean that the opportunity for a contemplated marriage is lost. As long as there are not easily available remedies in case of delays, the system cannot be satisfactory.

(2) Our procedures have been conceived for the Western world with long standing legal traditions and with easy access to courts. But in other regions where the communications are difficult, people are poor, there are few if any trained lawyers, or, where the government is constantly interfering with the church, it is virtually impossible to have an efficient tribunal system to follow canonical procedures. To the faithful who live in such regions (and there are many such regions), canon law offers little help.

(3) Whenever a case is brought before a tribunal, it is likely that the parties are in need of understanding, compassion and guidance, perhaps more than ever before in their lives. They come to the church as the people of Galilee came to Jesus, for healing. So there is an opportunity to proclaim to them the saving power of God. In reality, they are often given something else. They are exposed to a procedure that originated in adversary litigation and was not designed to heal their wounds. They are subjected to rigid formalities that can be correct judicially but otherwise bring no help to them. (Of course, there are many tribunals where the judges and others do their utmost to help their petitioners; but here we are concerned with the structures, norms and rules.)

By way of conclusion:

* Marriage tribunals have existed for such a long time (since the tenth century?) and are so deeply embedded in the canonical tradition of the church that to think of their abolition is unrealistic. Rarely did canon law develop by leaps and bounds.
* A more realistic approach would be to see how the tribunals can be gradually transformed even structurally into an instrument of pastoral care. As it is, the institution is still very legal in character; the only qualification the judges must possess is an academic degree in canon law. But there is much more to a marriage case than the norms of the Code. Perhaps the church should think of special schools where future judges could get an all-round training, with less law and more hman sciences. The art of forming a legal judgment, *ius dicere*, is not the art of healing. It is interesting that in

recent years there has been a great deal of discussion whether or not *jurisdiction* is required to judge a marriage case; there has not been much discussion whether or not the capacity to heal is necessary.

A note on a connected issue: Often enough one hears the question whether or not the Catholic church should make use of the institution of *oikonomia* in handling marriage cases. *Oikonomia* in the Eastern tradition means a radical power in the church, entrusted to the episcopate, to heal an otherwise hopeless situation. To use *oikonomia* would mean not to pronounce on the initial validity or invalidity of a marriage but to acknowledge that in the case of a marriage through human failure the divine plan has not been fulfilled and, if necessary, after appropriate remedies, such as the imposition of a serious penance, to give the opportunity for a new beginning. To equate this deeply religious approach with civil divorce and remarriage would be unfair and unjust to the Eastern church.

The question may not be mature for an answer in the Latin church; nor is it really a question about marriage. It concerns the nature of the power of the church, given by Christ and sustained by the Spirit. Vatican Council II made extraordinary strides in understanding and explaining this power, for instance as it is possessed by the episcopal college. There is no reason to think that there will not be further developments, through an ecumenical council or even outside of it. The wise Christian attitude is to wait and keep our lights burning.

Question 13: Could persons living in irregular marriages be admitted into eucharistic communion?

The terms of the question should be clarified. Clearly, we are speaking of Catholics, otherwise in communion with the church. A marriage could be irregular for several reasons; the point here being that it cannot be rectified in canon law, in most cases, because there has been a previous marriage that remains valid. Eucharistic communion here means the reception of the eucharist, which is the fullness of communion in the Christian church.

It seems not, *videtur quod non:* The International Theological Commission summed up the arguments against it in their Statement on Marriage, 1977:

The incompatibility of the state of remarried divorced persons with the precept and mystery of the paschal love of the Lord makes it impossible for these people to receive the sign of unity with Christ in the Eucharist. Access to eucharistic communion can only come through penance, which implies detestation of the sin committed and the firm purpose of not sinning again. (5.2; *see* in CPM, p. 32)

This seemingly severe position, however, is further qualified in the same statement:

They are not dispensed from the numerous obligations stemming from baptism, especially the duty of providing for the Christian education of their children. The paths of Christian prayer, both public and private, penance, and certain apostolic activities remain open to them. (5.4; CPM, p. 32)

John Paul II in his Apostolic Exhortation *Familiaris consortio* upheld the prohibition:

... the church insists on the custom, rooted in the very Sacred Scriptures, not to admit to the eucharistic communion those faithful who after divorce entered into a new marriage. In fact, they impede themselves, because their state and their condition of life are objectively opposed to that union of love between Christ and the church that is signified and made present by the eucharist. There is also a particular pastoral reason: if such persons were admitted to the eucharist, the faithful would be misled and confused about the doctrine of the church concerning the indissolubility of marriage. (84; AAS 74 (1982) pp. 185-186)

He, too, however, qualified his statement:

Together with the Synod we strongly exhort the pastors and the whole community of the faithful to help those who failed through divorce; to be careful with solicitous charity not to regard them as separated from the church because they [*the divorced*] can, even must, as baptized participate in its life. Moreover, they should be exhorted to hear the Word of God, to be present at the sacrifice of the mass, to persevere in prayer, to help the charitable works and the undertakings of the community for justice, to instruct their children in the Christian faith, to cultivate the spirit and the works of penance, to implore thus the grace of God every day. (*Ibid.*, p. 185)

The two documents are clearly not on the same level; one is a statement issued by a group of theologians with no formal authority, the other is an apostolic exhortation by the pope who has authority. The form he has chosen for his document has its own theological significance: it is an exhortation. There is no doubt, however, that the position taken by the commission and the pope are virtually identical.

From a theological point of view both see the divorced and remarried as constituting a special group in the church, with their own rather well defined status. They are not separated; therefore they are in communion. Their communion appears as full, except for the actual reception of the eucharist, although they are entitled to be present at its celebration. They are bound by their baptismal promises, and they are exhorted to share in the prayer life and the charitable works of the community.

This status of the divorced and remarried appears new and unusual. It would be difficult to find a precedent for a group of faithful to be invited to participate in the devotional, charitable, even apostolic life of the church and at the same time to be barred from the reception of the eucharist because they are public sinners. Further, ordinarily we assume that the gift of life received at baptism must be nourished by the eucharist; now this group of persons is called to lead a full Christian life in every way, but without the strength that normally is given through the eucharist.

Further, again and again it is hinted that, once repentant, the grace of God may be with such persons. If that is true, they can hardly be stubborn sinners who do not want to mend their ways.

Clearly, the two documents testify that the church is moving away from a severe and rigid stance, judging the divorced and remarried as public sinners, and is moving toward appreciating them, provided they are of contrite heart, as recipients of God's grace. The very content of the documents indicates that we are in the midst of a development that has not reached its final goal yet. The status of such a couple, participating in everything in the life of the community, except in the reception of the eucharist, appears so anomalous that one wonders if it could be sustained for any length of time, without causing serious tensions to both the persons involved and the community.

A seemingly obvious advice to remedy this situation is sometimes given: the couple should separate, and then they will be able to receive the eucharist.

In some cases, however, a genuine conflict-of-duties situation may have developed. From the second marriage children may have been born; children who have a natural right to be educated, not just in the abstract, but in a warm and loving home. Such education cannot be accomplished without the loving union of the parents. There is just too much evidence to show what happens to children of broken homes. So, the parents may have a duty to stay together for the sake of the children.

An answer to this problem can also be found in manuals of moral theology and canon law: the parents should commit themselves to live as brother and sister. A thoughtful psychologist, however, is likely to find fault with this answer; he will point out that the truth is different: they are not brother and sister, and nature does not tolerate false pretenses. The natural dynamics, physical and psychological, between a brother and sister are unique and different from any other relationship between a man and a woman.

The authors who advocate this solution are simply using a euphemism to say that couple should commit themselves not to have sexual relations. But then logically, if they are not married, they should not be allowed to enjoy any *consortium* either; after all consortium and procreation together are the specific ends of marriage, and of marriage only. How could a couple be allowed to have one part of true marriage, the *consortium*, but not the other, the procreation? After all, we are consistently told that sexual union should be an expression of a deeper spiritual union. There seems to be a built-in logical inconsistency in the so-called brother-and-sister solution, apart from all the problems that it may cause psychologically to those involved.

There are therefore arguments to the contrary, sed contra est:

Weighing the complex problems involved, a significant number of scholars reached the conclusion that there are circumstances in which divorced and remarried persons could and should be admitted to the eucharist. Although such writings appeared in many countries, the arguments and conditions were perhaps most carefully presented by a number of German theologians, especially by

Walter Kasper (University of Tübingen), Franz Böckle (University of Bonn), and Joseph Ratzinger (*then,* University of Regensburg). Their positions are virtually identical; none of them advocates a wholesale pardon, all of them plead for granting communion to individual couples provided that they are of contrite heart. Böckle states this succinctly in the form of a thesis:

> The eucharistic communion must not and should not be denied to those who, after having lived in a marriage that legally and sacramentally appears valid, divorced, and now live in a second marital union, provided they have repented of their fault and in a spirit of faith they proved themselves and are doing what they can by way of reparation.[23]

Ratzinger describes the conditions, and does it in the context of ancient traditions:

> The demand that a second marriage must prove itself over a longer period as the source of [*container of*] genuine moral values, and that it must be lived in the spirit of faith, corresponds factually to that type of indulgence [*leniency*] that can be found in Basil's teaching; there it is stated that after a longer penance, communion can be given to a *digamus* (= to someone living in a second marriage), without the suspension of the second marriage; this in confidence in God's mercy who does not leave penance without an answer. Whenever in a second marriage moral obligations have arisen toward the children, toward the family and toward the woman, and no similar obligations from the first marriage exist; whenever also the giving up of the second marriage is not permissible [*not fitting*] on moral grounds, and continence does not appear as a real possibility in the practical order (*magnorum est,* says Gregory II [*that is, it is beyond the ordinary strength of the parties*]); it seems that the granting of full communion, after a time of probation, is nothing less than just, and is fully in harmony with our ecclesiastical traditions. The concession of communion in such a case cannot depend on an act that would be either immoral or factually impossible.[24]

The same conditions can be put more systematically:

(1) the previous marriage cannot be retrieved any more;

[23]Franz Böckle, "Die gescheiterte Ehe," in *Ehe und Ehescheidung* (München: Kösel, 1972), p. 130.
[24]Joseph Ratzinger, "Zur Frage nach der Unauflösigkeit der Ehe," in *Ehe und Ehescheidung* (München: Kösel, 1972), p. 55.

(2) the present invalid union produced and supports important human values which would be destroyed by separation;

(3) the couple has repented and shown visible signs of "conversion" for a fairly long time;

(4) perpetual abstinence is not a practical possibility;

(5) the couple has shown willingness to participate in the life of the Christian community; to which one more condition should be added:

(6) the community is properly instructed to receive the couple without being unduly disturbed or confused about the evangelical precept of life-long fidelity.

So much for the stance of these theologians. But how do they support their proposal?

All of them state that what they propose in no way conflicts with the doctrine of indissolubility. On that point they stand firm. Rather, they all make an appeal to a radical power in the church that can go beyond the ordinary rules and can provide forgiveness and healing when most needed. Kasper puts it in this way:

> A broken marriage is not simply canceled out. It continues to exist, even though it can be compared with a ruin. It is therefore not possible to replace it with a second marriage equal to the first. What is possible, however, and in many cases necessary for survival, is some kind of emergency accommodation. This image would seem to be in accordance with the way in which God acts in the history of human salvation. He often writes straight on crooked lines.[25]

Ratzinger is more mindful to put his proposed solution into the context of our traditions:

> The anathema [of the Council of Trent] against a teaching that claims that foundational structures [forms] in the church are erroneous or that they are only reformable customs remains binding with its full strength. Marriage is a sacrament; it consists of an unbreakable structure, created by a firm decision. But this should not exclude the grant of ecclesial communion to those persons who acknowledge this teaching as a principle of life but find themselves in an emergency situation of a specific kind, in which they have a particular need to be in communion with the body of the Lord.[26]

---

[25] Walter Kasper, *Theology of Christian Marriage* (New York: Seabury, 1980), pp. 67-68.

[26] Joseph Ratzinger, *ibid.*, pp. 55-56.

These approaches are very close to the Eastern practice of *oiko-nomia*, a mysterious and undefinable power given by Christ to his church, which empowers it to heal and redress a situation that cannot be helped in any other way.

An Eastern theologian would prefer to rest the issue there and not to inquire any further. The Western mind, however, being much more analytically inclined, will want to know the nature of the second union: is it a marriage? Could it be a sacramental marriage?

There is no way of answering such questions with precision in our present state of knowledge; nor is it necessary to answer them before action can be taken. Many times in history the church has taken positions relying on its own grace-filled instinct; the explanations arrived later, sometimes centuries later. This is a sound enough position.[27]

---

[27]Nonetheless, a search for some explanation can be attempted, perhaps by simply raising a few questions.

Is it conceivable that after human sinfulness destroyed a union destined to be permanent in the plan of God, the church can accept the fact of failure (as God has accepted the Fall) and out of the power given to it by Christ, authorize a new beginning? (Tibor Horvath, a Canadian theologian, holds this view, noting that before the second union can be allowed, serious penance must be done; *see* Horvath in Bibliography.)

Is it conceivable that after the first marriage became irretrievably lost, its capacity to be a sign of the union of Christ to his church is lost as well? Ordinarily a sign must operate in the concrete order, it must be real and not nominal; it must be addressed to a determined public, which should be able to read it. But a lost marriage speaks to no one, the union is purely nominal and so is the sign; no one can read its meaning. (Horvath draws a comparison between the eucharist and marriage: if the eucharistic symbols, the bread and the wine, are destroyed, there is no eucharist anymore; if there is no unity between the man and woman, the sign is destroyed, therefore, there cannot be any marriage either.)

Is it conceivable that after a consummated sacramental marriage has been destroyed a non-sacramental marriage could come into existence? (There have been speculations in earlier times that when the nuptial blessing was not given, as in the case of a second marriage after the death of the first partner, the second marriage was natural and not sacramental (*see* our Historical Introduction).

Such questions are, of course, not affirmations, no less than the questions of Thomas Aquinas above each chapter of his *Summa* are affirmations. The mark of good research is that in the beginning it abounds in questions, until gradually the bad ones are discarded and the few that remain lead to the right answers. But how can a question be proved bad, unless it is raised and examined?!

SELECTED AND ANNOTATED BIBLIOGRAPHY

The purpose of this bibliography is manifold: besides listing the principal sources of the law and some useful reference books, it wants to acquaint the reader with a selection of books and articles on the historical development of the doctrine and law of the sacrament of matrimony; as well as with the contemporary literature on the theology and canon law of marriage.

Consequently, our list of books is selective, not comprehensive. In historical works we looked, as an ideal, for good documentations, in exegetical and reflective works for original insights as well as for well reasoned conclusions, in others, at least, for a certain abundance of information. On disputed issues we did our best to find authors who represent different points of view.

As a rule, we did not list well known encyclopedias, dictionaries, manuals and journals which can be easily found in specialized libraries.

Sources of the Law

Friedberg, Aemilius, ed. *Corpus Iuris Canonici,* 2 vls, reprint of the 1879 original ed. Graz: Akademische Druck- u. Verlagsanstalt, 1959.

> The source book for canon law before the first Code. *The first volume* is the *Decree of Gratian,* a systematic and critical collection (about 1140) of legally important documents; it has never become the official law of the church but enjoyed great authority for its intrinsic value; *the second volume* contains five

compilations (1234-1503) of decretal letters (mostly decisions given in individual cases) and other documents issued by the popes ; they have become official sources of the law.

Codex Iuris Canonici. Pii X Pontificis Maximi iussu digestus Benedicti Papae XV auctoritate promulgatus. Roma: Typis Vaticanis, 1917.

> The first Code of Canon Law ever; a milestone in the history of the church. The complete edition contains references to sources and an analytical index.

Codex Iuris Canonici. Auctoritate Ioannis Pauli Pp. II promulgatus. Vatican City: Libreria Editrice Vaticana, 1983.

> The second Code of Canon Law. It ought to be read with the official corrections published in the AAS 75 (1983) pp. 321-324. Eventually a new edition with an index and with references to sources is expected.

Code of Canon Law: Latin-English Edition. Washington, DC: CLSA, 1983.

> Translation prepared under the auspices of the *Canon Law Society of America* and approved by the National Conference of Catholic Bishops of the USA. The approval does not confer authenticity on the translation; the Latin text remains the official text.

The Code of Canon Law in English Translation. London: Collins, 1983.

> Translation prepared by *The Canon Law Society of Great Britain and Ireland* in association with *The Canon Law Society of Australia and New Zealand* and *The Canadian Canon Law Society*, approved by the Episcopal Conferences of Australia, Canada, England and Wales, India, Ireland, New Zealand, Scotland and Southern Africa. Again, the episcopal approvals do not confer authenticity on the translation.

Reference Works

Abbot, Walter M. *The Documents of Vatican II.* New York, Herder and Herder, 1966.

> The most widely used English translation of the documents of Vatican Council II.

Alberigo, Joseph, and Others, eds. *Conciliorum Oecumenicorum Decreta*, 3d ed. Bologna: Istituto per le Scienze Religiose, 1973.

> A complete collection of the decisions of the twenty-one ecumenical councils, from Nicea to Vatican II, in Greek and Latin. Extensive indices.

Bauer, Walter. *A Greek-English Lexicon of the New Testament.* Chicago: University of Chicago, 1968.

> A widely recognized dictionary, first published in German in 1937; translated into, and adapted to, the English language.

Bouscaren, T. Lincoln, ed. vols. 1-3;
Bouscaren, T. Lincoln, and O'Connor, James I., eds. vols. 4-6;
O'Connor, James I., ed. vols. 7-9. *The Canon Law Digest*, 9 vols. to date. Vols. 1-6: Milwaukee: Bruce, 1934, 1943, 1954, 1958, 1963, 1969; vols. 7-9: Chicago: CLD, 1975, 1978, 1983.

> A collection, in English translation, of legally important documents, published after the promulgation of CIC/17. It is judiciously selective, not comprehensive. It contains also a number of private replies communicated to the editors by the recipients.

Denzinger, Henricus, and Schönmetzer, Adolfus, eds. *Enchiridion Symbolorum*, 34th rev. ed. Freiburg im Breisgau: Herder, 1967.

> The indispensable reference book of documents concerning doctrine. Vast historical knowledge is required to reconstruct correctly the authority and meaning of each document.

Glare, P.G.W., ed. *Oxford Latin Dictionary.* Oxford: Clarendon Press, 1985.

The best and the most up to date Latin-English dictionary. The explanations are so comprehensive and the quotes from ancient literature so numerous that many entries have become detailed outlines of a study on the meaning of a word. It includes legal terms used in antiquity up to and including Justinians's Digest; it does not include special words and expressions used by Christian writers.

Gordon, Ignatius, and Grocholewski, Zenon, eds. *Documenta recentiora circa rem matrimonialem et processualem.* Roma: Universitas Gregoriana, 1977.
Grocholewski, Zenon, ed. *Documenta recentiora circa rem matrimonialem et processualem.* Roma: Universitas Gregoriana, 1980.

These two volumes contain a collection of documents, published or promulgated mostly by the Holy See concerning marriage and procedures to be followed in marriage cases. They cover the period between the end of Vatican Council II and the year 1979. Each group of documents is preceded by a historical introduction and followed by references to subsequent commentaries.

Index to the Code of Canon Law in English Translation. Prepared by the Canon Law Society of Great Britain and Ireland. London: Collins, 1984.

A companion volume to *The Code of Canon Law in English Translation.*

Ochoa, Xaverius. *Index verborum ac locutionum Codicis Iuris Canonici,* 2d ed. Roma: Libreria Editrice Lateranense, 1984.

A concordance of CIC/83 on the pattern used in biblical concordances. Apart from minor particles, every word is listed in its context; the average length of a quote being 5 or 6 words. There is no better *index* available; an indispensable tool for researchers.

Ochoa, Xaverius. *Leges Ecclesiae post Codicem Iuris Canonici editae,* 5 vols to date. Roma: Commentarium pro Religiosis, 1966, 1969, 1972, 1974, 1980.

The most complete collection of official Roman documents (of varying degrees of authority); each in its original language (mostly Latin, of course). Besides the ordinary references to sources, the editor provides references to commentaries in the periodical literature; also indices of various types. The five volumes published to date, *in folio*, contain some eight thousand columns (two per page). A monumental enterprise; to be continued.

Schlick, Jean, and Zimmermann, Marie, eds. *Marriage and Divorce: International Bibliography*, 1978-1980, RIC Supplement 57-58. Strasbourg: CERDIC, 1980.

> CERDIC is the acronym for the *Centre de Recherches et Documentation des Institutions Chrétiennes* (University of Strasbourg); well known for its research concerning ecclesiastical institutions, canon law and ecumenical issues. Its published bibliographies have become indispensable tools.

Zimmermann, Marie. *Marriage and Code of Canon Law: International Documentation*, 1975-1983. Strasbourg: CERDIC, 1983.

> A list of publications, books and articles, canon by canon (CIC/83). Especially important for the preparatory period of the new Code. It includes also a concordance of CIC/17, SCH/75, 80, REL 82, and CIC/83.

Commentaries on CIC/17

Cappello, Felix. *De matrimonio*, 7th rev. ed. Torino: Marietti, 1961.

> A systematic exposition of the law of CIC/17 with vast erudition; it is one of the most widely used reference works. The author's approach to the law is neither original nor critical but virtually no issue escapes his attention.

Gasparri, Petrus. *Tractatus canonicus de matrimonio*, 2 vols., new ed. Civitas Vaticana: Typis Vaticanis, 1932.

> One of the most important commentaries on CIC/1917 by the person who was its main architect. Gasparri had many of the gifts of the great classical Roman lawyers; especially balance in

> judgment and clarity in exposition. This work contains also plentiful information about the transition from the law of the Decretals of that of the first Code.

Wernz, Franciscus X., and Vidal, Petrus. *Ius canonicum: De matrimonio*, 3d ed. Roma: Universitas Gregoriana, 1946.

> Wernz was one of the best commentators of the law of Decretals. Vidal revised his works after the promulgation of CIC/17.

Commentaries on CIC/83

Aznar Gil, Frederico R. *El Nuevo Derecho Matrimonial Canonico*. Salamanca: Universidad Pontificia de Salamanca, 1983.

> The approach of the author is strictly juridical, very detailed, tending to casuistry. The law appears as absolute, having no theological roots. There is no critical evaluation of the canons. He gives extensive lists of books and articles before every chapter without any annotations or evaluations.

Coriden, James; Green, Thomas; and Heintschel, Donald, eds. *The Code of Canon Law: A Text and Commentary* Mahwah, NJ: Paulist Press, 1985.

> A reference work by 23 contributors, intended for a wider public than specialists in canon law; commissioned by the Canon Law Society of America. The canons are given in English translation. The part on marriage is the work of Thomas P. Doyle, pp. 737-833.

de Echeverria, Lamberto, ed. *Codigo de Derecho Canonico*. Biblioteca de Autores Christianos, vol. 442. Madrid: Editorial Catolica, 1984.

> A cooperative work by six professors of the Pontifical University of Salamanca. The canons are given in Latin and in Spanish, the comments are in the footnotes, which on the

average take up the half of every page. They are written in a
concise encyclopedic style; problems are mentioned but rarely
discussed. Proportionally, marriage has received less than it
deserves; see pp. 502-565.

Heimerl, Hans, and Pree, Helmut. *Kirchenrecht: Allgemeine Normen und Eherecht*. Wien-New York: Springer, 1983.

> A well designed and organized textbook of canon law on the
> General Norms and Marriage, intended for the use of university
> students. The method of exposition is systematic; the text of the
> canons is not given. The authors are clearly aware of many
> problems but they do not wish to discuss them in an introductory manual.

Listle, Joseph; Müller, Hubert; and Schmitz, Heribert, eds. *Handbuch des katholischen Kirchenrechts*. Regensburg: Pustet, 1983.

> A systematic exposition of the content of CIC/83 in 117 small
> chapters by 46 contributors. The theological foundations of the
> law are stressed and briefly explained. On the whole, it is more a
> presentation of legal concepts and institutions than a commentary on the canons, of which the text is not given. Within its own
> genre, it is a fine work. Seven authors contributed to the chapter
> on "The Sacrament of Marriage," pp. 730-836.

Lombardia, Pedro, and Arrieta, Juan Ignacio, eds. *Codigo de Derecho Canonico*. Pamplona: Universidad de Navarra, 1983.

> This work is similar in method and style to the BAC commentary but overall of lesser quality both in its content and its·
> external outlay. It gives the canons in Latin and Spanish. The
> comments are in the footnotes. They tend to simplify issues;
> they do not display much doctrinal or historical awareness.

Lüdicke, Klaus, ed. *Münsterischer Kommentar zum Codex Iuris Canonici*. Essen: Ludgerus, 1984.

> This commentary is being published in parts, in loose-leaf
> form; all to be contained in a large binder. It gives the canons in
> Latin and German, the comments are well organized under each
> canon; they tend to be pragmatic and practical. The part on
> marriage is already available.

Paralieu, Roger. *Guide pratique du Code de droit canonique: Notes pastorales.* Bourges: Tardy, 1985.

> A very concise commentary with a strong practical and pastoral orientation "in the spirit of Vatican Council II." To date, it is the only comprehensive commentary in French; it is all too short on marriage, *see* pp. 315-338.

Pinto, Pio Vito, ed. *Commento al Codice di Diritto Canonico.* Roma: Università Urbaniana, 1985.

> The work of 29 commentators. It gives the canons in Latin and Italian. The comments are intended mainly for the "practitioners" of the law. The spirit of the contributions vary; some are narrowly legal, others include valuable theological insights. On marriage: pp. 617-680; the subject would have deserved a more extensive treatment.

Schwendenwein, Hugo. *Das neue Kirchenrecht: Gesamtdarstellung.* Graz: Styria, 1983.

> A concise presentation of the content of the canons in CIC/83, without giving their text but following closely their order in the Code.

Sebott, Reinhold. *Das neue kirchliche Eherecht.* Frankfurt am Main: Knecht, 1983.

> An introduction into the new law of marriage. It gives the canons in Latin and German, followed by concise explanations.

Zapp, Hartmut, and Mosiek, Ulrich. *Kanonisches Eherecht.* 6th rev. ed. Freiburg im Breisgau: Rombach, 1983.

> This is a widely used textbook in German speaking countries, clear and comprehensive. It remains within a strict juridical horizon, with little ambition to examine the canons critically. After every chapter there is an extensive but neither selective nor annotated bibliography.

Marriage in the Scriptures

de Vaux, Roland. *Ancient Israel*, vol. 1. New York: McGraw-Hill, 1965.

> Christian beliefs concerning marriage have their origins in the traditions of Israel. There is both continuity and contrast between the ancient laws of the Jews and the new laws of the Christians. de Vaux's book is a classic, a mine of information, without being overloaded with technical details. See especially the chapter on "Family Institutions," pp. 19-64.

Fitzmyer, Joseph A. "Matthean Divorce Texts." *Theological Studies*, 37 (1976), 197-226.

> Excellent, thorough, nuanced. It gives a good overview of the present state of the question. It is uniquely strong in exploring the Jewish background of the problem. The notes give ample bibliography for further study. The author holds that *porneia* refers to illicit marital unions within the degrees of kinship forbidden by the Mosaic laws.

Grelot, Pierre. *Man and Wife in Scripture*. New York: Herder and Herder, 1964.

> The author covers the Old and New Testaments, describes the evolution of ideas. He is familiar with relevant data coming from other religious beliefs. A good summary survey.

Langevin, Paul-Emile, ed. *Bibliographie biblique*; vol. I: 1930-1970 (Roman Catholic works); Vol. II: 1930-1975 (R.C. and non-R.C. works). Quebec: Université Laval, 1972, 1978.

> A virtually complete yet easily manageable bibliography of studies on the Bible. All titles, classifications, topics, indices, etc. are in five languages. There is a large number of entries under the heading *Marriage*.

Schlier, Heinrich. *Der Brief an die Epheser*, 7th ed. Düsseldorf: Patmos, 1971.

> The author of the Epistle to the Ephesians has left us the most penetrating reflections on the meaning of Christian marriage (5:21-6:9). Schlier, in his commentary, first published in 1957

and now in its seventh edition, gives us a lucid and thorough exegesis of the text, with that sensitivity to theological issues that is truly his own and exceptional even among biblical scholars. The passage quoted is explained in the chapter *Das Haus des Christen*, best translated perhaps as "The Christian Household" (pp. 250-288).

Marriage in Roman Law

Corbett, Percy Ellwood. *The Roman Law of Marriage*. Aalen: Scientia, 1979.

> Clear and comprehensive; nothing better is available in English on the law of marriage. A reprint of the original edition by Clarendon Press, Oxford, 1930.

Diosdi, György. *Contract in Roman Law: From the Twelve Tables to the Glossators*. Budapest: Akademia, 1981.

> A highly original work of legal history. It gives a good background for the understanding of marriage as "consensual contract."

Hallett, Judith P. *Fathers and Daughters in Roman Society: Women and the Elite Family*. Princeton, NJ: Princeton University, 1984.

> There is much more in this book about daughters than about fathers. It is a scholarly study of the position of women in Roman society. The author shows that their influence often was "formidable," well beyond what their legal position would suggest. This is a good book to read in order to realize how the Romans lived; it can balance the one sided information that comes from the study of their laws.

Robleda, Olis. *El matrimonio en Derecho Romano*. Roma: Università Gregoriana, 1970.

> A well documented systematic and historical study of the Roman law of marriage.

Historical Works

Barberena, Tomas Garcia, ed. *El Vinculo Matrimonial: Divorcio o indisolubilidad?* Madrid: BAC, 1978.

> A very comprehensive survey by eleven contributors of the issue of divorce and indissolubility in the Scriptures, Fathers, ancient and medieval legal texts, Councils of Trent and Vatican II. There is a long special chapter by Urbano Navarrete on the historical origins and development of the "privilege of the faith"-type dispensations; also, by Clemente Pujol, on divorce in the Orthodox Church. An altogether remarkable documentary. The historical inquiries however, were not carried out with sufficient awareness of their theological dimensions.

Berman, Harold J. *Law and Revolution: The Formation of the Western Legal Tradition.* Cambridge, MA: Harvard University Press, 1983.

> A book of admirable erudition and of penetrating historical insights. It has two parts, in the first, *The Papal Revolution and the Canon Law*, the author shows how much the Western legal tradition owes to medieval theologians and canonists; in the second, *The Formation of Secular Legal Systems*, he covers the birth and growth of different national systems in Europe. Some chapter headings in themselves speak of the exceptional and creative role that canon law played in the formation of the secular systems. e.g.: "The Origin of the Western Legal Tradition in the Papal Revolution" — the revolution in question being that of Gregory VII, which radically transformed the social fabric of the church and of the secular society. Or, "The Origin of Western Legal Science in the European Universities" the first university mentioned is that of Bologna. Then, "Canon Law: the First Modern Western Legal System"-first among the modern ones because there was in the church "something more than legality in the *Rechtsstaat* sense, something more akin to what the English later called "the rule of law." Food for thought. In such environment the structures of the medieval marriage laws were created.

Beumer, Johannes. *Die theologische Methode*, Handbuch der Dogmengeschichte, Band I. Freiburg: Herder, 1972.
Söll, Georg. *Dogma und Dogmenentwicklung*, Handbuch der Dogmengeschichte, Band I, Faszikel 6. Freiburg: Herder, 1971.

Neither of these books is on marriage, but they can help enormously to carry on the search toward understanding the mystery of Christian marriage.

In the same series, a specific volume is in preparation on the evolution of the doctrine concerning the sacrament of matrimony. Once published, we shall have a rich source of information that is likely to give a new impetus to theological reflections.

Boelens, Martin. *Die Klerikerehe in der Gesetzgebung der Kirche: Eine rechtsgeschichtliche Untersuchung.* Paderborn: Schöningh, 1968.

It would be difficult to doubt that the pessimistic theories about marriage and sexuality, especially as they were represented by Augustine, influenced the church's legislation concerning clerical celibacy. Therefore, the study of that legislation may be helpful to understand better the inspiration that guided the development of the doctrine and law of marriage.

Boelens's work, a study in legal history in the strict sense of the term, covers the period from the beginning of the Christian church to 1139. It is written in the style of an encyclopedia article; it is detailed and probably as comprehensive as any such study can be. He shows that the legislation imposing compulsory celibacy on the regular clergy was slow in developing. It had no scriptural foundation; besides in the early centuries the majority of deacons, priests and bishops were married *(waren meistens verheiratet).* The practice of regularly ordaining married men continued without interruption until 1139 when Lateran Council II through a combination of various prohibitions and with the help of the increased authority of the papacy succeeded in making the law universal and binding.

Bressan, Luigi. *Il canone Tridentino sul divorzio per adulterio e l'interpretazione degli autori.* Roma: Università Gregoriana, 1973.

Originally this was a doctoral dissertation presented at the Gregorian University in Rome. A genuinely scholarly work. Delicate historical situations are handled with sensitivity; texts are given every chance to speak their meaning. The author's conclusions are nuanced and moderate; he does not aim for clarity at all costs. He is equally secure in presenting certainties and uncertainties.

Bressan, Luigi. *Il divorzio nelle Chiese orientali: Ricerca storica sull' atteggiamento cattolico.* Bologna: Edizioni Dehoniane, 1976.

> This book is a well researched historical work. The author produces ample evidence to show that the churches of the East and of the West, during the first millennium, were not very different in their approach to divorce and remarriage. Both were quite steady in preaching and trying to enforce indissolubility. Both displayed hesitations and not rarely showed compassion in resolving practical cases. The schism and the mutual distancing of the two churches, however, eventually had their impact on the evolving understanding of marriage within each community. Yet, in these matters, no conflict arose between the Greeks and the Latins until the twelfth century. Then theologians and canonists from the West began to criticize the Easterners for their practice of admitting divorce and remarriage. But, even then, the Latins refrained from accusing the Greeks of heresy. Some of them were even willing to tolerate "abuses" on the other side.

Cereti, Giovanni. *Divorzio, nuove nozze e penitenza nella chiesa primitiva.* Bologna: Edizioni Dehoniane, 1977.

> The author presents a couple of substantial "theses" on the basis of his research into history *(our summary)*: (1) the primitive church interpreted *porneia* in the Matthean clause of exception as meaning "adultery" and as indeed constituting an exception to the precept of life-long fidelity; therefore a second marriage was open to the innocent party; (2) if there was no adultery, the primitive church considered divorce and remarriage gravely sinful, warranting serious penance; once, however, the penance was completed, the couple of the second marriage was readmitted into the eucharistic communion. On several points the author opposes his interpertation of patristic texts and conciliar documents to that of Crouzel.

Duby, Georges. *Medieval Marriages: Two Models from Twelfth Century France.* Baltimore: Johns Hopkins University, 1978.

> The author is one of the most outstanding historians of the medieval civilization in France. In this book (originally three lectures at Johns Hopkins University), he contrasts two models of marriage in the twelfth century; the aristocratic and the ecclesial. A quote: "The entire history of marriage in Western Christendom amounts to a gradual process of acculturation, in

which the ecclesiastical model slowly gained the upper hand, not over disorder — as is too often claimed by those who blindly espouse the point of view of Churchmen whose testimony is almost all that has come down to us — but over a different order, one that was solidly entrenched and not easily dislodged." A remark: the story the author has to tell brings out forcefully how closely the theology of laity and the theology of marriage were intertwined. An interesting book.

Duby, Georges. *The Knight, the Lady, and the Priest: The Making of Modern Marriage in Medieval France.* New York: Pantheon Books, 1983.

> This study has grown out of the author's *Medieval Marriages*; it is the study of the institution of marriage, mainly in France, in its sociological and cultural context from the late ninth to the early thirteenth century. It is the period when the church through the use of newly formulated laws "appropriated marriage," and by doing so had a far reaching effect on the life and development of the medieval society.

Fransen, Piet F. *Hermeneutics of the Councils and Other Studies.* Leuven: University Press, 1985.

> An indispensable documentary for the understanding of the Tridentine canons on marriage (sess. 24). The extremely nuanced expositions and interpretations of Fransen (together with those of Lennerz; *see* Fransen's references) should put an end to the widely spread simplistic interpretations of canon 7 on indissolubility (e.g.: the canon is a dogmatic definition *or* the canon is a mere disciplinary decree). Fransen brings out the complex nature of those canons and shows how they can be understood only as important and authentic steps toward a fuller understanding of what is contained in divine revelation. His conclusions are already having a major impact on the interpretation of the documents of the Council of Trent — and of other councils.

Gaudemet, Jean. *Sociétés et mariage.* Strasbourg; CERDIC, 1980.

> This is a collection of studies by Jean Gaudemet on the history of marriage. Some of them deal with highly specific issues, such as the originality of Roman betrothals, the decision of Pope Callistus concerning clandestine marriages. Some cover a broad spectrum and give a very good idea of how the law

of marriage has developed, such as the essay "On the uncertainties of the high Middle Ages," or "On the interpretation of the principle of indissolubility in the first millennium," or "On the legacy of Roman law in matrimonial matters." The qualities that we have learned to associate with the works of Jean Gaudemet are all there: scrupulous attention to historical data, insights into trends that moved the external events, lucid expositions and critical judgments.

The book contains also an international bibliography on the history of marriage that leads us right up to the threshold of modern debates.

Godefroy, L.; Le Bras, G.; and Jugie, M. *Mariage*, DTC IX-2: 2044-2335.

> There is not a more comprehensive and at the same time a more detailed work available on the history of the doctrine and law of marriage than this article (now in need of completion) in the *Dictionnaire de Théologie catholique.*

Joyce, G.H. *Christian Marriage: An Historical and Doctrinal Study*. London: Sheed and Ward, 1933.

> Probably the most comprehensive work on the history of marriage in English. Although dated, it is still useful.

Kelly, William. *Pope Gregory II on Divorce and Remarriage*. Roma: Università Gregoriana, 1976.

> A doctoral dissertation, and an outstanding one. The author does much more than to attempt to reconstruct Pope Gregory II's doctrine on divorce and remarriage; he researches also on the interpretations of the pope's doctrine right into modern times. But not even such a thorough study can bring us certainty. He concludes:
> Therefore, although the possibility that Gregory permitted divorce and remarriage cannot be completely ruled out, the likelihood that he did so must be considered to be remote. As a final judgment about the text all one can say is that it is and will remain a problem text. (P. 315)

Kelly, Henry Ansgar. *The Matrimonial Trials of Henry VIII.* Stanford, CA: Stanford University 1976.

> Many know about the marital troubles of Henry VIII, but a few only are familiar with the legal intricacies of his three petitions to have his marriages declared null and void, one after the other. First, there was the case of *Henry versus Catherine of Aragon*, then followed *Henry versus Ann Boleyn*, and finally *Henry versus Anne of Cleves*. In this well researched and documented book, sixteenth century canon law comes alive with its certainties, hesitations, and doubts, as the case may be. And, for background, there is the Tudor court with its capricious imperialism; the Holy See gradually becoming aware of the immense problems that some new religious movements were raising in the sixteenth century; there are the legates and emissaries shuffling back and forth; universities drawing fine distinctions; and, witnesses, often enough, instructed as to what to say. Only a few dared to dissent, at a high price to themselves.
>
> This is a book that can greatly help students of canon law to develop an awareness of the historical dimensions of the law.

Lucas, Angela M. *Women in the Middle Ages: Religion, Marriage and Letters.* New York: St. Martin's Press, 1983.

> From the point of view of canon law, *Part Two* of this book on "Women and Marriage" is enlightening, especially for the history of matrimonial consent. From our modern vantage point, many of those medieval marriages appear invalid: "when a girl was deemed old enough, or if her father was dead, she had to marry, generally with little choice in the matter of a husband" (p. 85), or, "the Church refused to recognize the bond of marriage if contracted before the 'contracting' parties had turned seven" (p. 89) — meaning that when they did turn seven such recognition was possible.

Ritzer, Korbinian. *Formen, Riten und religiöses Brauchtum des Eheschliessung in den christlichen Kirchen des ersten Jahrtausends.* Münster: Aschendorff, 1962.

> This collection contains virtually all the information available today concerning the liturgy of marriage in the first millennium. The pessimism of Augustine may have dominated the

theological speculations but it could not suppress the joyful optimism of the faithful that has found expression in liturgical celebrations. An exceptionally important source book for the theology of marriage.

Sauerwein, Erich. *Der Ursprung des Rechtsinstitutes der päpstlichen Dispens von der nicht vollzogenen Ehe.* Roma: Università Gregoriana, 1980.

An important historical contribution concerning the development of the *consensus* theory in general, and of the papal power to dispense from a non-consummated marriage in particular.

Soto, Josè Maria. *El matrimonio "in fieri" en la doctrina de S. Ambrosio y S. Juan Crisostomo: Estudio comparativo.* Roma: Università Gregoriana, 1976.

A well rounded off doctoral dissertation, half of it on the doctrine of St. Ambrose, half on that of St. John Chrysostom, concerning marriage. The comparative part is rather meagre, since the two doctors had very similar views. For both, human love played an important role in the coming into being of the marriage covenant; for both, the covenant bound the parties to lifelong fidelity. Thus, man and woman, united in a mutual sharing of all aspects of their life, fulfill in marriage the divine plan of creation.

On Marriage in General, on Some Issues in Particular

Adnès, Pierre. *Le mariage*, 2d ed. Tournai: Desclée, 1961.

A textbook in French, very much on the scholastic pattern, published before the Council. The material is presented under theses, propositions, and affirmations. It contains a fair amount of historical information.

Doms, Herbert. *Du sens et de la fin du mariage*, 2d ed. Paris: Desclée de Brouwer, 1937.

Doms is the best-known representative of those theologians who, beginning in the 1930's, attempted to bring correction into the, then generally taught, doctrine of the ends of marriage. In particular, they tried to reverse the hierarchy of ends, putting mutual help in the first place.

The Holy Office explicitly condemned them in a decree dated March 29, 1944 (D-SCH 3838). Pius XII rejected their doctrine in two allocutions, one in 1944, another in 1951. The Rota also judged them adversely in 1944.

Vatican Council II, however, reversed the situation. The Council virtually cancelled out all condemnations and encouraged further investigation in the direction set by Doms and others. Adnès, in his textbook, *Le mariage*, gives a good bibliography concerning this dispute (pp. 119-120).

Through this book, Doms made an important contribution to our understanding of Christian marriage. Much of what he said, although first rejected, is now commonly accepted; in fact, it has become the main theme of many post-conciliar works on marriage.

Eigo, Francis A., ed. *The Sacraments: God's Love and Mercy Actualized.* Villanova, PA: Villanova University, 1979.

In a collection of essays on the sacraments, the one by Tibor Horvath, Professor of Theology at Regis College, Toronto, is interesting. He writes:

... there is no reason why, after having done all the penance, divorced persons could not be given another chance to gradually build again out of the fragments of their sacramental symbol the definitive symbol of the infallible love of God triumphing over the sinfulness of man. By doing this, the sacrament of marriage becomes indeed the actualization of God's love and mercy, who comes forward precisely through the fallible love of men as victorious redeemer who conquered the sin of man. (P. 172).

Please note that divorce is not simply condoned when culpable. It should be expiated by a sizable penance.

Evdokimov, Paul. *Sacrement de l'amour.* Paris: Editions de l'Epi, 1962.

A lucid book on marriage by an outstanding Orthodox theologian. First published in 1944, it has been reprinted many times. It contains the liturgical text for the celebration of marriage in the Orthodox Church.

Evenov, J. "Le mariage." In *L'Eglise en prière,*" new ed. by Aimé Georges Mortimort, vol. 3: *Les Sacrements,* pp. 201-224. Tournai: Desclée, 1984.

In this manual of the science and art of liturgy the rite of marriage is discussed in an insightful theological framework.

Henrich, Franz and Eid, Volker, eds. *Ehe und Ehescheidung.* Müchen: Kösel, 1972.

A collection of essays by outstanding theologians of the German-speaking countries. One of them is by Joseph Ratzinger (then Ordinary Professor of theology in Regensburg) who takes a firm position on the indissolubility of Christian marriage, but pleads with equal firmness for some way of readmitting into the eucharistic communion those whose first marriage is irretrievably lost and now live in an irregular second marriage—with a contrite heart.

Herrmann, Horst. *Ehe und Recht.* Freiburg: Herder, 1972.

The author examines critically the relationship between the theological understanding of marriage and the legislation for the same sacrament. He touches on all the main issues historically and systematically. His presentation is clear but somewhat summary throughout.

Hillman, Eugene. *Polygamy Reconsidered: African Plural Marriage and the Christian Churches.* Maryknoll, NY: Orbis Books, 1975.

The author raises the question if the Christian doctrine of marriage is compatible with polygamy in a culture radically different from the one in the West. He pleads for openness and attempts to show that there is no intrinsic contradiction between Christian teaching and polygamy. His handling of the historical and theological documents, however, leaves much to be desired; his method is not well grounded critically. He is pleading for a cause and marshals all the arguments in favor of it. The book is not an impartial scholarly study but a plea for a cause.

Huizing, Peter, ed. *Für eine neue kirchliche Eheordnung: Ein Alternativentwurf.* Düsseldorf: Patmos, 1975.

In this work, published before the promulgation of CIC/83 Peter Huizing proposed thirty eight new "canons," to become the new canon law of marriage. Here are some of his proposals: non sacramental marriages between baptized persons should be recognized, informal consultations should take the place of judicial procedures, the local community should play a role in receiving a divorced and remarried person into eucharistic communion, etc. Although such proposals did not find their way into the new Code, which in all probability the author never expected, the problems they tried to answer continue to exist. Consequently, the search for balanced solutions must go on. In the dialectics of this search Huizing's proposals may still play an important role.

Kasper, Walter. *Theology of Christian Marriage.* New York: Seabury, 1980.

A small book, just about a hundred pages, published in German in 1977, in English translation in 1980. It is not a comprehensive theology of marriage, but a collection of essays on some important themes such as human values in marriage, sacramentality, unity, indissolubility, the role of Christian marriage in contemporary society. The essays are somewhat loosely written, but their content is excellent. The author is obviously familiar with the relevant historical and scriptural studies; his views are sound and critically well grounded. He sees Christian marriage as indissoluble, yet he is looking for a compassionate solution for those whose first marriage has broken up and are living now in an irregular union. Short as this work is, it is theology at its best.

Kelly, Kevin T. *Divorce and Second Marriage: Facing the Challange.* London: Collins, 1982.

The author seeks a new understanding of marriage that would not weaken the traditional doctrine of indissolubility but would make possible the admission of divorced and remarried persons to the eucharist provided certain indispensable conditions are fulfilled: (1) the first marriage is irretrievably lost and cannot be restored, (2) all obligations originating in it have been satisfied, (3) the second marriage is being lived in good faith ("we see God's hand in it"), (4) the couple is motivated by faith.

Kleinheyer, Bruno. "Riten um Ehe und Familie." In *Gottesdienst der Kirche: Handbuch der Liturgiewissenschaft*, edited by Hans Bernhard Meyer, Teil 8:2 Sakramentliche Feiern II, pp. 67-156. Regensburg: Pustet, 1984.

> A scientific treatise on the liturgy of marriage and other sacred rites connected with the life of the family. It discusses modern practices and problems in an extensive and quite detailed historical background.

L'Huillier, Pierre, and Others. *Divorce et indissolubilité du mariage*. Paris: Cerf-Desclée, 1971.

> The book is a collection of papers given in 1970 at a *Congrès de l'Association de théologiens pour l'étude de la morale* at Chevilly-la-Rue, France. The papers are interesting as documentations of ongoing reflections on contemporary problems concerning Christian marriage, mainly on indissolubility and fidelity. The issues are handled from several points of view by authors of different specializations. "Canonical theology" is represented by Jean Bernhard from the Catholic Faculty of Strasbourg, editor of *Revue de Droit canonique*. He proposes a new hypothesis (he stresses that it is a tentative theory) that, for indissolubility, the marriage must be "consummated existentially and in faith." On the whole, the essays are rich in insights, but often in need of more thorough critical grounding. The value of the book has been summed up admirably by the intelligent statement released by the Chancery of the diocese of Paris and printed instead of an *imprimatur*; it deserves to be quoted in full:
>
> > The papers of this convention do not hesitate to deal with problems which have no solution at present. Their starting point is the present teaching of the Church which they intend to develop. They are the fruit of serious research, thus valuable, and for this reason worthy of being published.

Mackin, Theodore. *Marriage in the Catholic Church: What is Marriage?* New York: Paulist Press, 1982.

> A historical survey of the understanding of marriage in the Christian tradition. The author begins with the impact that Jewish and Roman customs and laws had on Christian practices, then continues with the exposition of relevant scriptural passages. Among the Fathers he gives much space to the doc-

trine of Augustine; rightly so. He examines the works of medieval theologians and canonists; perhaps he could have stressed more how Aquinas has corrected Augustine and yet, how the Augustinian approach has continued to dominate ecclesiastical thinking. He traces the development of modern canon law and the emerging corrective reflections which after having met strong resistance from church authorities were received and officially sanctioned by Vatican Council II.

A work of great industry and erudition; at times, however, the attention to less important detail overshadows and obscures the great trends of development. In the historical part more attention to the doctrine of the Eastern churches, especially as it was and is still expressed in their liturgies, would have enriched the book; there is a line of tradition that has not been influenced by the pessimism of Augustine. Also, a more extensive presentation of, the liturgical prayers of the West, would have shown that the joyful beauty of the scriptural approach was not entirely lost among narrow theological and canonical speculations and rulings.

Mackin, Theodore. *Marriage in the Catholic Church: Divorce and Remarriage.* New York: Paulist Press, 1984.

> A sequel to the author's previous work "What is Marriage?". The historical development of the understanding of marriage is covered again but now from the point of view of determining the church's attitude toward divorce and remarriage. The author gathered a great amount of material from primary sources; his final thesis is that a more compassionate approach to remarriage would be consonant with our Christian traditions.

Malone, Richard, and Connery, John R., eds. *Contemporary Perspectives on Christian Marriage: Propositions and Papers from the International Theological Commission.* Chicago: Loyola University 1984.

> An important and valuable documentation on the work of, and on the positions taken by, the International Theological Commission concerning marriage, which was the topic of their meeting in 1977. Their final statement is divided into five chapters, each containing a certain number of propositions (assertions): marriage as institution, as sacrament, as contract/covenant, indissolubility and remarriage. We are told that "these propositions have received the absolute majority of

votes of the members" (p.6), which raises a serious methodological question: can truth be determined by majority vote? Note that here we are not dealing with an ecumenical council where the fathers take their stance with the assistance of the Spirit (*placuit Spiritui sancto et nobis* — as the old formula goes) but with a meeting of theologians where reason enlightened by faith must provide the criteria. No one would think to determine the truth of a physical theory by majority vote (most pioneers would have lost in the first round), yet such approach is extensively used in theology — with no conceivable justification. If there is a commission, minority opinions with attached reasoning should be published just as well as majority ones.

The proposals of the Commission form a good introduction into the theology of marriage, even if at times they display illogical conflicts (not unusual in papers produced by committees). E.g. after stating that divorced and remarried persons cannot be prophetic witnesses to the union of Christ with his church, the proposals say that "certain apostolic activities remain open to them" (cf. pp. 31-33, n.5).

The theses by G. Martelet were not officially adopted by the commission but "approved in general by the absolute majority of the members" (p.318, n.14). They are significant and inspiring as systematic theological insights but some of them not well grounded critically. Martelet pushes the *analogy* between the relationship of Christ to his church and the relationship of one spouse to the other to an extreme; he seems to claim that the two relationships are *identical.* In such conception we can only call the Eastern practice of allowing remarriage after adultery a practice inspired by heresy, and of course, the Catholic practice of granting dispensations from the bond of a non-consummated sacramental marriage should be condemned too.

The most insightful of the position papers is the one by Wilhelm Ernst on "Marriage as Institution and the Contemporary Challenge to It": he identifies correctly most of the problems that beset us today. A few contributors appear to be preoccupied with combatting errors (Caffarra, Descamp), others are more positively inspired (Ernst, Lehmann).

The position papers by various members of the Commission are valuable summaries of the known; they do not contain hitherto unknown historical data, or new insights into the "mystery."

Metz, René and Schlick, Jean, eds. *Le lien matrimonial.* Strasbourg: CERDIC, 1970.

A collection of eleven essays covering a great deal: marriage in different cultures, historical evolution of Christian marriage, and marriage in different theologies — Protestant, Orthodox, Catholic. The historical essays by Gaudemet, Fransen, and Huizing are probably the most important and the most remarkable.

Meyendorff, John. *Byzantine Theology: Historical Trends and Doctrinal Themes*, 2d ed. New York: Fordham University, 1979.

This book is a clear and concise exposition of the traditions of the Byzantine church. Canon lawyers would particularly benefit from reading the chapter on sacramental theology (pp. 191-201): there is another understanding of marriage that would burst our canons! The pages on *oikonomia* (88-90) are enlightening. No one can read this book without marvelling at the riches of the Orthodox tradition.

Meyendorff, John. *Marriage: An Orthodox Perspective*. Crestwood, NY: St. Vladimir Seminary, 1975.

A good introduction into the teaching and practices (including canon law) of the Orthodox church concerning marriage. Their liturgies display great and ancient beauty. A short and readable book.

Moore, Garth E. *An Introduction into English Canon Law*. Oxford: Clarendon, 1967.

A short survey of the canon law of the Church of England. Much of the part on marriage is given to the discussion of the tense situations that often arise due to the conflict between the secular approach of the state and the religious approach of the church to marriage; *see* "Holy Matrimony," pp. 82-96.

Navarrete, Urbanus. *Quaedam problemata actualia de matrimonio*, 3d rev. ed. Roma: Università Gregoriana, 1979.

The book contains sixteen essays, all of them published previously in various periodicals or symposia, on contemporary problems concerning marriage. On the whole they provide a good introduction into the method and ideas of the author. He perceives canon law as far more independent from theology than the nature and role of the two sciences postulate. Hence, in the handling of theological issues, he tends to come to firm conclusions on the basis of law only.

Orsy, Ladislas. *The Evolving Church and the Sacrament of Penance*. Denville, NJ: Dimension Books, 1978.

This is not a book on marriage, but its Chapter Two on the development of doctrine and Chapter Three on the evolution of mentalities are relevant for our purposes. Besides, the book is an attempt to discover a method that would help us to make good laws built on theological foundations. The sacraments of matrimony is as much in need of such a new methodological approach as penance is.

Orsy, Ladislas. "The Interpreter and his Art," *The Jurist*, 40 (1980), 27-56.
"The Interpretation of Laws: New Variations on an Old Theme," *Studia Canonica*, 15 (1983), 95-133.

The two articles account for the method of interpretation used in this book.

Richstatter, Thomas. *Liturgical Law: New Style, New Spirit*. Chicago: Franciscan Herald Press, 1977.

The author provides a thorough documentation about the development of liturgical norms in recent times. He searches for the new spirit that must animate it. A useful reference work.

Robinson, Geoffrey. *Marriage, Divorce and Nullity: A Guide to the Annulment Process in the Catholic Church*. Melbourne: Dove Communications, 1984.

A concise, clear and eminently practical guidebook.

Schillebeeckx, Edward. *Christ the Sacrament of the Encounter with God*. New York: Sheed and Ward, 1973.

A classical work on the understanding of the Christian sacraments.

Schillebeeckx, Edward. *Marriage: Human Reality and Saving Mystery*. New York: Sheed and Ward, 1965.

A well known historical and systematic treatise on marriage.

Sequeira, John Baptist. *Tout mariage entre baptisés est-il néces-sairement sacramentel? Etude historique, théologique et canonique sur le lien entre baptême et mariage.* Paris: Cerf, 1985.

> The issue the author has investigated is theological although it has momentous consequences in canon law. He handles it in an exemplary way, first by carefully gathering the relevant historical facts, then by evaluating them according to proper theological criteria, and finally by drawing the consequences for canon law. He suggests that the paragraph on the identity of the contract and the sacrament (1055 § 2) should be suppressed together with the canon on the compulsory canonical form (1108).

Walgrave, Jan. *Unfolding Revelation: The Nature of Doctrinal Development.* Philadelphia, PA: Westminster, 1972.

> If the development of doctrine is a problem for theologians, it is even more of a problem for those who participate in the making of laws, in their implementation and interpretation. But, why should development be more of a problem for lawyers than for theologians? Because theologians, on the whole, have discovered that much of the development takes place through intuitive knowledge, "by the light of the faith," before it is articulated in precise concepts. Canon law is, in many ways, the translation of beliefs and theological insights into practical rules. But legal norms cannot easily spring from an intuition. They require conceptual premises; hence, it is not an uncommon phenomenon in our modern Church to find the intuitive understanding of the community to be ahead of the laws based on pedestrian concepts.
>
> Keeping this in mind, it is easy to see why it took nearly twenty years after Vatican Council II to have a new Code; also, why it takes a long time to translate new theological insights concerning the mystery of marriage into new structures and laws.
>
> To handle.with wisdom the tensions that are bound to arise from such situations, a good understanding of the process of evolution in the church is necessary. Although Walgrave's primary object is to explain doctrinal development, much of what he says is helpful toward understanding, judging and promoting the development of canon law.

Weiler, Rudolf, and Zsifkovits, Valentin, eds. *Familie im Wandel.* Freiburg: Herder, 1975.

A collection of essays "on the family" by different authors. Each writes from a particular point of view: philosophy, economics, anthropology, sociology, theology, etc. The chapter on the family in different cultures is remarkably informative. The majority of essays are empirical studies; they report on the state of families.

Weinrich, A.K.H. *African Marriage in Zimbabwe and the Impact of Christianity*. Gweru: Mambo Press, 1982.

The author is a sociologist. She examines the changing pattern of marriage in Zimbabwe, and pays special attention to the central signficance of fertility. She presents and interprets the sociological data with the help of Marxist categories; her aim being "to point the way for a concrete cross fertilization of Christian and Marxist aspirations." Her findings show how much the "human reality of marriage" can be different from one continent to another.

Wrenn, Lawrence G. *Annulments*, 4th rev. ed. Washington, DC: CLSA, 1983.

A detailed guidebook revised on the basis of CIC/83, intended mainly for tribunal personnel.

Zirkel, Adam, and Limbeck, Meinrad. *Kirchliche Ehegerichstsbarkeit und biblisches Rechsverständnis*. Mainz: Grünewald, 1981.

The two essays by the two authors are complementary. Zirkel examines the theory and practice of marriage tribunals and finds them wanting under several aspects; Limbeck suggests that the way out of the difficulties is in turning to the Scriptures for inspiration and in making the law an instrument of mercy and compassion.

Psychology

Conn, Walter E. *Conscience: Development and Self-Transcendence*. Birmingham, AL: Religious Education Press, 1981.

An interdisciplinary study of personality development: the author brings together discoveries and insights from the field of empirical psychology (Erikson, Piaget, Kohlberg), philosophy (Lonergan), and offers some conclusions of importance for Christian anthropology and in particular for ethics.

Dominion, Jack. *Marriage, Faith and Love: A Basic Guide to Christian Marriage.* New York: Crossroad, 1981.

A guide written by a highly respected psychiatrist; useful for canon lawyers as general background reading. After reflecting on the nature of contemporary marriage and describing its development from the time of "personal encounter" to the "later years," the author dedicates a long chapter to marital break-downs.

Johnson, Robert A. *WE: Understanding the Psychology of Romantic Love.* San Francisco: Harper & Row, 1983.

An explanation of romantic and non-romantic love in Jungian categories. It is interesting to note that Jung's understanding of true marital love comes very close to Aquinas' definition of *amor benevolentiae*, love that wants the welfare of the other.

Jung, Carl Gustav. *Aion: Researches into the Phenomenology of the Self*, Bollingen Series. Princeton, NJ: Princeton University Press, 1979.

The theory of Jung on the *animus* and *anima* as integral parts of every human self, and on the role they play in man-and-woman relationship, can bring much enlightenment not only for the understanding of marital problems but also for knowing better the necessary conditions for a happy marriage. *Animus* and *anima* are explained in this work in the context of the whole self. More on them can be found in Jung's *Two Essays on Analytical Psychology* and *Aspects of the Feminine*, both in the same series.

Kegan, Robert. *The Evolving Self: Problem and Process in Human Development*. Cambridge, MA: Harvard University, 1982.

> The development of a human person is a slow and complex process. At times it happens that someone is able to advance with the years in physical strength and intellectual achievement, yet, remains retarded or even stationary at some early stage of overall personality development. When such a situation arises, there is the puzzling phenomenon of a person who is able to carry out narrowly circumscribed professional responsibilities yet unable to be a good partner in marriage. In simpler terms someone may be of thirty years of age physically and intellectually but only twelve in overall personality development. Classical canon law has not known such complications. And, needless to say, such an advanced-and-retarded person (all at once) projects sharply contradictory images about himself or herself. Developmental psychology in general, and Kegan's work in particular, can help to understand and judge such situations.

Porot, Antoine, ed. *Manuel Alphabétique de Psychiatrie*, 5th ed. Paris: Presses Universitaires de France, 1975.

> An excellent concise reference work, used throughout French-speaking countries. Since the science of psychiatry and its language is conditioned more than any other branch of medicine by the national character, to learn how the other half of the world thinks, speaks, and works or fails to do so, can be an enriching experience.

Singer, June. *Boundaries of the Soul: The Practice of Jung's Psychology*. Garden City: Doubleday, 1973.

> To handle the issue of consent judiciously, especially to apply canon 1095, a basic understanding of the human psychology is indispensable. But the name of psychological schools is legion; nothing is easier than to get lost among them. It is wise therefore for a canon lawyer to get thoroughly acquainted with the ideas of one school; not to support it uncritically, but to use it as a point of reference and comparison when hearing and learning about the others. Jung's school is eminently suitable for this purpose; Singer's book is a good introduction into it.

EPILOGUE

This epilogue is not meant to be a conclusion, rather an opening of new perspectives. There is a principle as yet not mentioned in this book. It should really govern the making, the implementing and the interpreting of the laws in the church; yet, it has not been much explored to date. It is that every individual person in the believing community, and the community as a whole, is ultimately in the service of a person — that is, of God. All juridical relations are subordinated to person-to-person relations.

To understand this, it may help to contrast civil law with canon law. The system of civil law is a closed one, it does not point to anyone or anything beyond the constitutional authorities of the state; the system of canon law exists to create an environment for the believers to honor and worship God. If follows that God's own self revelation is normative for our laws. They must somehow reflect God's personality: his greatness, his magnanimity, his compassion, his dedication to failing human being. Since he stands for authentic values, in his Kingdom there is no place for legalism or formalism, which is nothing else than nominalism in disguise. There cannot be any anarchy either because he stands for peace and progress. Rigorism is excluded, because he wants to manifest his mercy.

The Scriptures, especially the New Testament, are appropriate guides in these matters. Jesus displayed a far greater preoccupation with the preaching of the good news of salvation than with giving precise instructions about future structures.

This is not to say that the Christian community was wrong in developing a legal system. But it is to say that laws can never mirror perfectly the wisdom of God and his love for his creatures. They are human constructs, carrying the limitations of our humanity in their very substance.

Thus a fundamental question for a believer in dealing with the law should always be: How far a norm, a decision or an interpretation is in harmony with the personality of our God as he revealed himself in our history? There is the supreme rule of canonical hermeneutics. The new Code does not deny this; in fact, it ends with the words "the salvation of the souls ... must be the supreme law in the church" (canon 1752). This should not be taken as a merely pious phrase. It means that after we have done our best to clarify the meaning of the canons, we should recall that they are indeed subordinated to a superior law that was promulgated nearly two thousand years ago in the valleys and on the mountains of the land of Israel by the One who *reflected the glory of God and bore the very stamp of his nature* (cf. Heb 1:3).

Good order postulates that our historically conditioned and man made laws should be always subject to the grace-filled and timeless norms of the evangelical message.

> For my thoughts are not your thoughts,
> neither are your ways my ways, says the Lord.
> For as heavens are higher than the earth,
> so are my ways higher than your ways
> and my thoughts than your thoughts (Is 55:8-9).

INDEX OF PERSONS

(Includes historical and bibliographical entries)

326

INDEX OF STRUCTURES AND TOPICS IN THE LAW OF MARRIAGE

(Refers to the Chapters on the Canons and on the Disputed Questions)